# ALSO AVAILABLE FROM ☁ TOKYOPOP®

## MANGA

*INDICATES TITLE IS IN THE RIGHT-TO-LEFT FORMAT

### ACTION

ANGELIC LAYER*
CLAMP SCHOOL DETECTIVES* (April 2003)
DIGIMON (March 2003)
DUKLYON: CLAMP SCHOOL DEFENDERS* (September 2003)
GATEKEEPERS* (March 2003)
GTO*
HARLEM BEAT
INITIAL D*
ISLAND
JING: KING OF BANDITS* (June 2003)
JULINE
LUPIN III*
MONSTERS, INC.
PRIEST
RAVE*
REAL BOUT HIGH SCHOOL*
REBOUND* (April 2003)
SAMURAI DEEPER KYO* (June 2003)
SCRYED* (March 2003)
SHAOLIN SISTERS* (February 2003)
THE SKULL MAN*

### FANTASY

CHRONICLES OF THE CURSED SWORD (July 2003))
DEMON DIARY (May 2003)
DRAGON HUNTER (June 2003)
DRAGON KNIGHTS*
KING OF HELL (June 2003)
PLANET LADDER*
RAGNAROK
REBIRTH (March 2003)
SHIRAHIME:TALES OF THE SNOW PRINCESS* (December 2003)
SORCERER HUNTERS
WISH*

### CINE-MANGA™

AKIRA*
CARDCAPTORS
KIM POSSIBLE (March 2003)
LIZZIE McGUIRE (March 2003)
POWER RANGERS (May 2003)
SPY KIDS 2 (March 2003)

### ANIME GUIDES

GUNDAM TECHNICAL MANUALS
COWBOY BEBOP
SAILOR MOON SCOUT GUIDES

### ROMANCE

HAPPY MANIA* (April 2003)
I.N.V.U. (February 2003)
LOVE HINA*
KARE KANO*
KODOCHA*
MAN OF MANY FACES* (May 2003)
MARMALADE BOY*
MARS*
PARADISE KISS*
PEACH GIRL
UNDER A GLASS MOON (June 2003)

### SCIENCE FICTION

CHOBITS*
CLOVER
COWBOY BEBOP*
COWBOY BEBOP: SHOOTING STAR* (June 2003)
G-GUNDAM*
GUNDAM WING
GUNDAM WING: ENDLESS WALTZ*
GUNDAM: THE LAST OUTPOST*
PARASYTE
REALITY CHECK (March 2003)

### MAGICAL GIRLS

CARDCAPTOR SAKURA
CARDCAPTOR SAKURA: MASTER OF THE CLOW*
CORRECTOR YUI
MAGIC KNIGHT RAYEARTH* (August 2003)
MIRACLE GIRLS
SAILOR MOON
SAINT TAIL
TOKYO MEW MEW* (April 2003)

### NOVELS

SAILOR MOON
SUSHI SQUAD (April 2003)

### ART BOOKS

CARDCAPTOR SAKURA*
MAGIC KNIGHT RAYEARTH*

### TOKYOPOP KIDS

DISNEY CLASSICS (June 2003)
STRAY SHEEP (September 2003)

# VOLUME 4

## BY
## MIN-WOO HYUNG

TOKYOPOP®

LOS ANGELES ★ TOKYO

Translator - Jessica Kim
English Adaptation - Jake Forbes
Cover Artist - Raymond Swanland
Graphic Designer - Anna Kernbaum
Layout- Melissa Hackett

Senior Editor - Jake Forbes
Production Manager - Jennifer Miller
Art Director - Matt Alford
VP Production - Ron Klamert
President & C.O.O. - John Parker
Publisher - Stuart Levy

email: editor@TOKYOPOP.com
Come visit us online at www.TOKYOPOP.com

A 　TOKYOPOP® MANGA

TOKYOPOP® is an imprint of Mixx Entertainment, Inc.
5900 Wilshire Blvd., Ste. 2000, Los Angeles, CA 90036

ISBN: 1-59182-088-X

First TOKYOPOP Printing: January 2003

. 10 9 8 7 6 5 4 3 2

Manufactured in the USA.

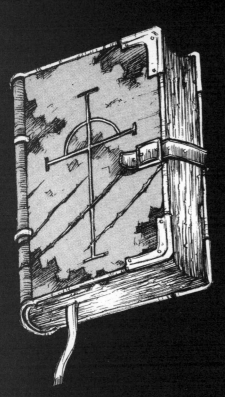

# THE STORY SO FAR...

In the frontier of the American West, a forgotten war was waged between the followers of Temozarela, an angel of blood fallen from heaven, and those who stood against the darkness. And somewhere in between walked Ivan Isaacs, a dead priest who sold his soul to the devil Belial for a second chance at life and the power to get his revenge. While Ivan hunted down Temozarela's followers, he kept a detailed log of his tragic journey. Now his journal has fallen into the hands of Father Simon, a modern day religious scholar who had been looking for this kind of miraculous proof of the divine to fortify his faith. Simon was summoned to the Heshion, a holy prison where the soul of Temozarela is sealed to this day, along with the soul of Ivan Isaacs. But before Simon can understand the evil that has been discovered in the present, he must first learn about the man who trapped it.

# PRIEST

## 프리스트

### 4

## HARBINGER'S SONG

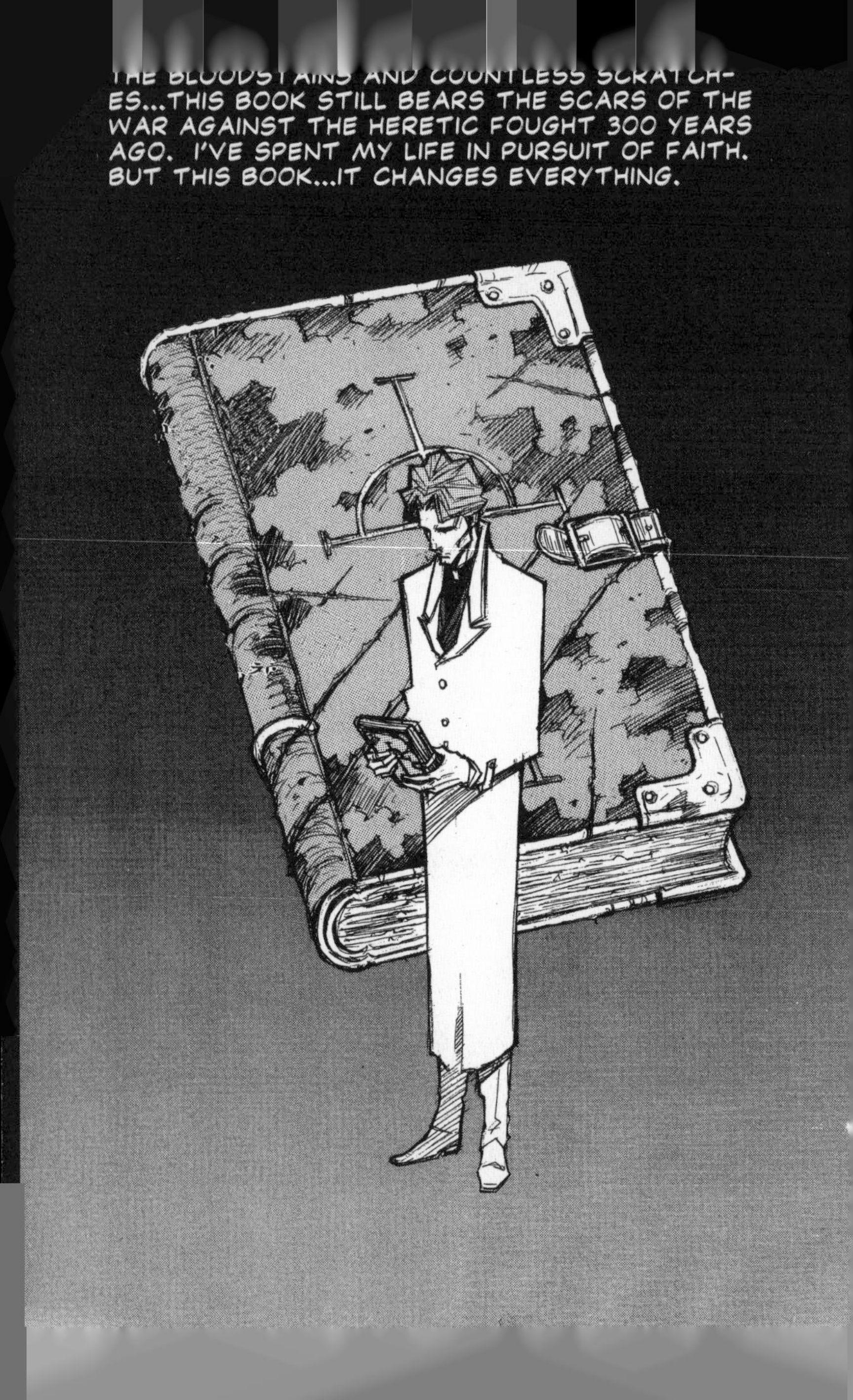
THE BLOODSTAINS AND COUNTLESS SCRATCHES...THIS BOOK STILL BEARS THE SCARS OF THE WAR AGAINST THE HERETIC FOUGHT 300 YEARS AGO. I'VE SPENT MY LIFE IN PURSUIT OF FAITH. BUT THIS BOOK...IT CHANGES EVERYTHING.

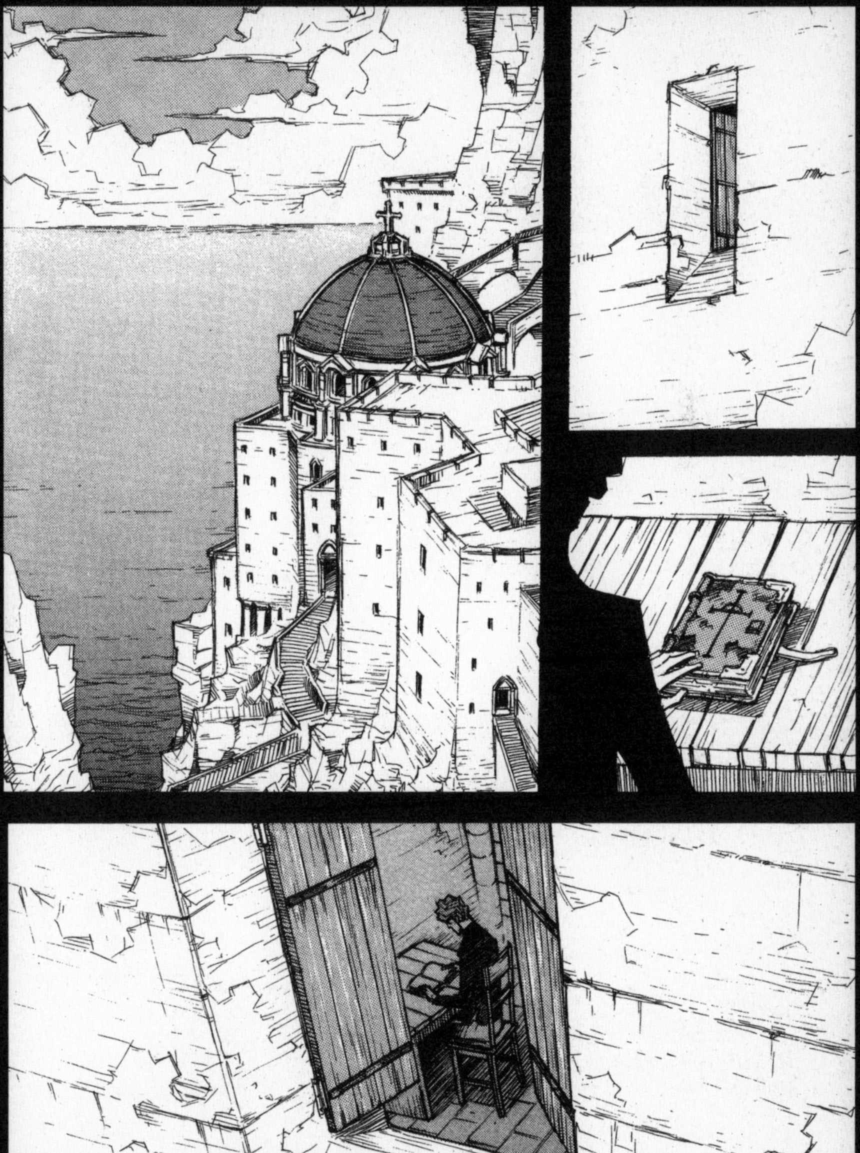

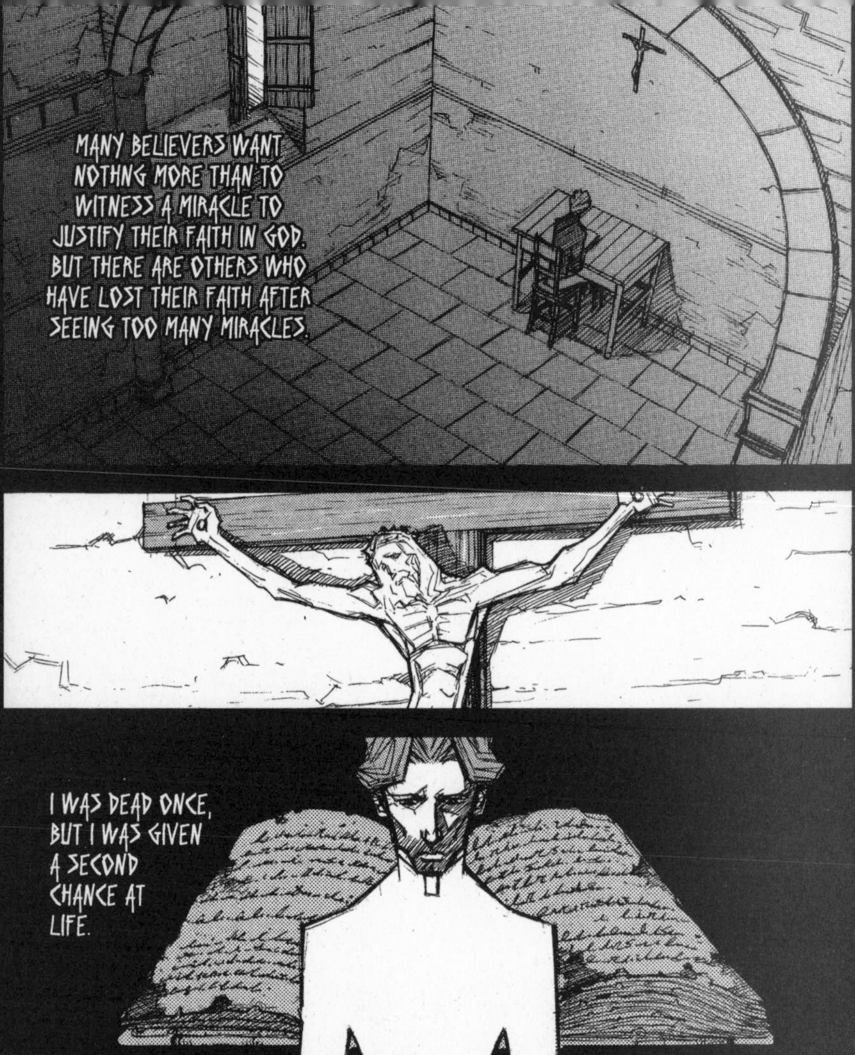
MANY BELIEVERS WANT NOTHNG MORE THAN TO WITNESS A MIRACLE TO JUSTIFY THEIR FAITH IN GOD. BUT THERE ARE OTHERS WHO HAVE LOST THEIR FAITH AFTER SEEING TOO MANY MIRACLES.
I WAS DEAD ONCE, BUT I WAS GIVEN A SECOND CHANCE AT LIFE.

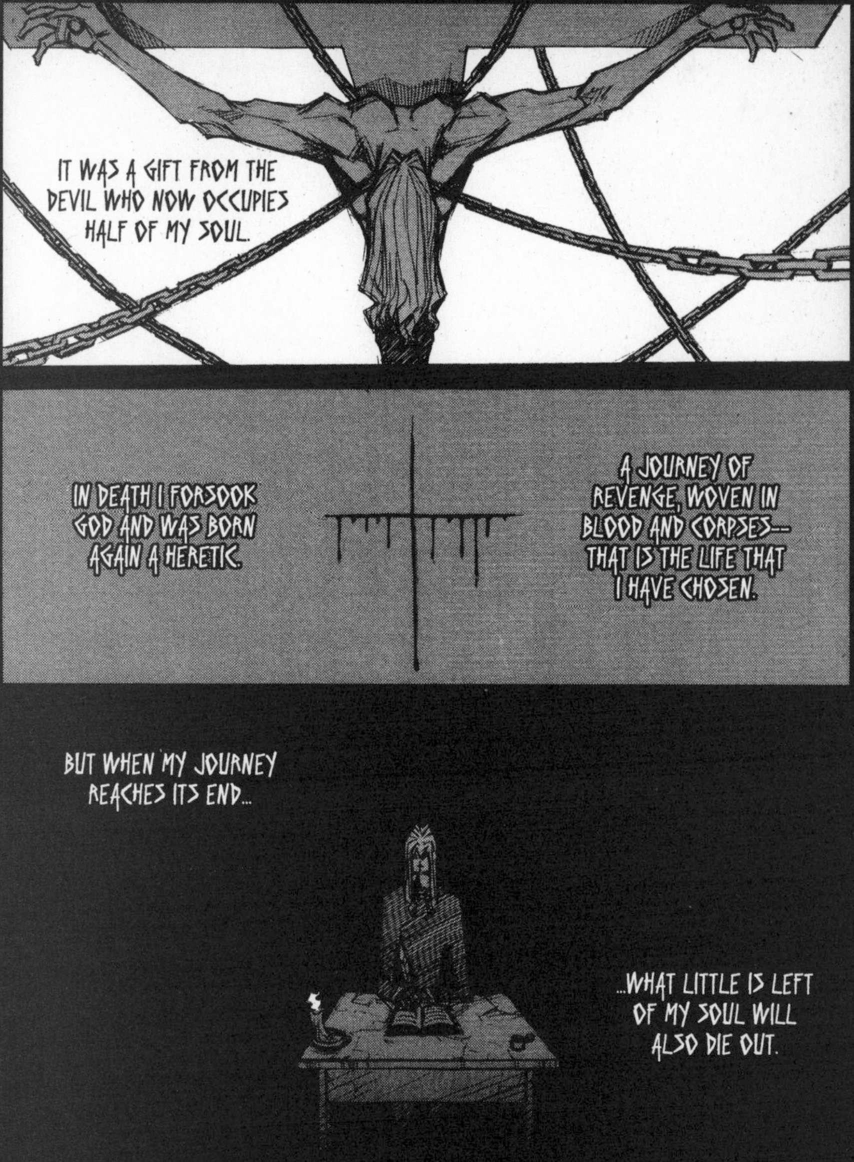
IT WAS A GIFT FROM THE DEVIL WHO NOW OCCUPIES HALF OF MY SOUL.
IN DEATH I FORSOOK GOD AND WAS BORN AGAIN A HERETIC.
A JOURNEY OF REVENGE, WOVEN IN BLOOD AND CORPSES--THAT IS THE LIFE THAT I HAVE CHOSEN.
BUT WHEN MY JOURNEY REACHES ITS END...
...WHAT LITTLE IS LEFT OF MY SOUL WILL ALSO DIE OUT.

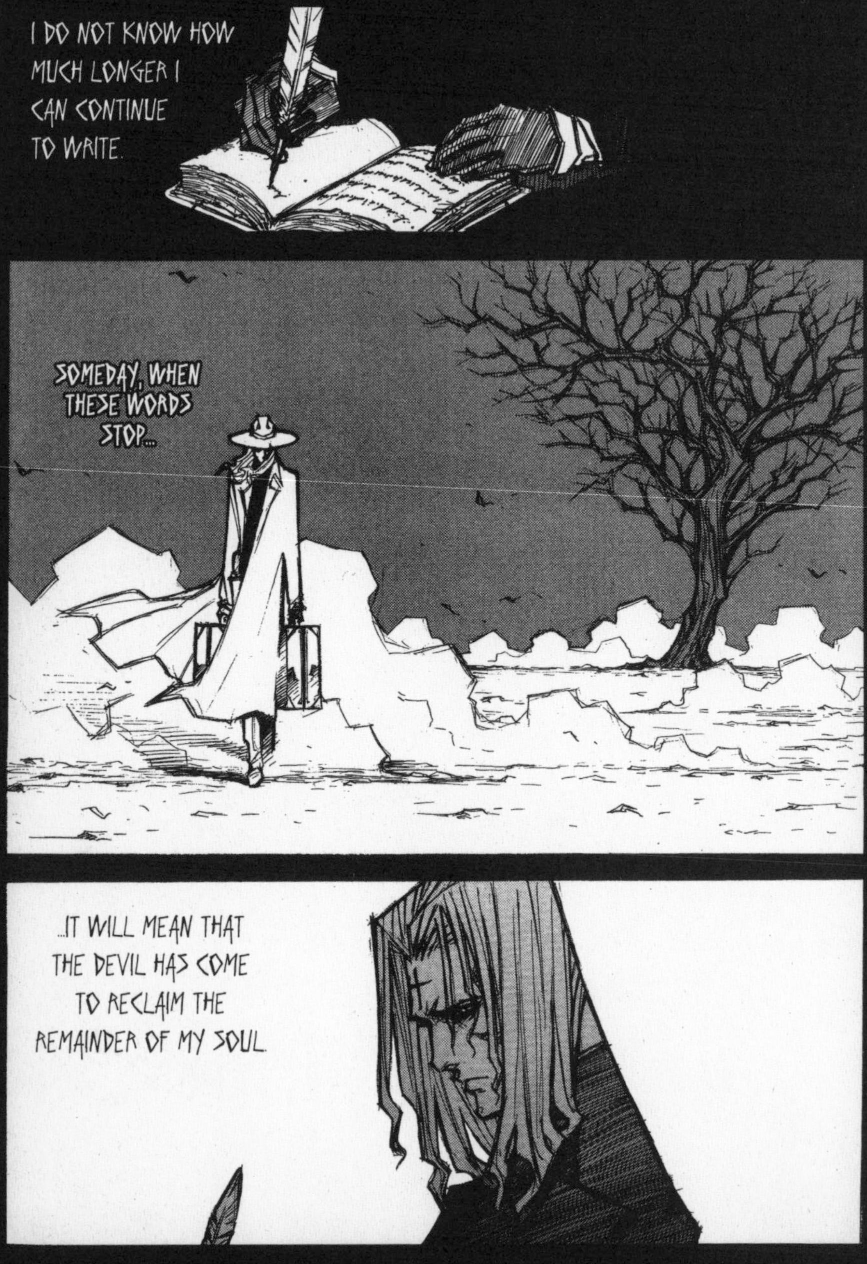
I DO NOT KNOW HOW MUCH LONGER I CAN CONTINUE TO WRITE.
SOMEDAY, WHEN THESE WORDS STOP...
...IT WILL MEAN THAT THE DEVIL HAS COME TO RECLAIM THE REMAINDER OF MY SOUL.

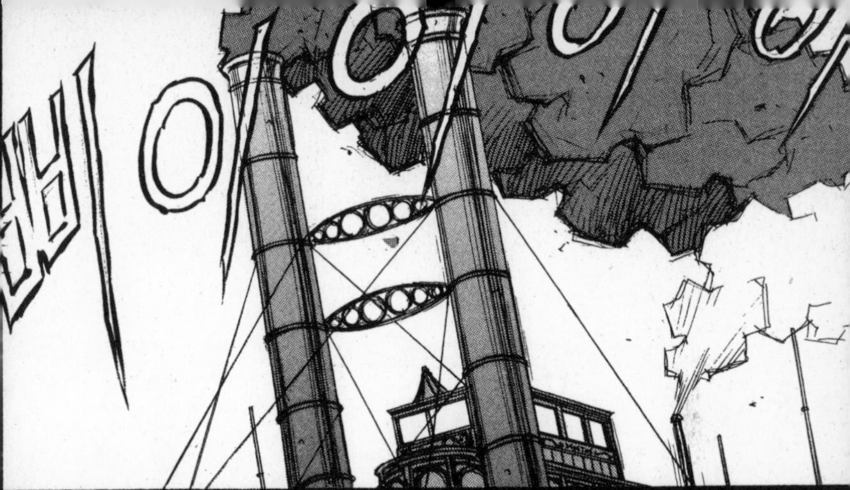

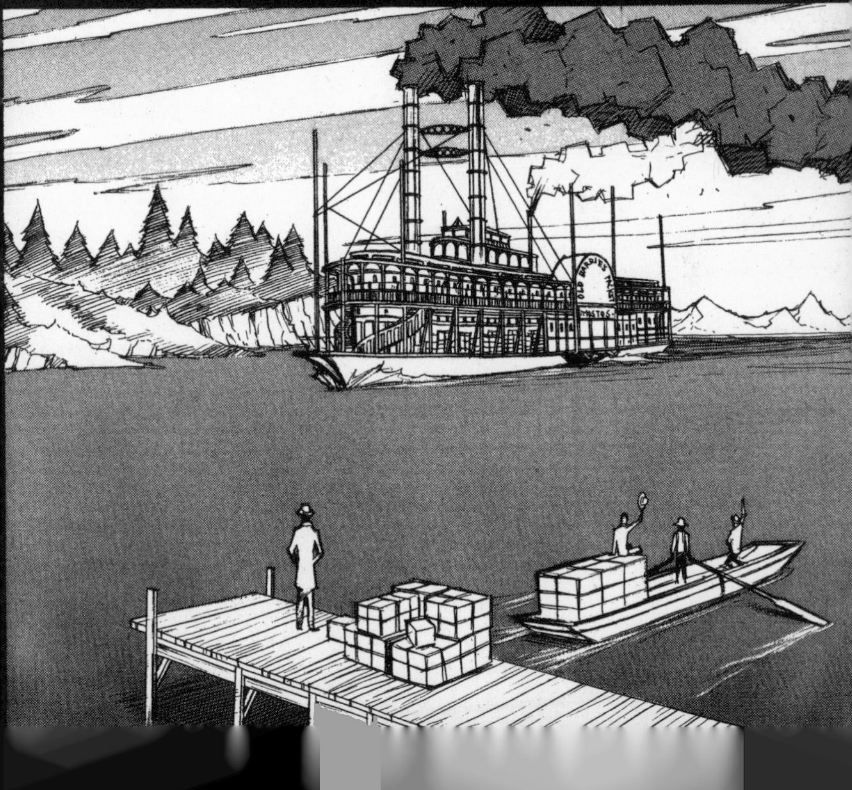

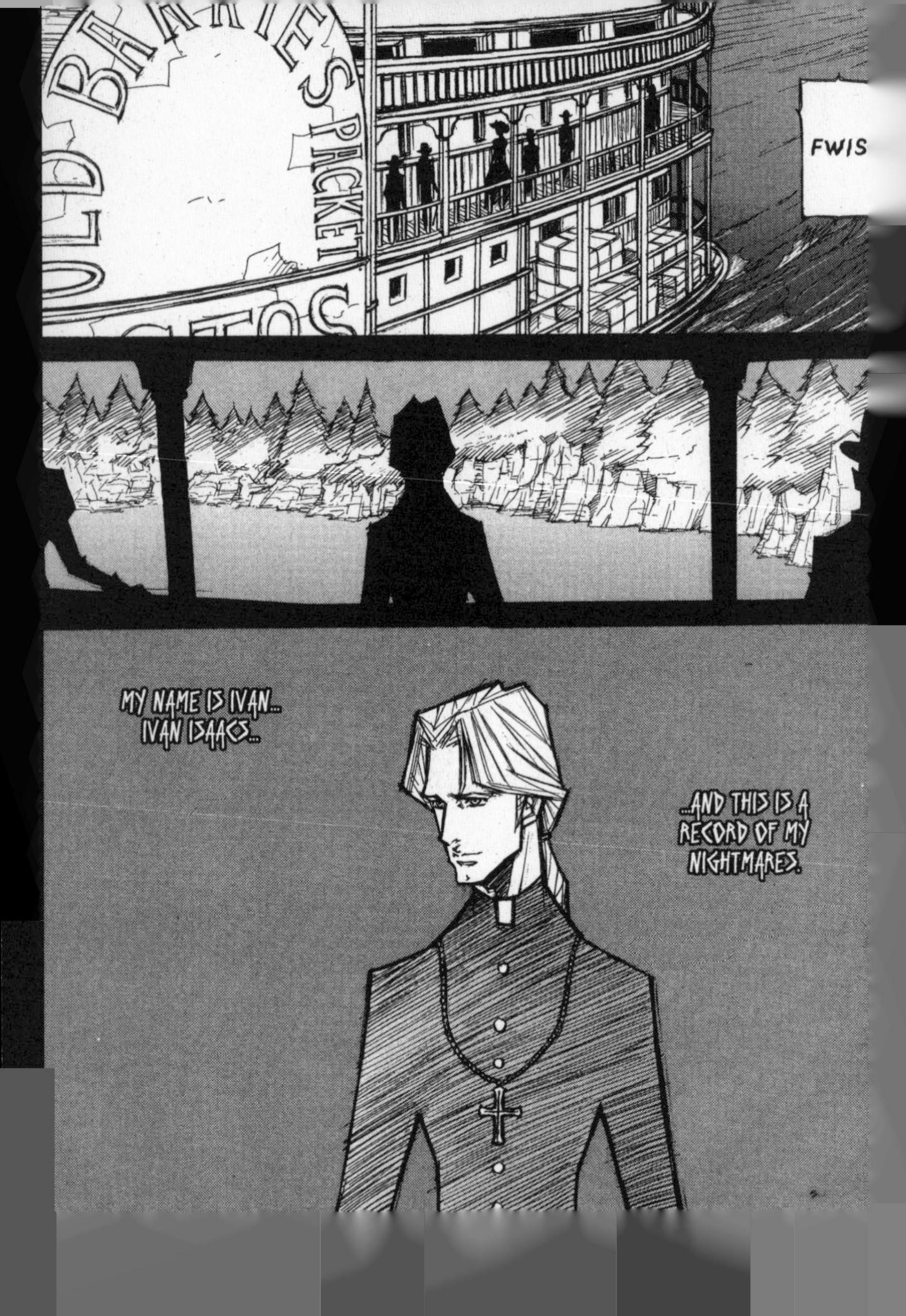
OLD BARRIES PACKET
FWIS
MY NAME IS IVAN... IVAN ISAACS...
...AND THIS IS A RECORD OF MY NIGHTMARES.

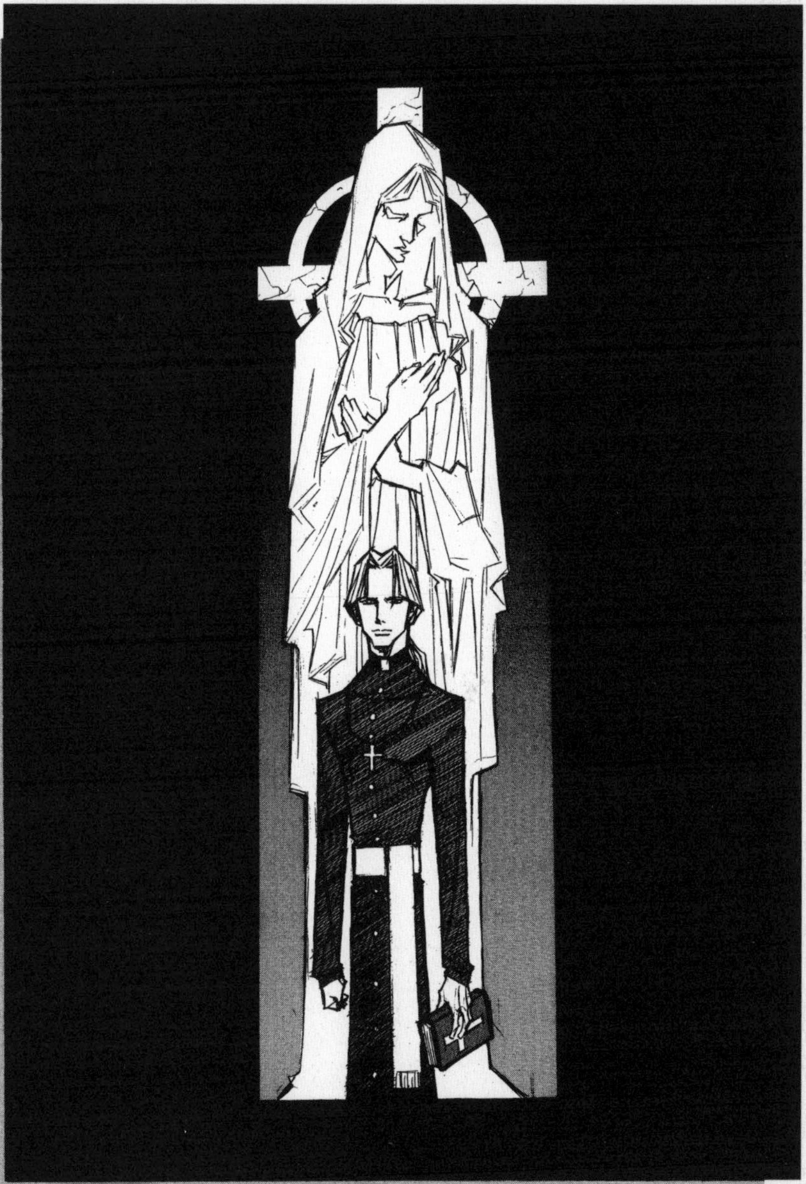

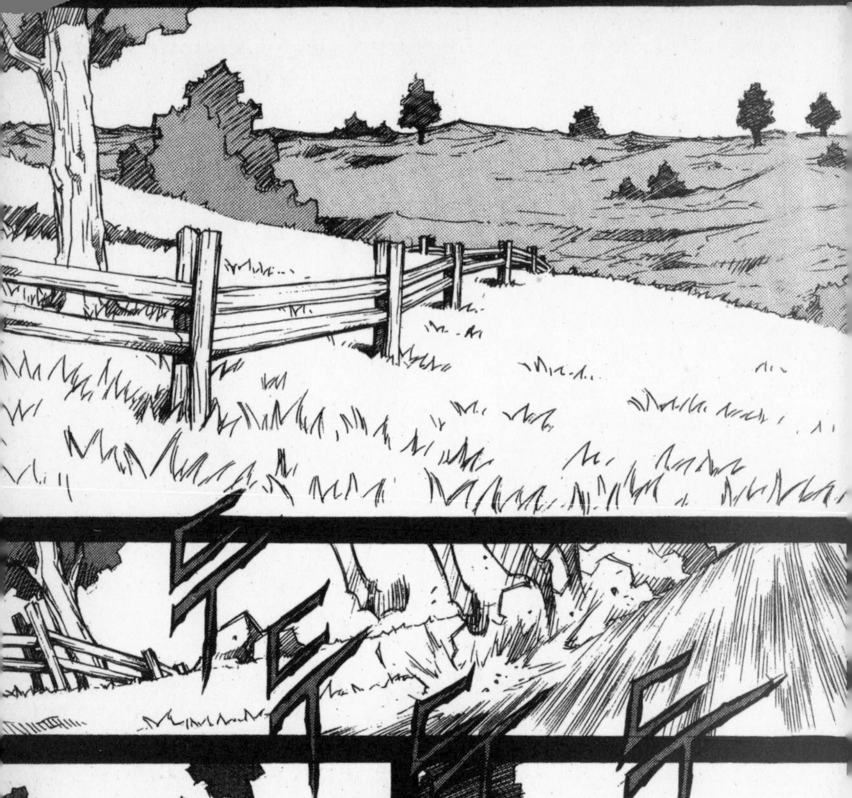
TROM

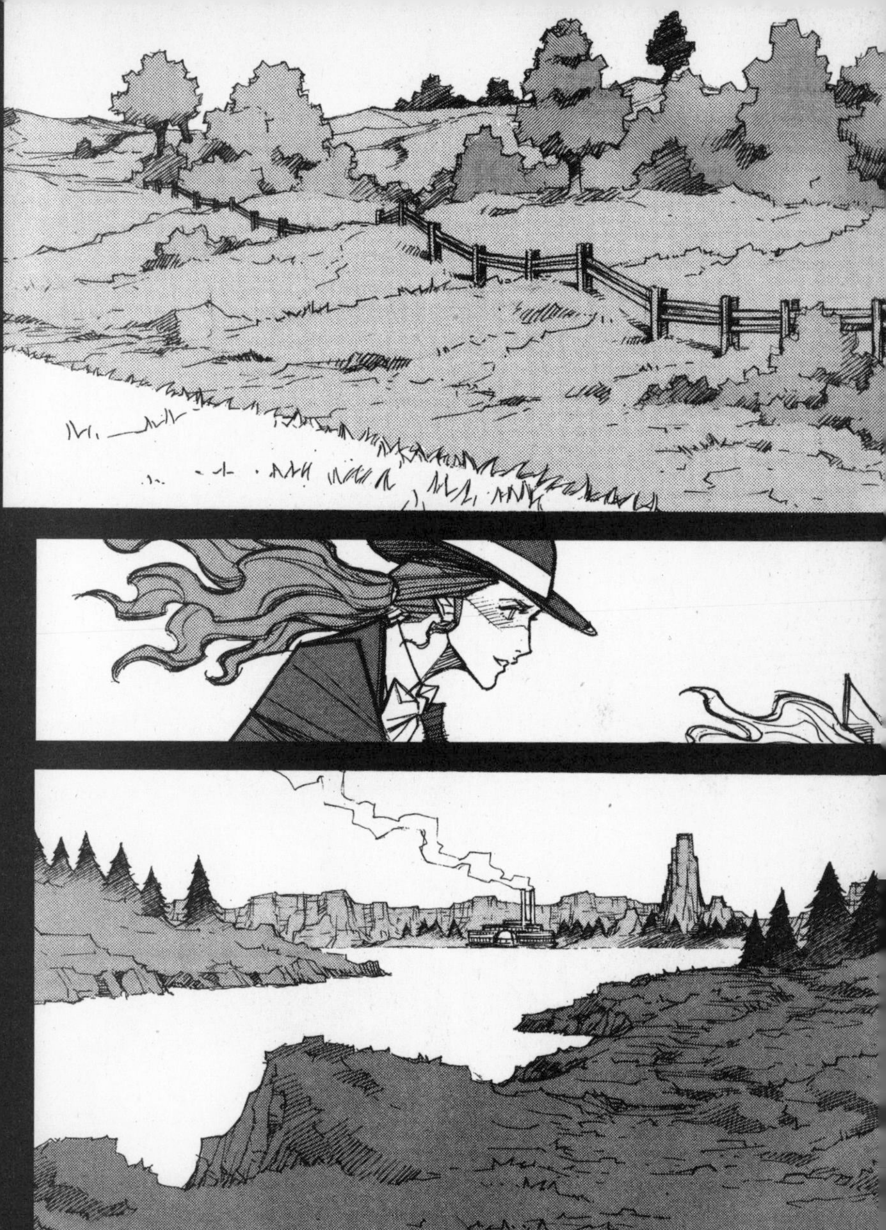

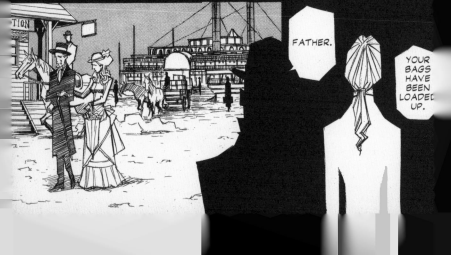

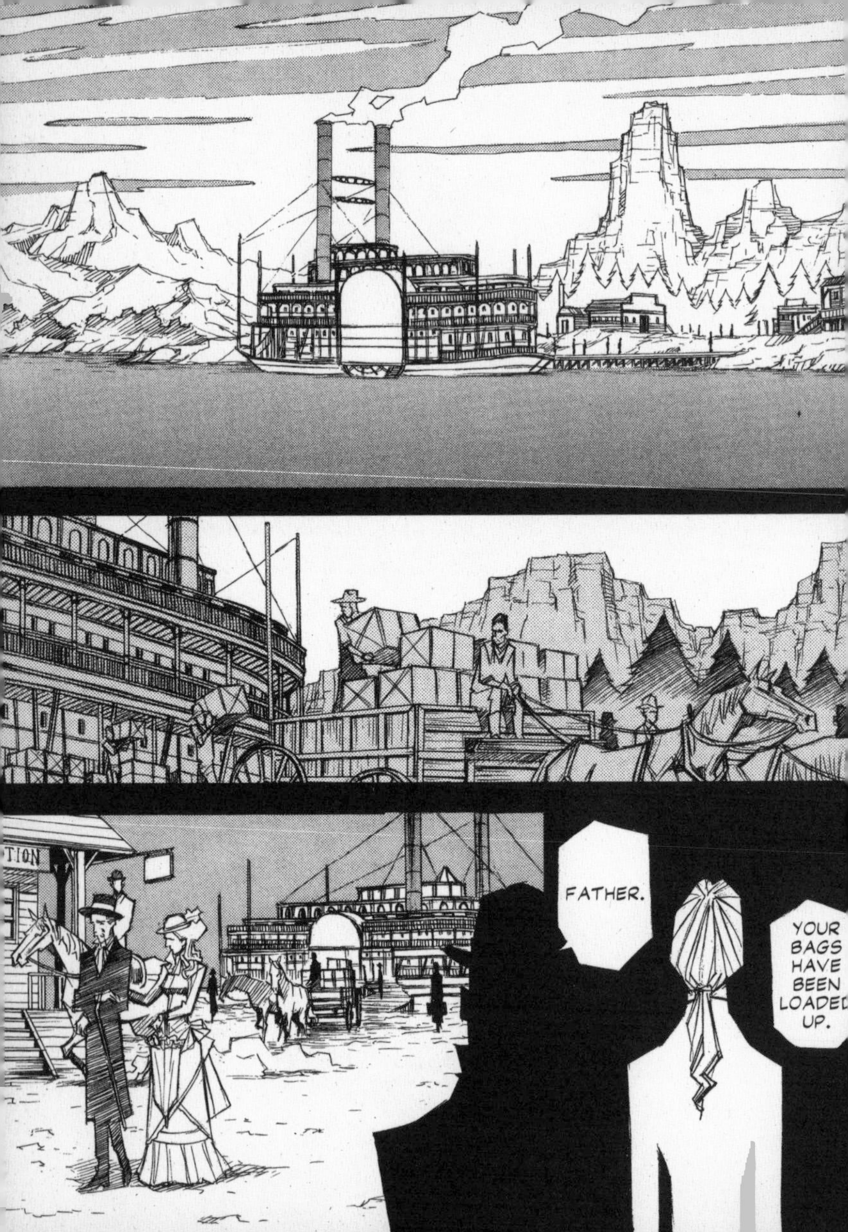
FATHER.
YOUR BAGS HAVE BEEN LOADED UP.

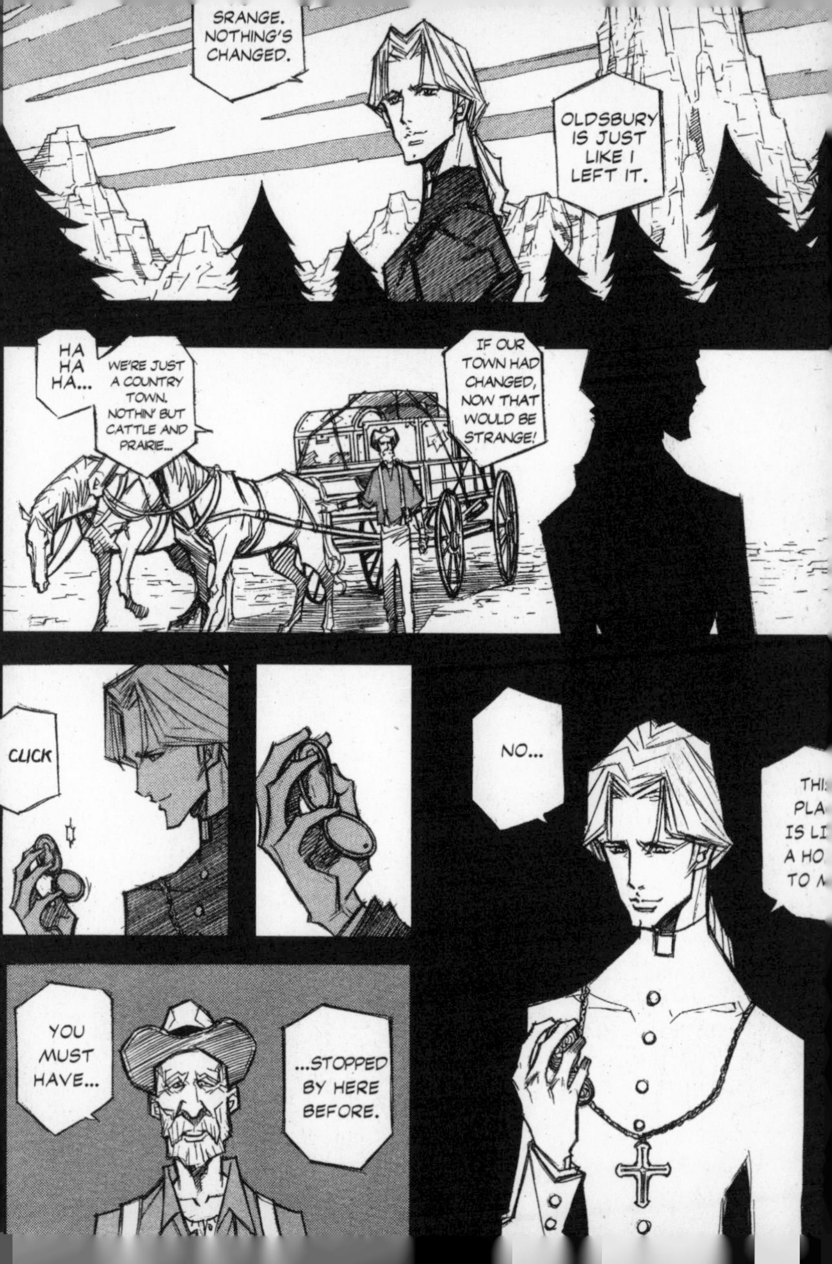
SRANGE. NOTHING'S CHANGED.
OLDSBURY IS JUST LIKE I LEFT IT.
HA HA HA...
WE'RE JUST A COUNTRY TOWN. NOTHIN' BUT CATTLE AND PRAIRIE...
IF OUR TOWN HAD CHANGED, NOW THAT WOULD BE STRANGE!
CLICK
NO...
YOU MUST HAVE...
...STOPPED BY HERE BEFORE.

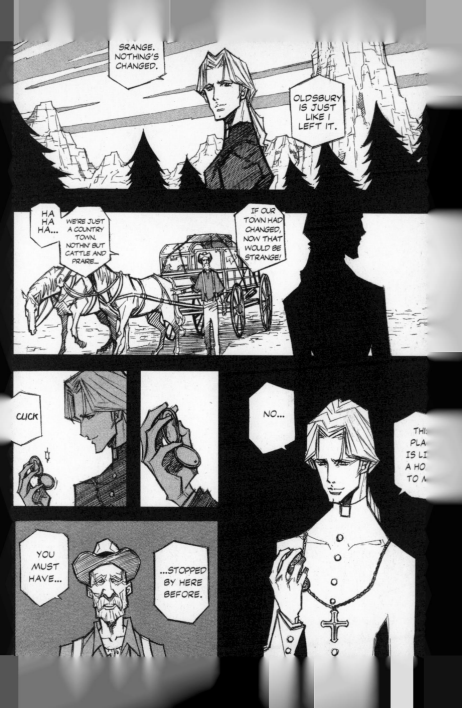

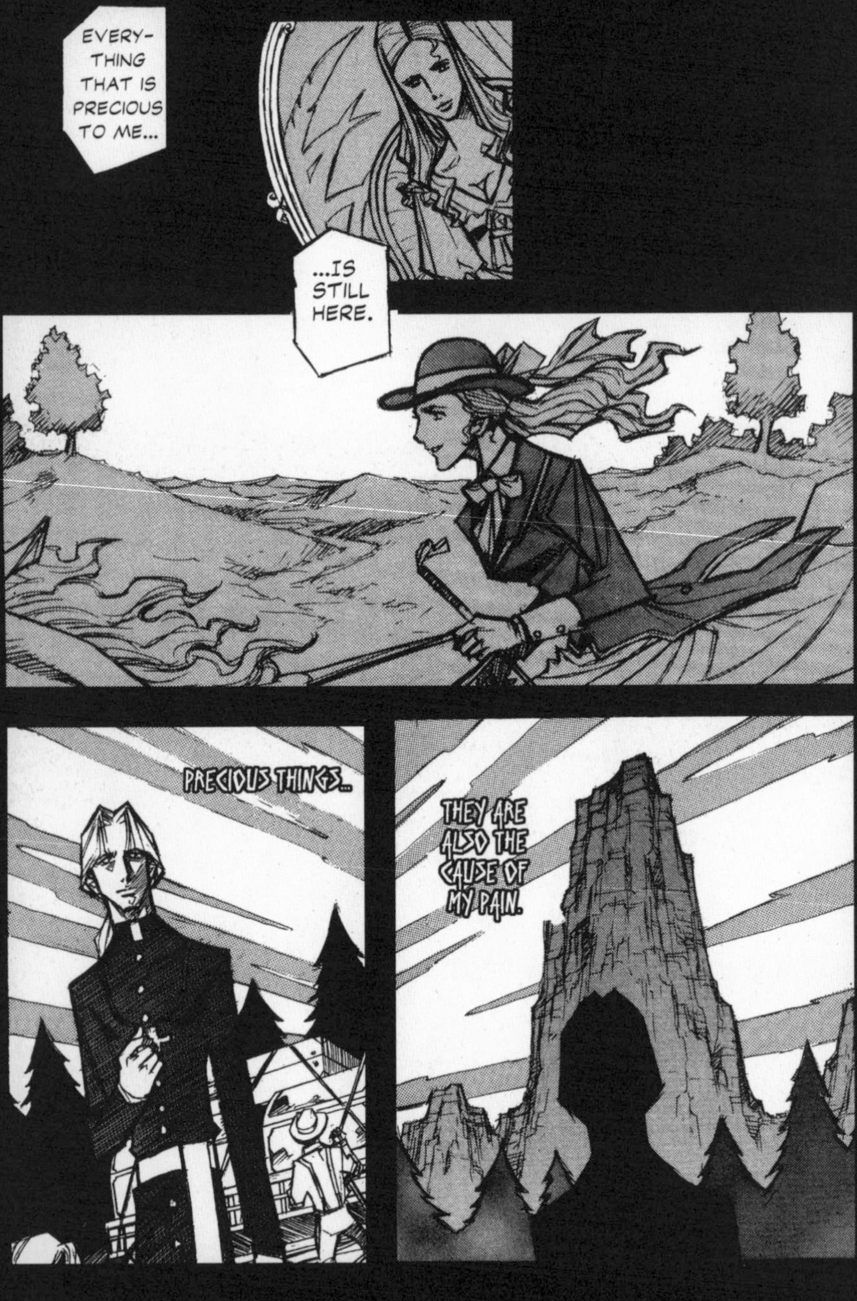
EVERY-THING THAT IS PRECIOUS TO ME...
...IS STILL HERE.
PRECIOUS THINGS...
THEY ARE ALSO THE CAUSE OF MY PAIN.

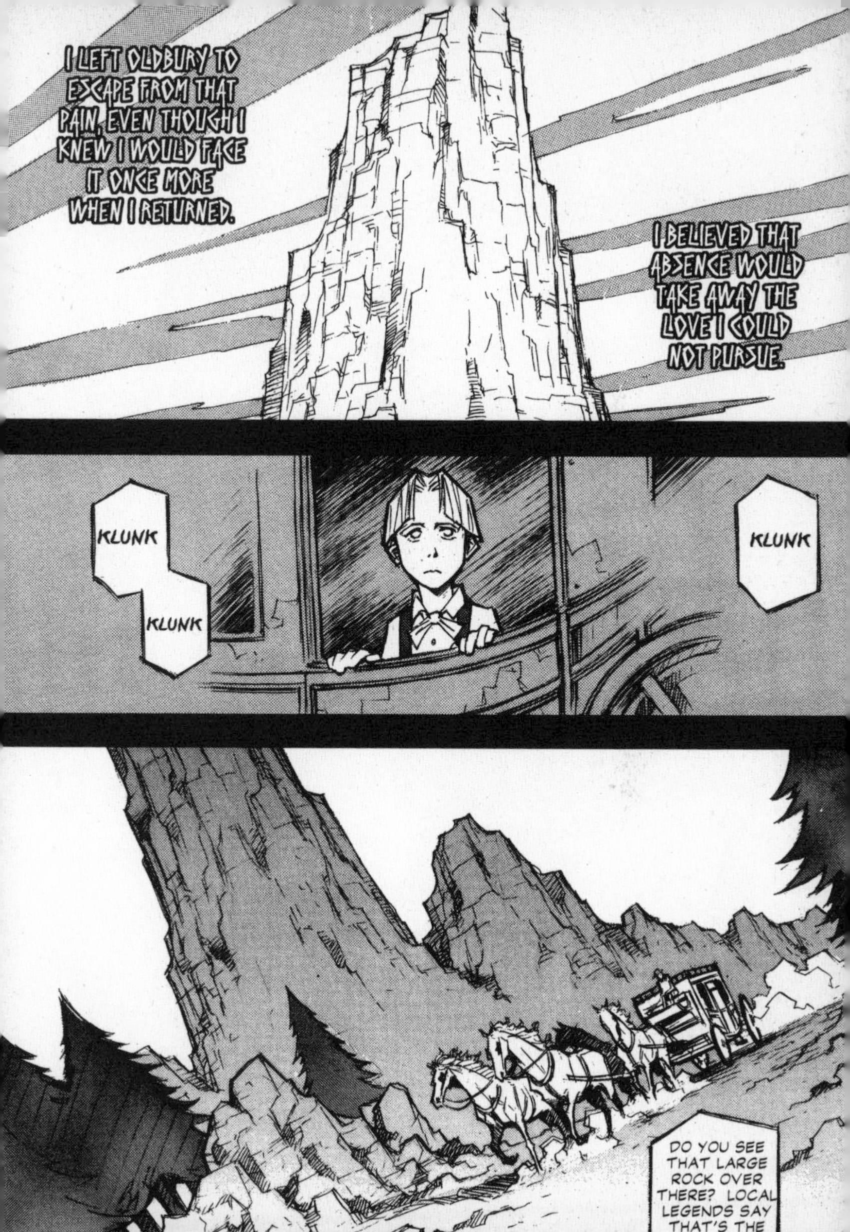
I LEFT OLDBURY TO ESCAPE FROM THAT PAIN, EVEN THOUGH I KNEW I WOULD FACE IT ONCE MORE WHEN I RETURNED.
I BELIEVED THAT ABSENCE WOULD TAKE AWAY THE LOVE I COULD NOT PURSUE.
KLUNK
KLUNK
KLUNK
DO YOU SEE THAT LARGE ROCK OVER THERE? LOCAL LEGENDS SAY THAT'S THE

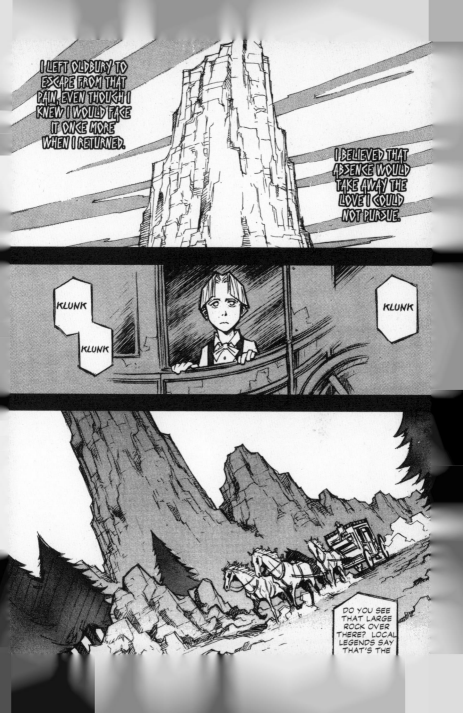

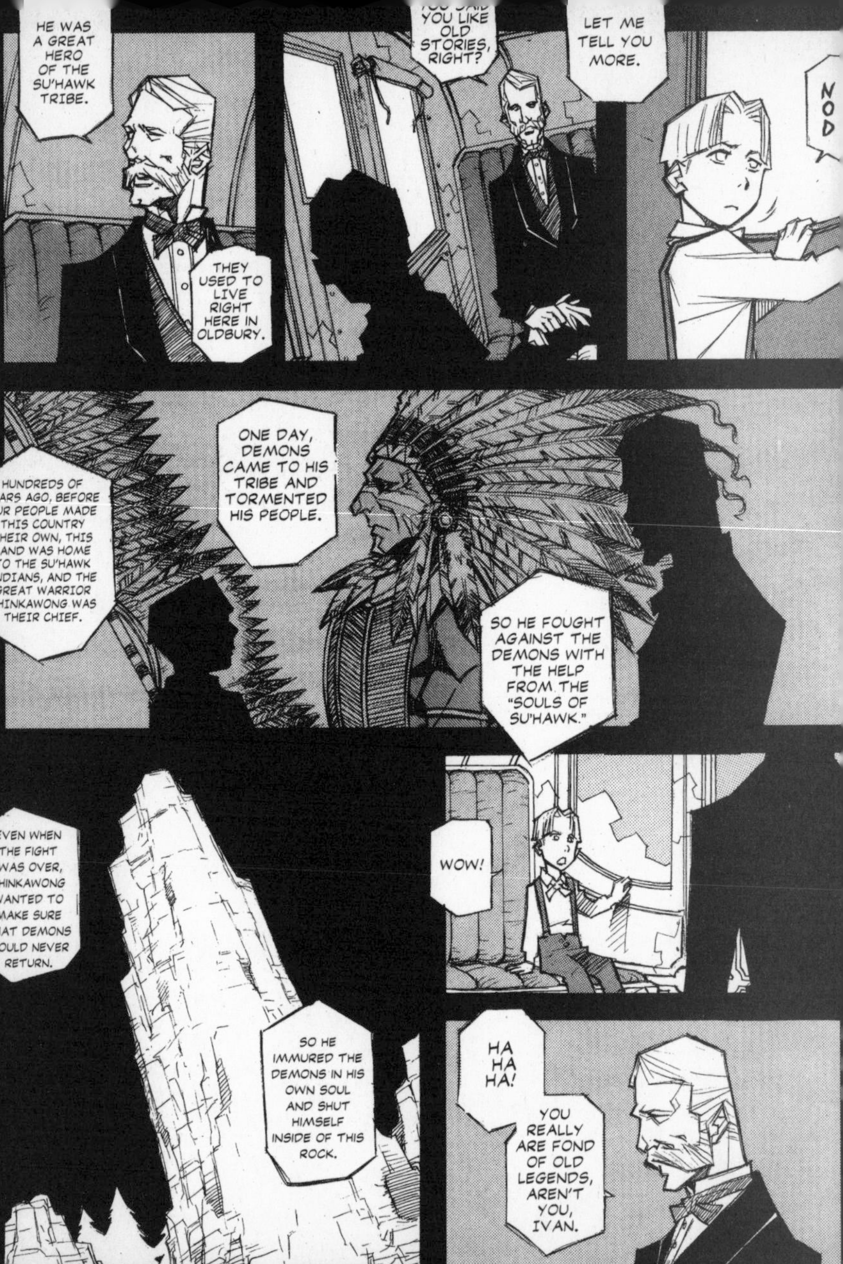
HE WAS A GREAT HERO OF THE SU'HAWK TRIBE.
THEY USED TO LIVE RIGHT HERE IN OLDBURY.
YOU LIKE OLD STORIES, RIGHT?
LET ME TELL YOU MORE.
NOD
HUNDREDS OF YEARS AGO, BEFORE OUR PEOPLE MADE THIS COUNTRY THEIR OWN, THIS LAND WAS HOME TO THE SU'HAWK INDIANS, AND THE GREAT WARRIOR CHINKAWONG WAS THEIR CHIEF.
ONE DAY, DEMONS CAME TO HIS TRIBE AND TORMENTED HIS PEOPLE.
SO HE FOUGHT AGAINST THE DEMONS WITH THE HELP FROM THE "SOULS OF SU'HAWK."
EVEN WHEN THE FIGHT WAS OVER, CHINKAWONG WANTED TO MAKE SURE THAT DEMONS WOULD NEVER RETURN.
SO HE IMMURED THE DEMONS IN HIS OWN SOUL AND SHUT HIMSELF INSIDE OF THIS ROCK.
WOW!
HA HA HA!
YOU REALLY ARE FOND OF OLD LEGENDS, AREN'T YOU, IVAN.

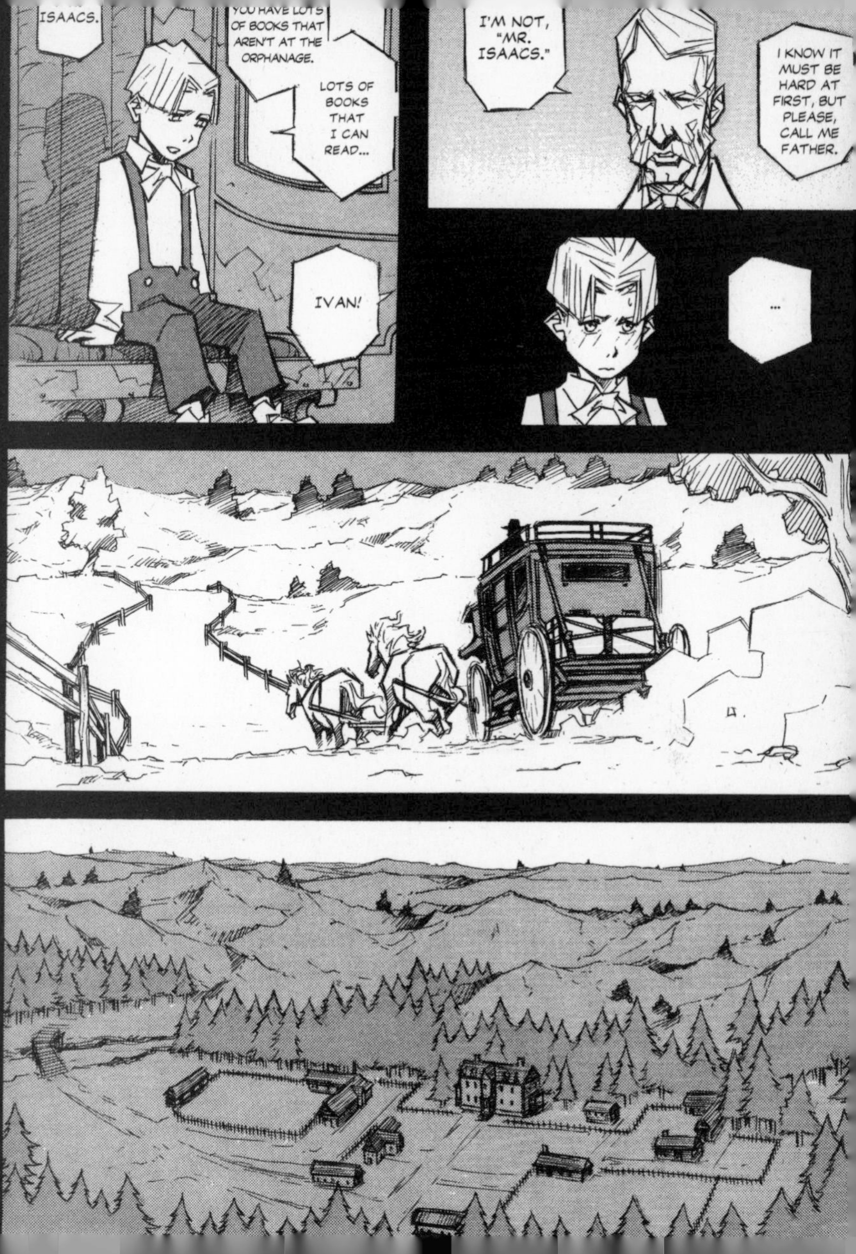
ISAACS.
YOU HAVE LOTS OF BOOKS THAT AREN'T AT THE ORPHANAGE.
LOTS OF BOOKS THAT I CAN READ...
IVAN!
I'M NOT, "MR. ISAACS."
I KNOW IT MUST BE HARD AT FIRST, BUT PLEASE, CALL ME FATHER.
...

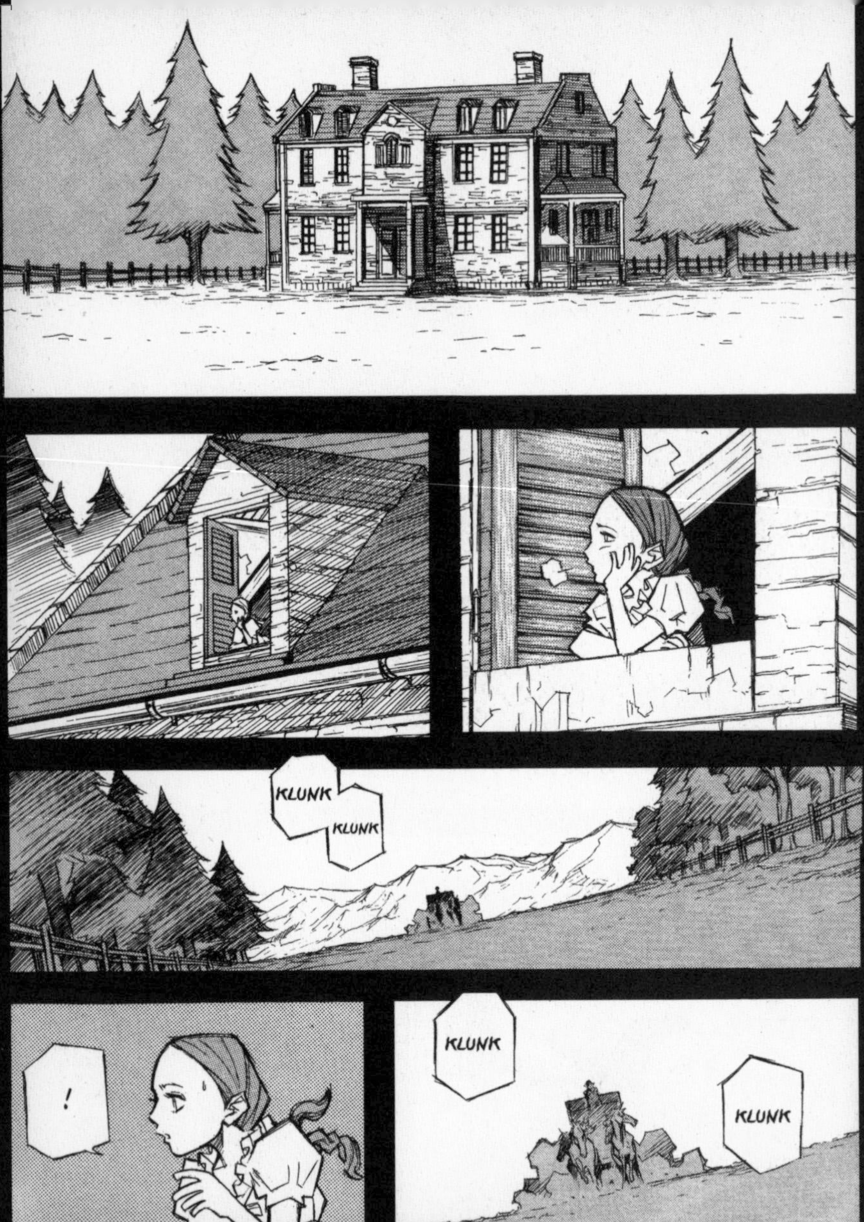
KLUNK
KLUNK
!
KLUNK
KLUNK

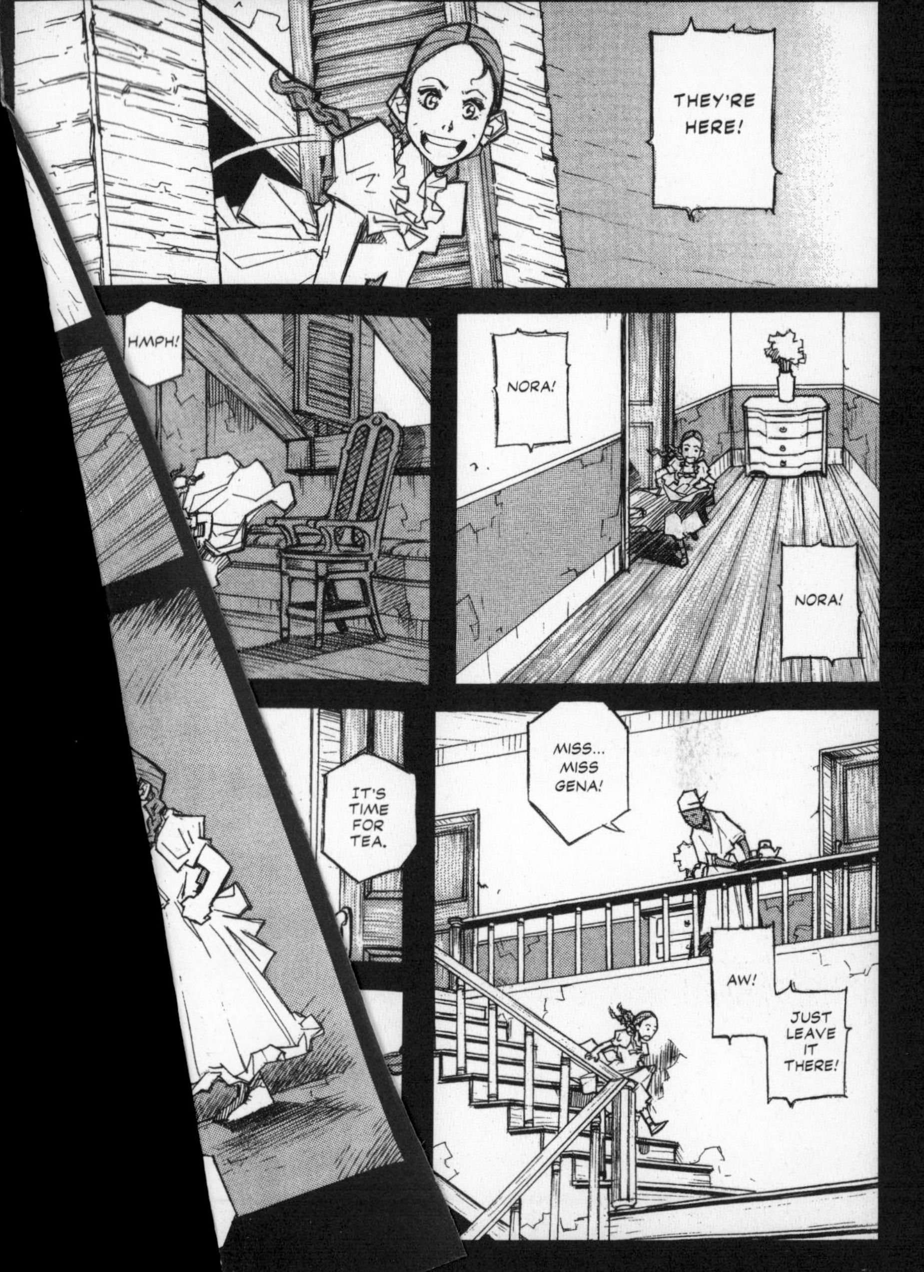
THEY'RE HERE!
HMPH!
NORA!
NORA!
IT'S TIME FOR TEA.
MISS... MISS GENA!
AW!
JUST LEAVE IT THERE!

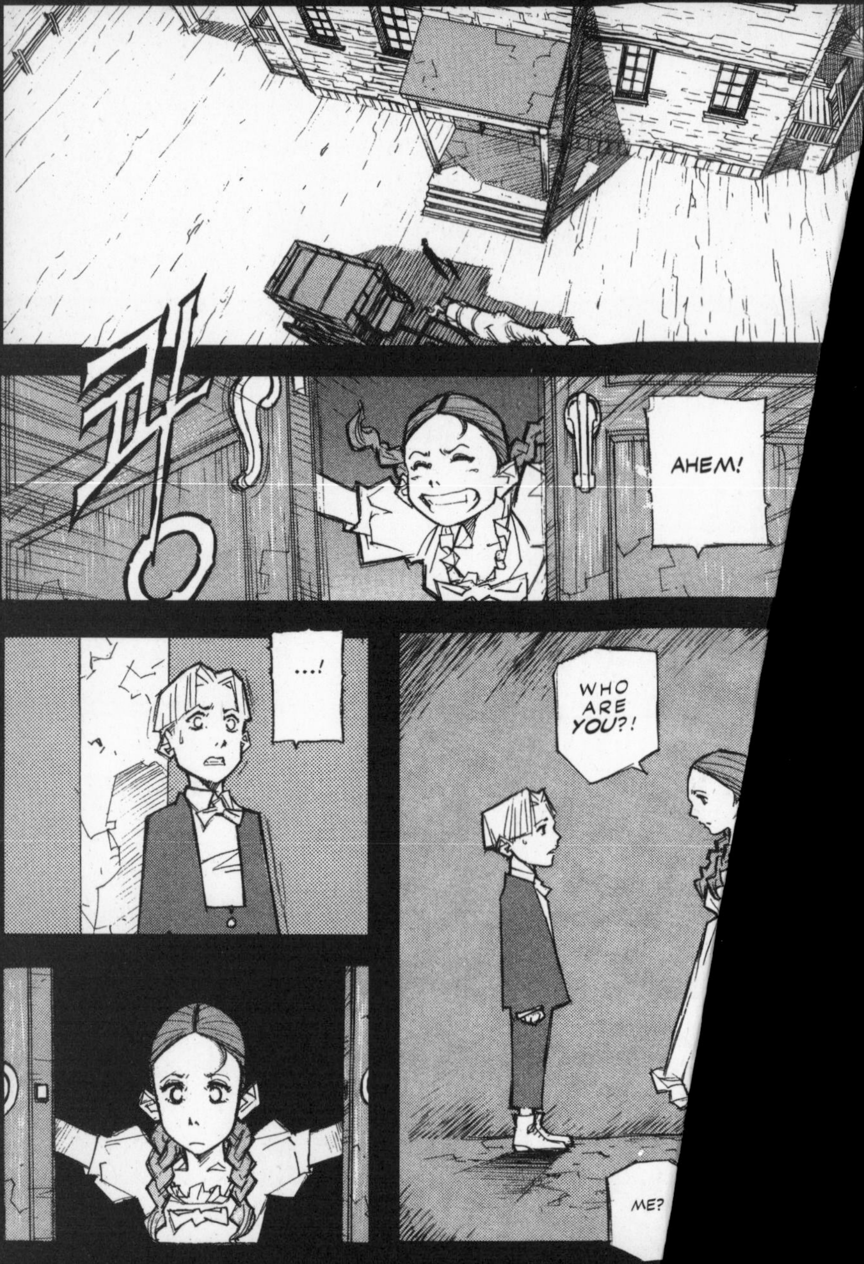
AHEM!
...!
WHO ARE YOU?!
ME?

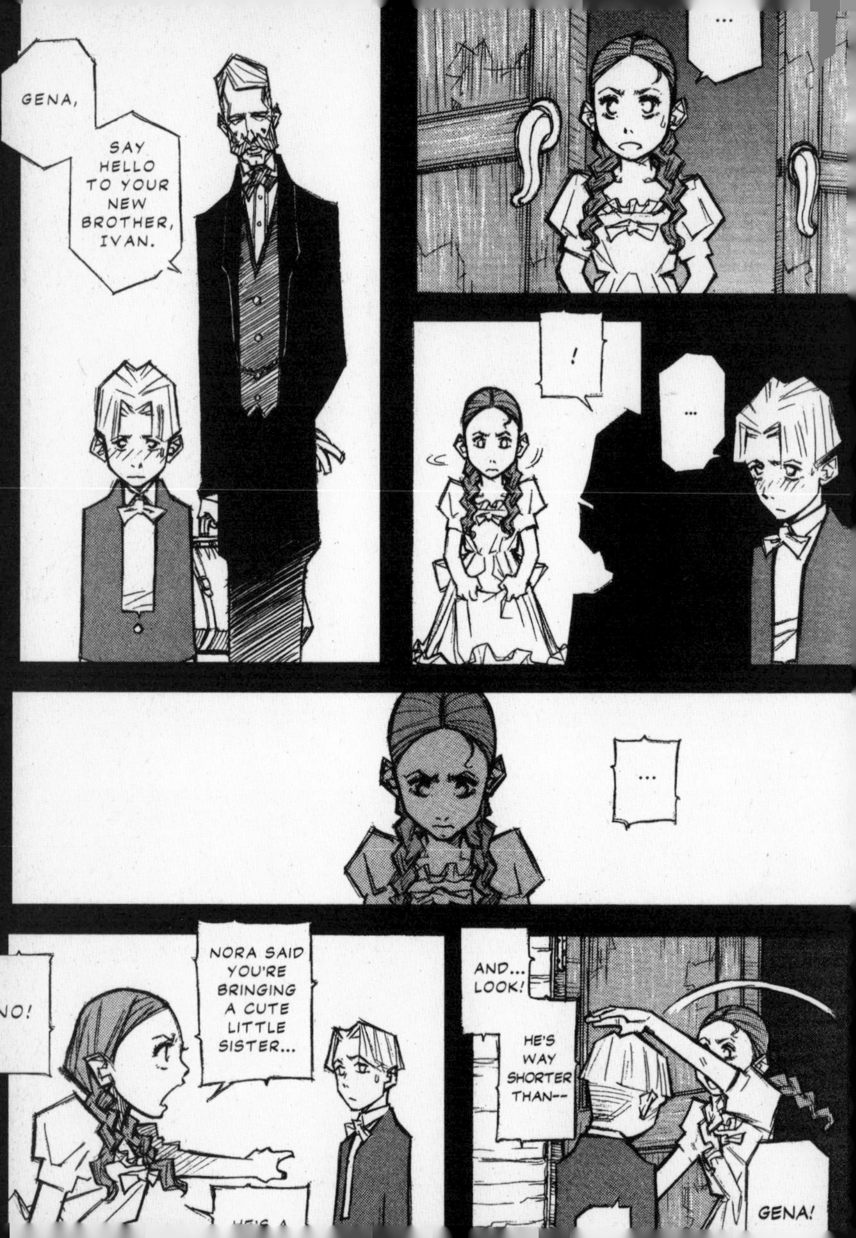
GENA,
SAY HELLO TO YOUR NEW BROTHER, IVAN.
...
!
...
...
NO!
NORA SAID YOU'RE BRINGING A CUTE LITTLE SISTER...
AND... LOOK!
HE'S WAY SHORTER THAN--
GENA!

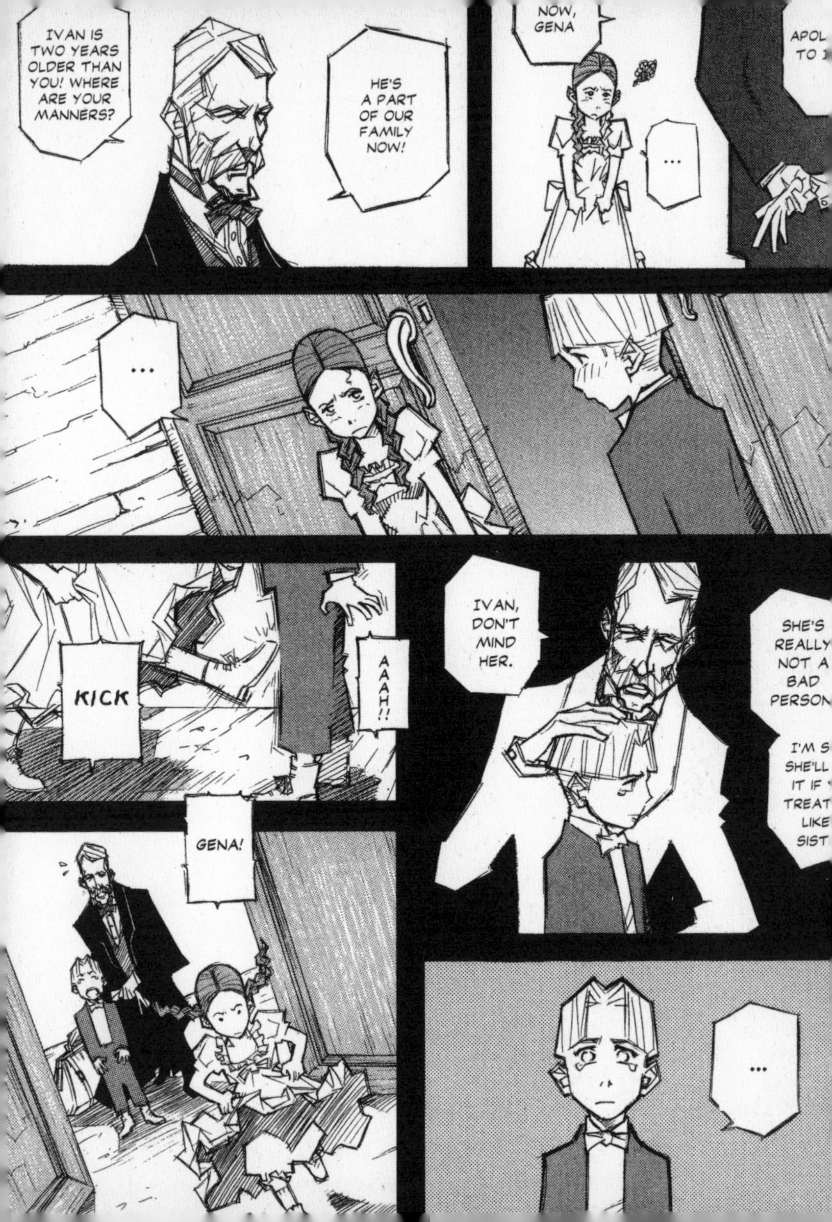
IVAN IS TWO YEARS OLDER THAN YOU! WHERE ARE YOUR MANNERS?
HE'S A PART OF OUR FAMILY NOW!
NOW, GENA
...
...
KICK
AAAAH!!
GENA!
IVAN, DON'T MIND HER.
SHE'S REALLY NOT A BAD PERSON
...

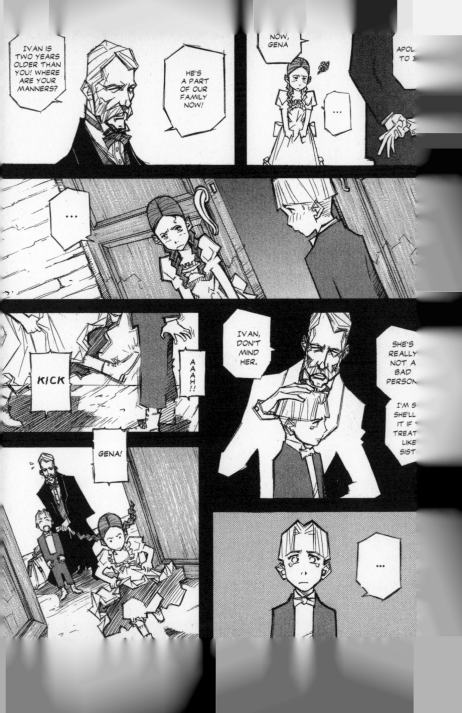

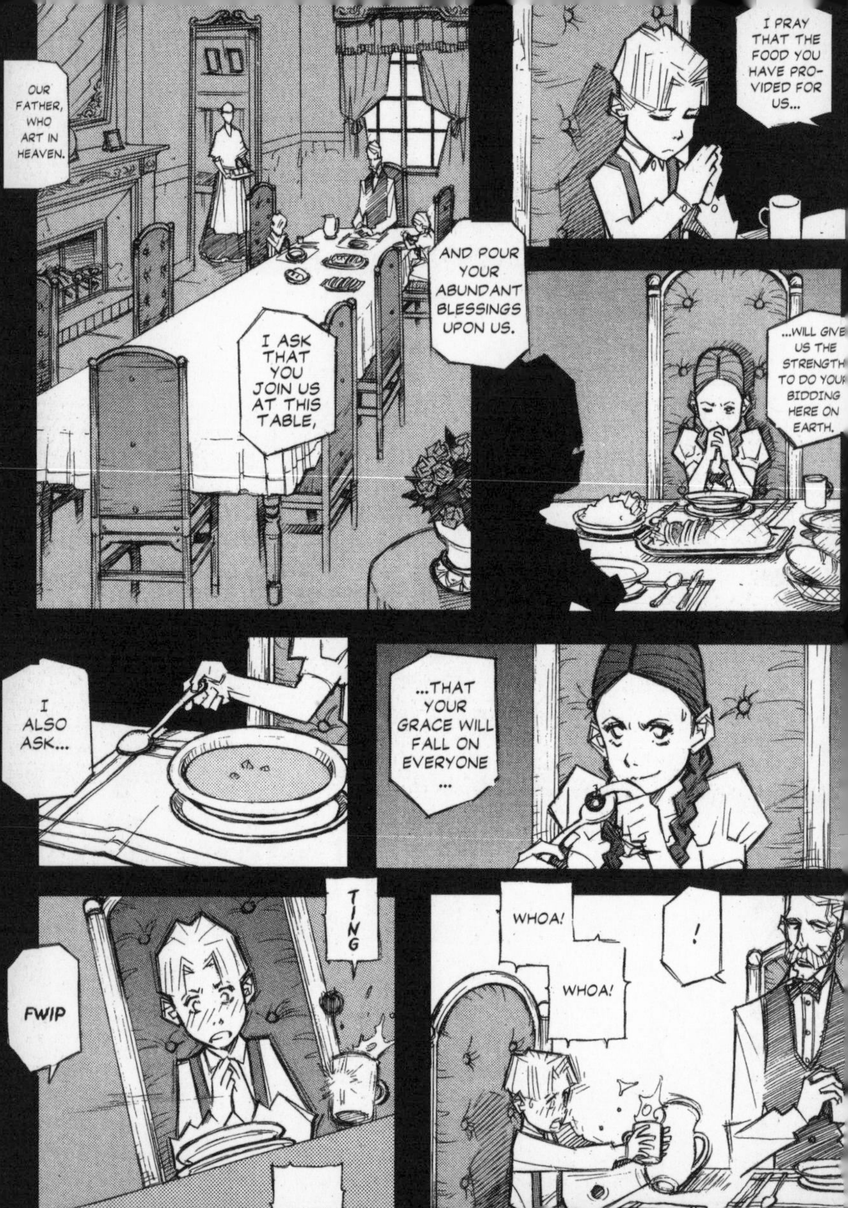
OUR FATHER, WHO ART IN HEAVEN.
I ASK THAT YOU JOIN US AT THIS TABLE,
AND POUR YOUR ABUNDANT BLESSINGS UPON US.
I PRAY THAT THE FOOD YOU HAVE PRO-VIDED FOR US...
...WILL GIVE US THE STRENGTH TO DO YOUR BIDDING HERE ON EARTH.
I ALSO ASK...
...THAT YOUR GRACE WILL FALL ON EVERYONE ...
FWIP
TING
WHOA!
WHOA!
!

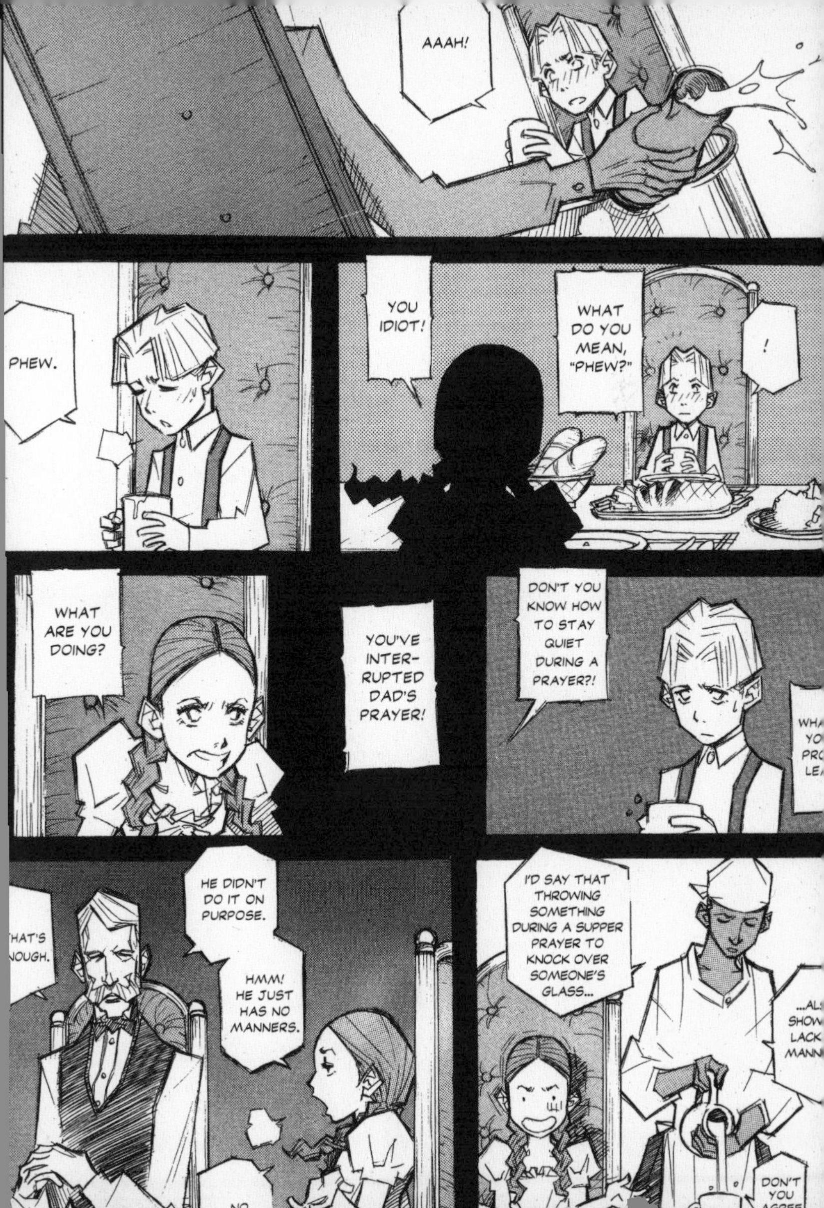
AAAH!
PHEW.
YOU IDIOT!
WHAT DO YOU MEAN, "PHEW?"
!
WHAT ARE YOU DOING?
YOU'VE INTER-RUPTED DAD'S PRAYER!
DON'T YOU KNOW HOW TO STAY QUIET DURING A PRAYER?!
WHA YO PRO LEA
HAT'S NOUGH.
HE DIDN'T DO IT ON PURPOSE.
HMM! HE JUST HAS NO MANNERS.
NO
I'D SAY THAT THROWING SOMETHING DURING A SUPPER PRAYER TO KNOCK OVER SOMEONE'S GLASS...
...ALS SHOW LACK MANN
DON'T YOU

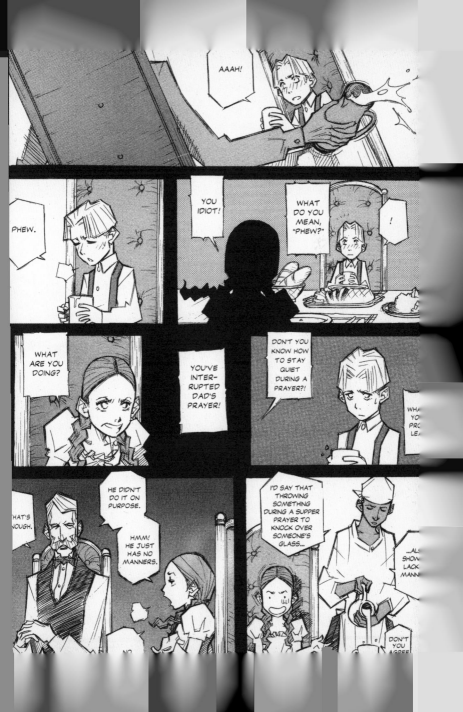

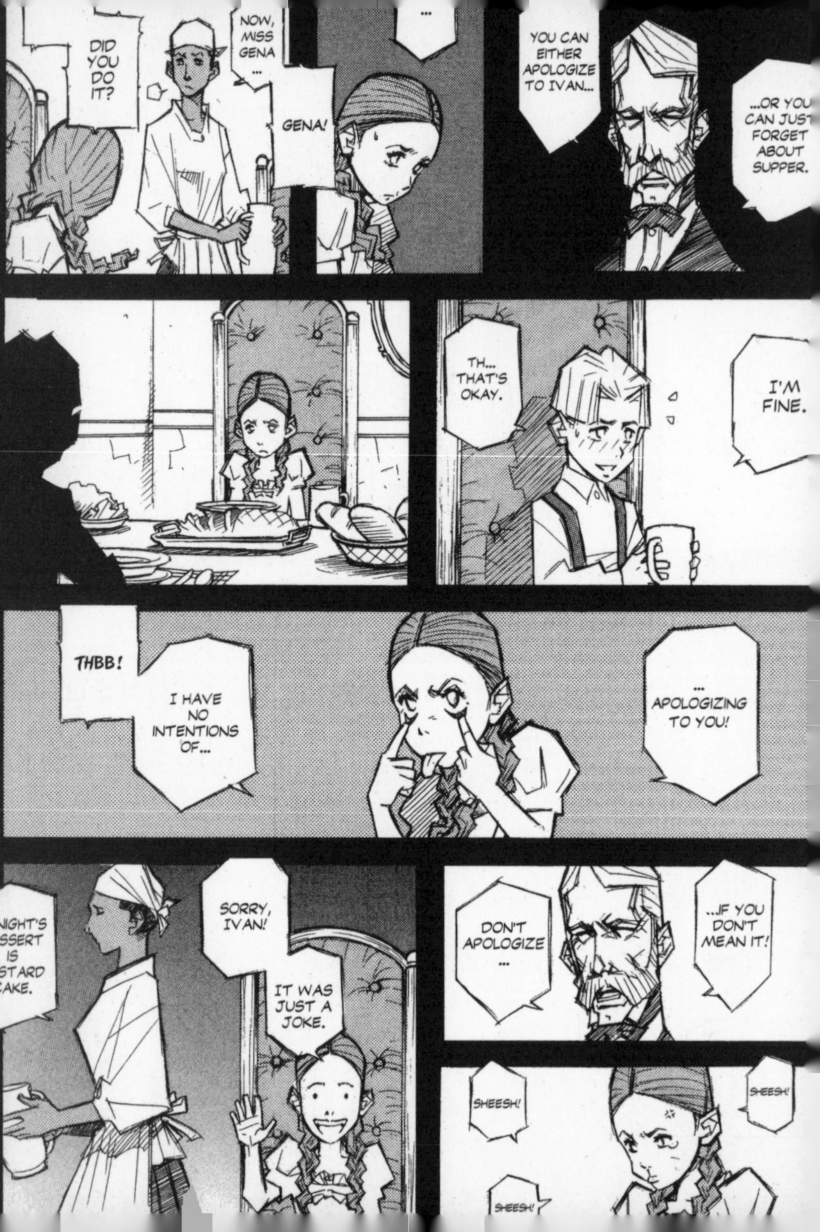
DID YOU DO IT?
NOW, MISS GENA ...
GENA!
...
YOU CAN EITHER APOLOGIZE TO IVAN...
...OR YOU CAN JUST FORGET ABOUT SUPPER.
TH... THAT'S OKAY.
I'M FINE.
THBB!
I HAVE NO INTENTIONS OF...
... APOLOGIZING TO YOU!
TONIGHT'S DESSERT IS CUSTARD CAKE.
SORRY, IVAN!
IT WAS JUST A JOKE.
DON'T APOLOGIZE ...
...IF YOU DON'T MEAN IT!
SHEESH!
SHEESH!
SHEESH!

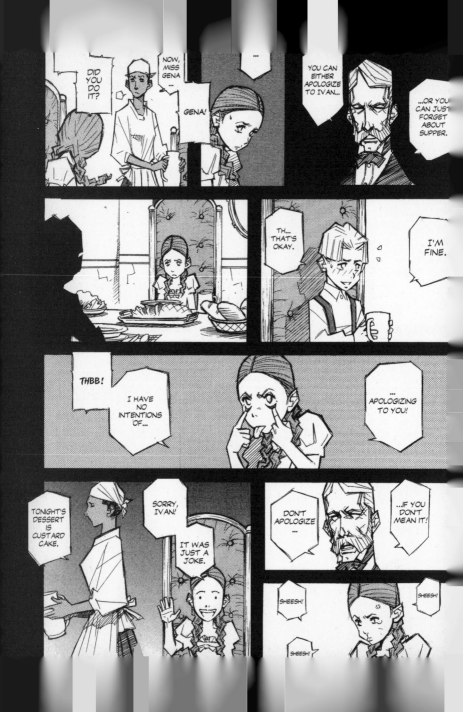

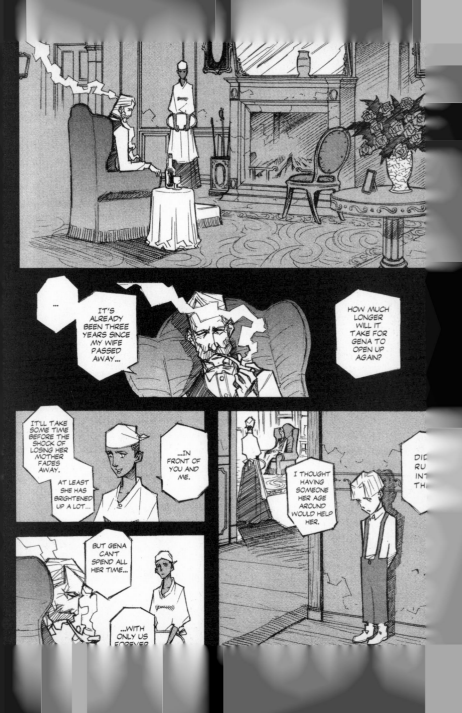

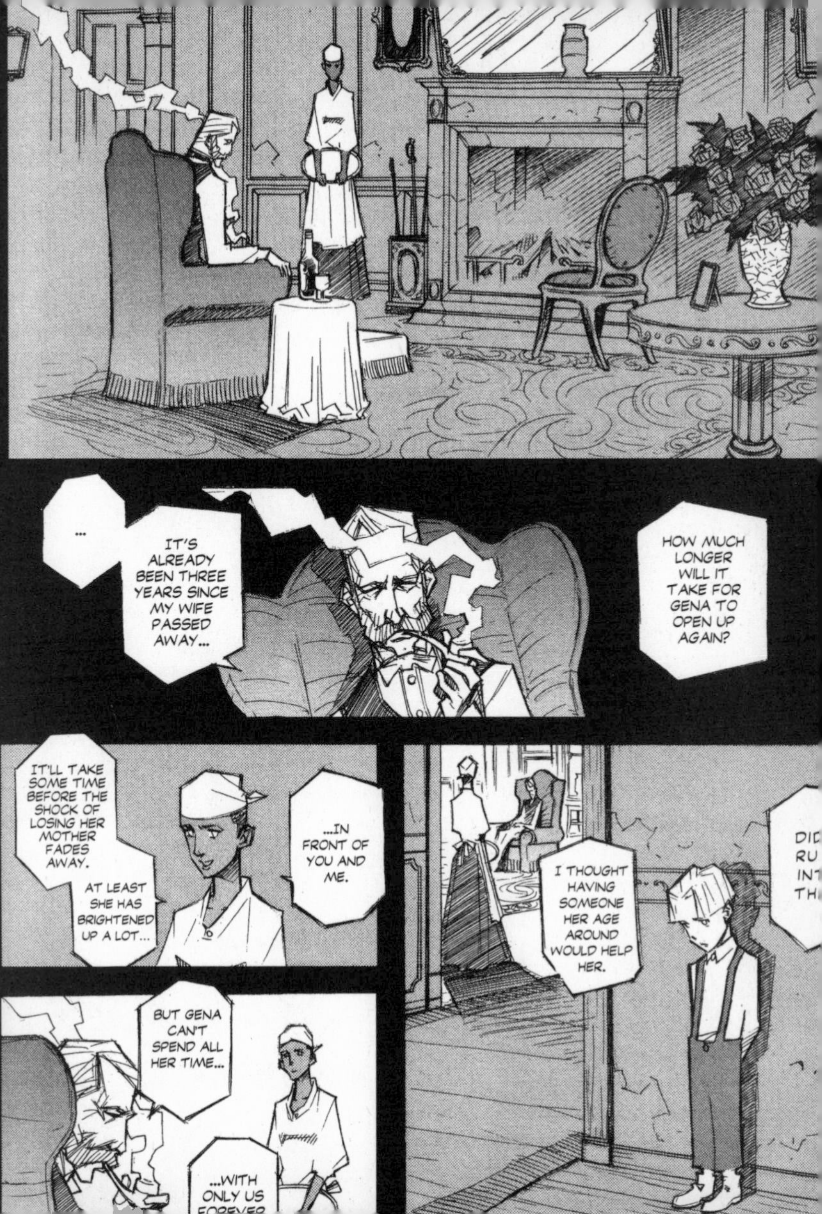
...
IT'S ALREADY BEEN THREE YEARS SINCE MY WIFE PASSED AWAY...
HOW MUCH LONGER WILL IT TAKE FOR GENA TO OPEN UP AGAIN?
IT'LL TAKE SOME TIME BEFORE THE SHOCK OF LOSING HER MOTHER FADES AWAY.
AT LEAST SHE HAS BRIGHTENED UP A LOT...
...IN FRONT OF YOU AND ME.
BUT GENA CAN'T SPEND ALL HER TIME...
...WITH ONLY US
I THOUGHT HAVING SOMEONE HER AGE AROUND WOULD HELP HER.

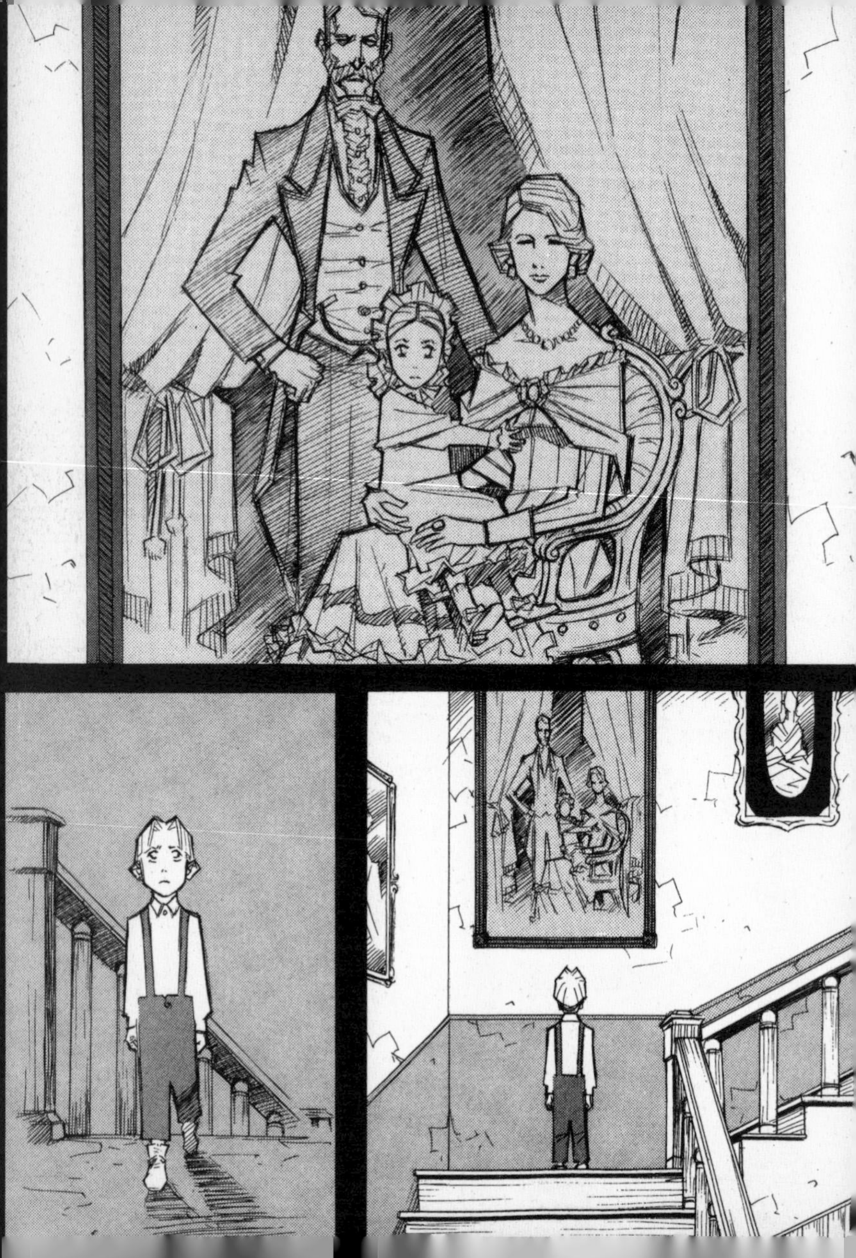

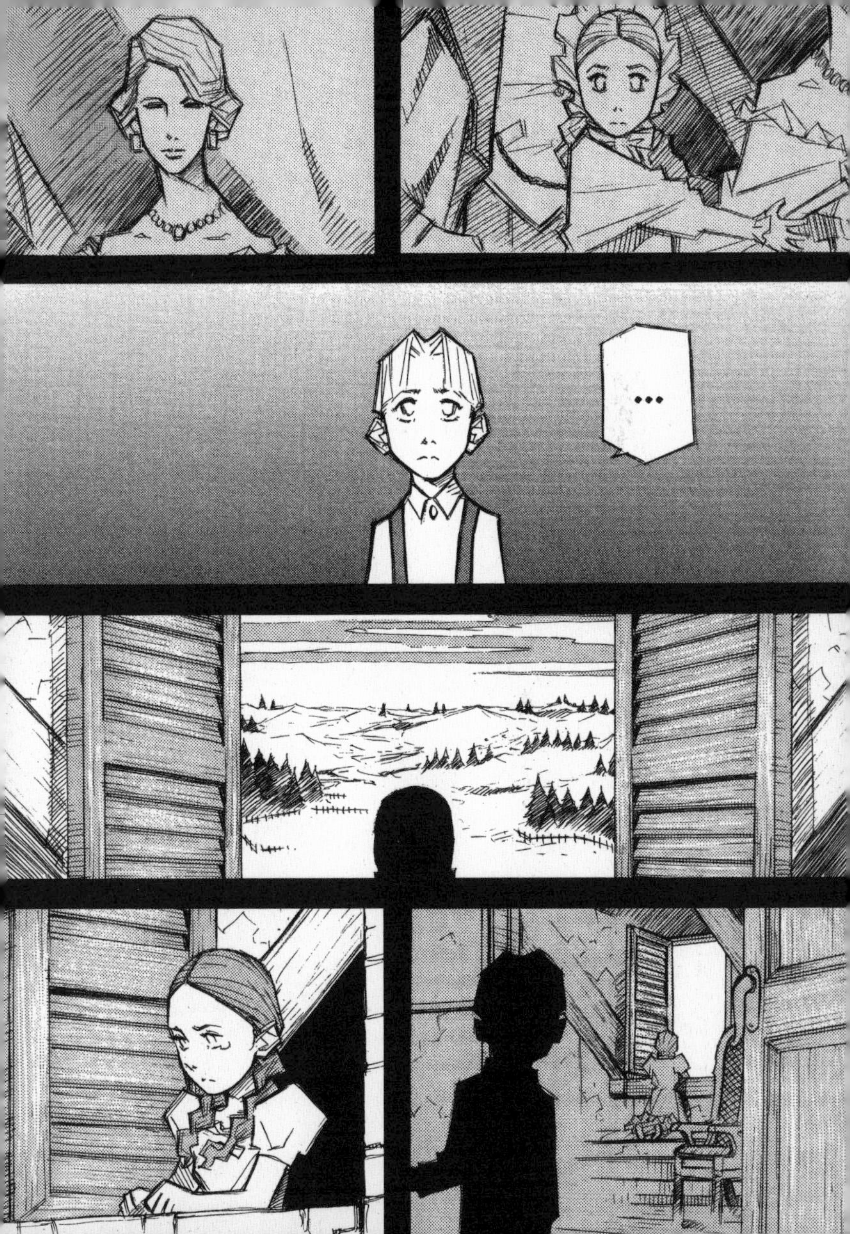
...

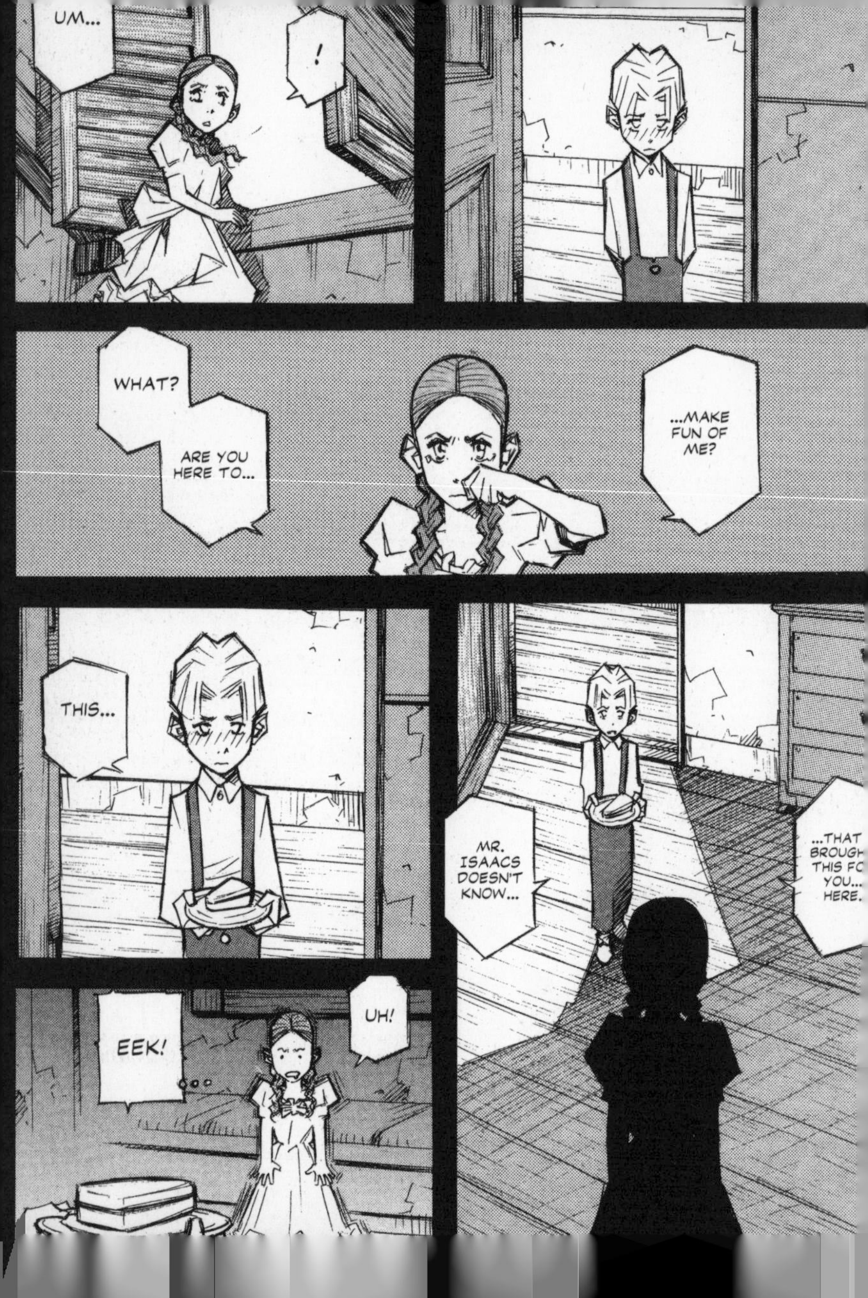
UM...
!
WHAT?
ARE YOU HERE TO...
...MAKE FUN OF ME?
THIS...
MR. ISAACS DOESN'T KNOW...
...THAT BROUGH THIS FO YOU... HERE.
EEK!
UH!

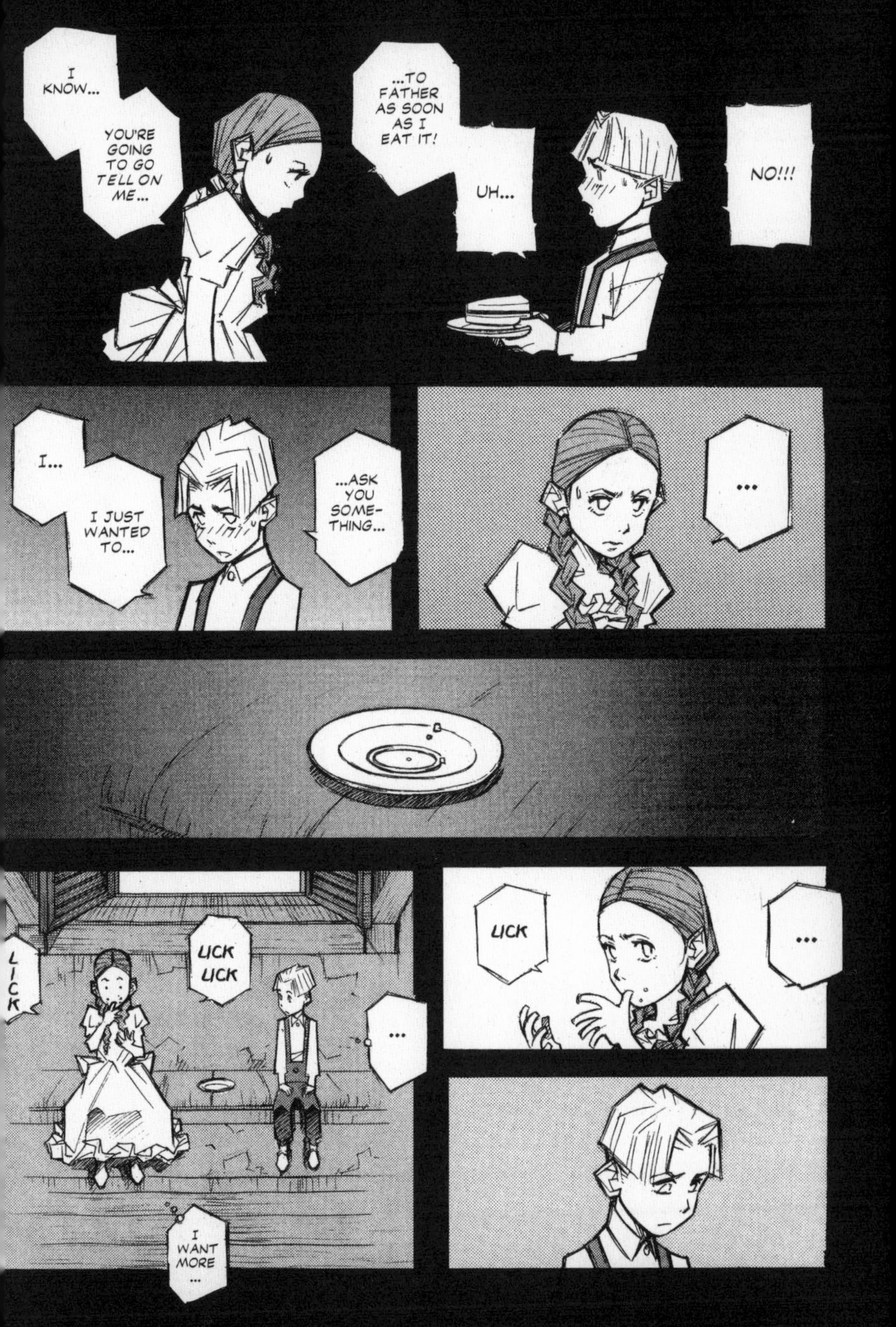
I KNOW...
YOU'RE GOING TO GO TELL ON ME...
...TO FATHER AS SOON AS I EAT IT!
UH...
NO!!!
I...
I JUST WANTED TO...
...ASK YOU SOME-THING...
...
LICK
LICK LICK
...
I WANT MORE ...
LICK
...

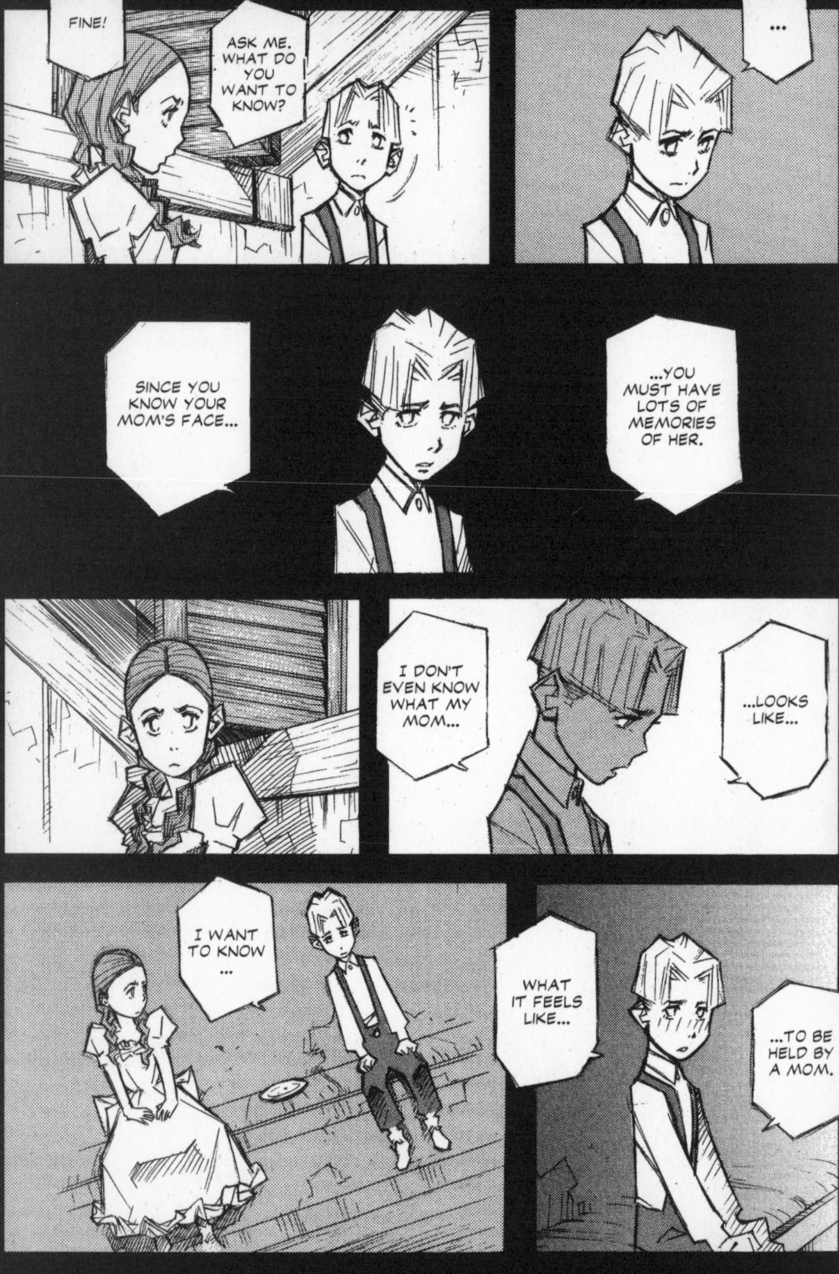
FINE!
ASK ME. WHAT DO YOU WANT TO KNOW?
...
SINCE YOU KNOW YOUR MOM'S FACE...
...YOU MUST HAVE LOTS OF MEMORIES OF HER.
I DON'T EVEN KNOW WHAT MY MOM...
...LOOKS LIKE...
I WANT TO KNOW ...
WHAT IT FEELS LIKE...
...TO BE HELD BY A MOM.

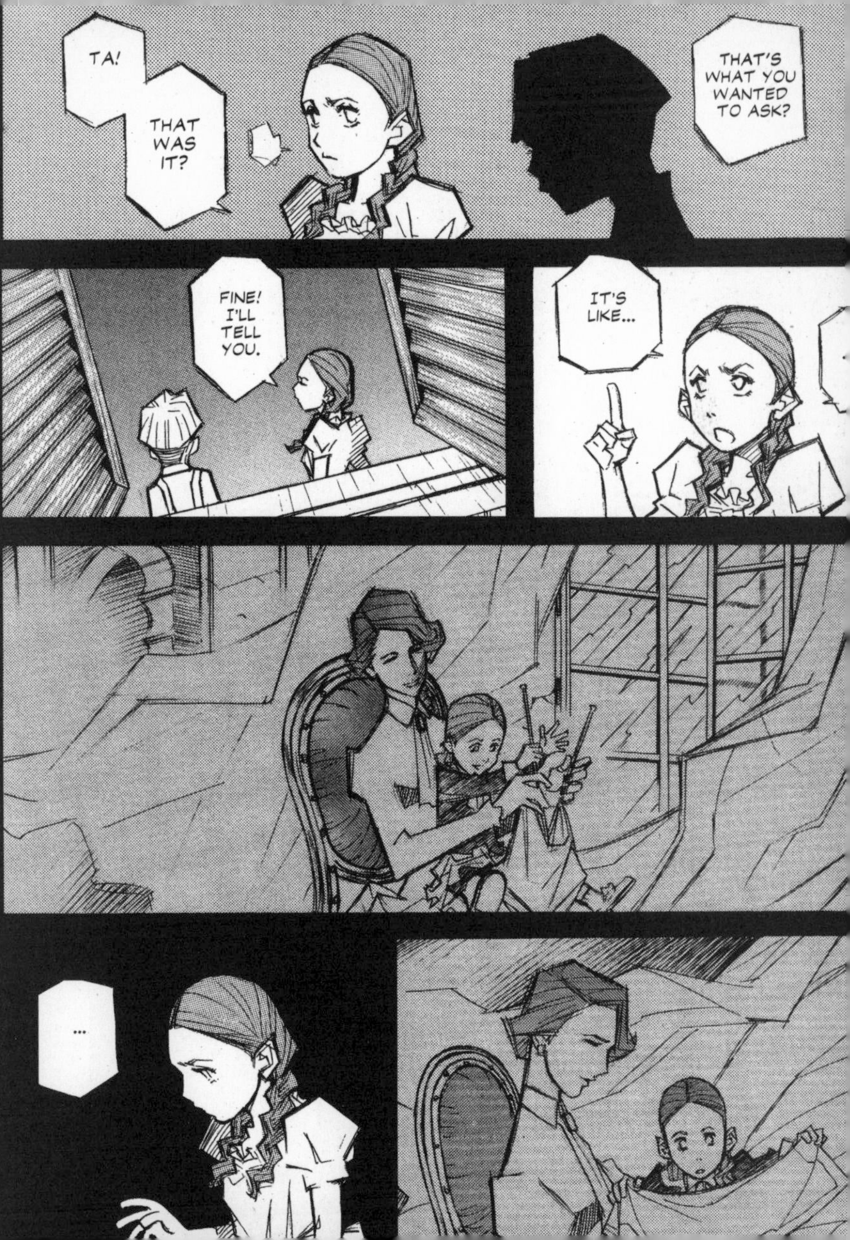
TA!
THAT WAS IT?
THAT'S WHAT YOU WANTED TO ASK?
FINE! I'LL TELL YOU.
IT'S LIKE...
...

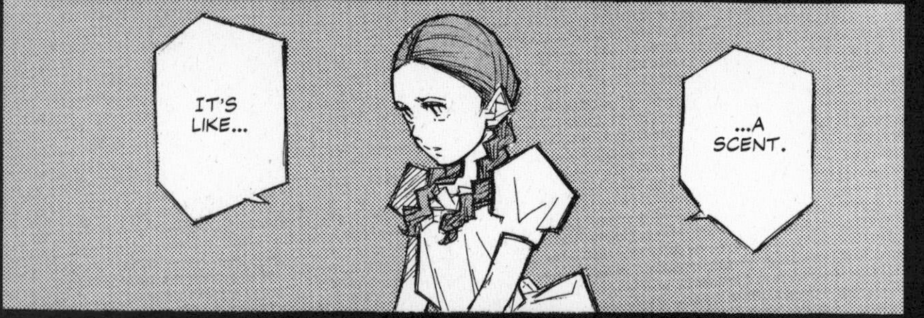
IT'S LIKE...
...A SCENT.
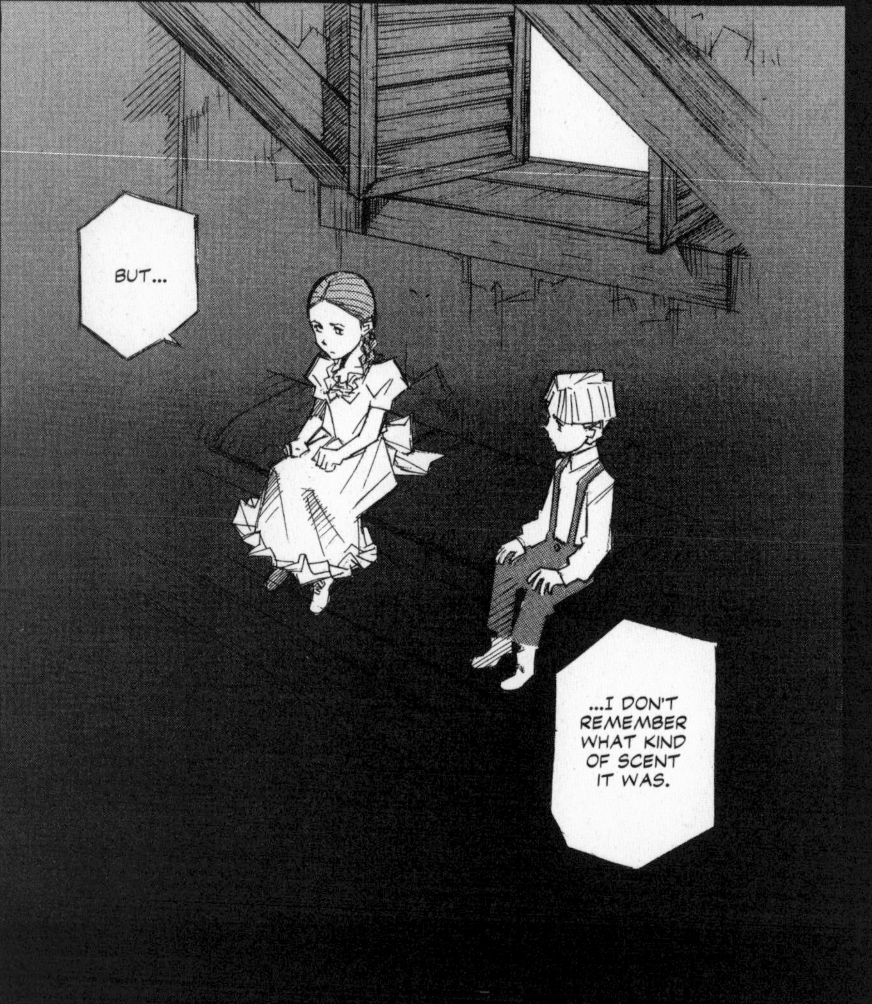
BUT...
...I DON'T REMEMBER WHAT KIND OF SCENT IT WAS.

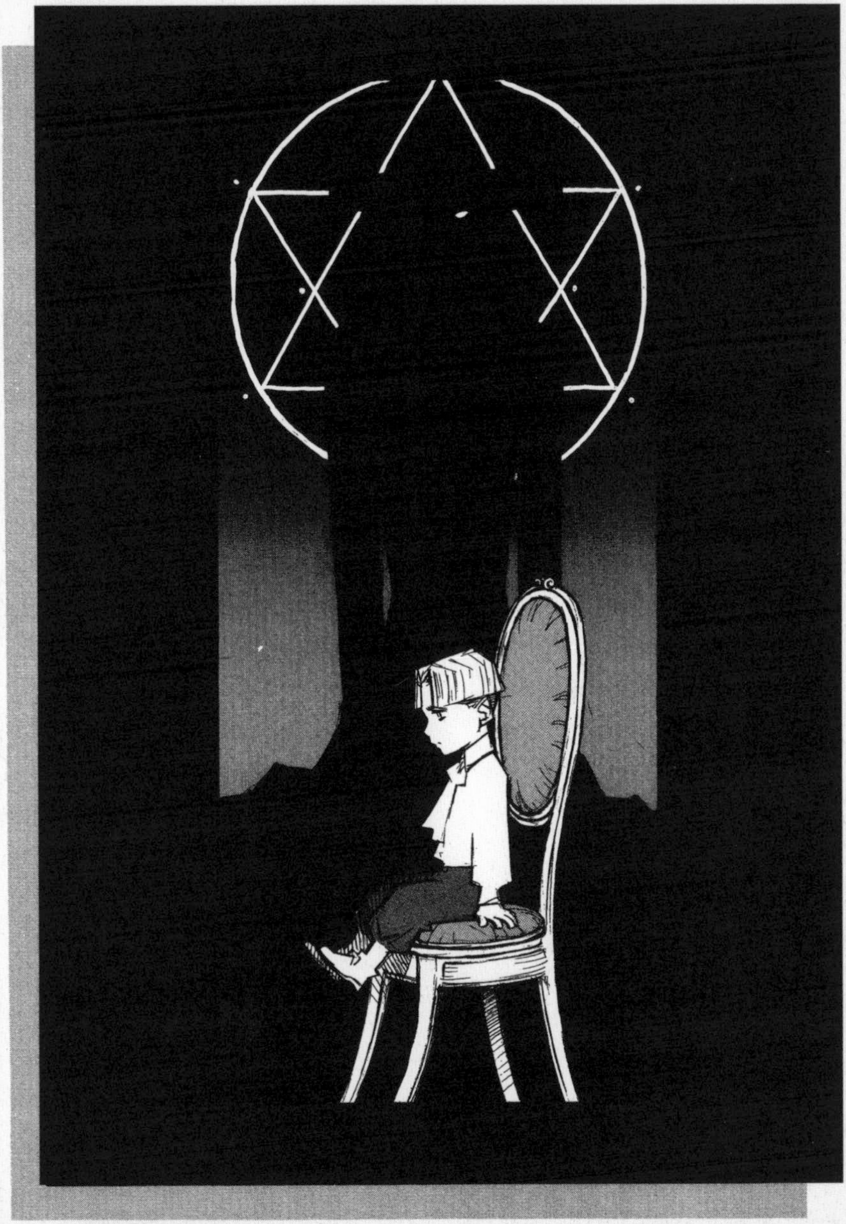

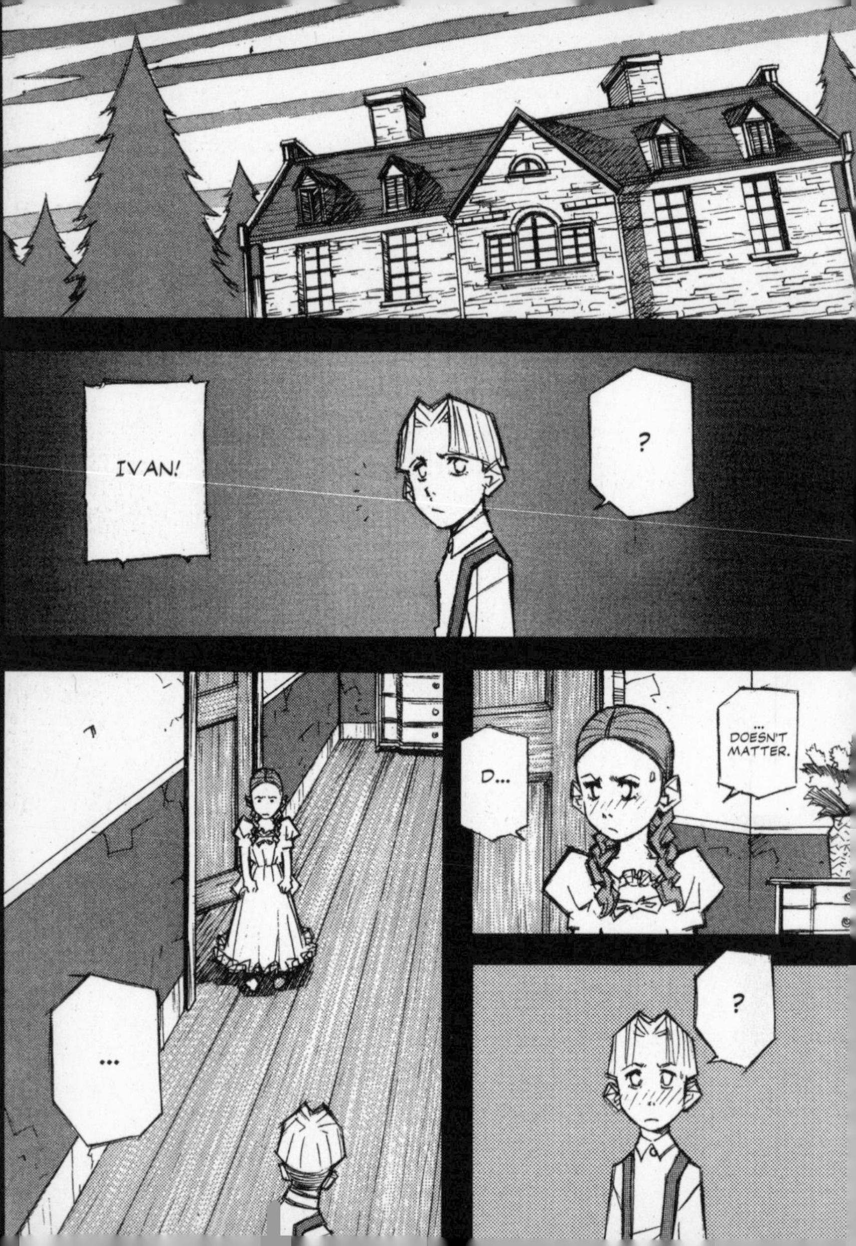
IVAN!
?
...
D...
... DOESN'T MATTER.
?

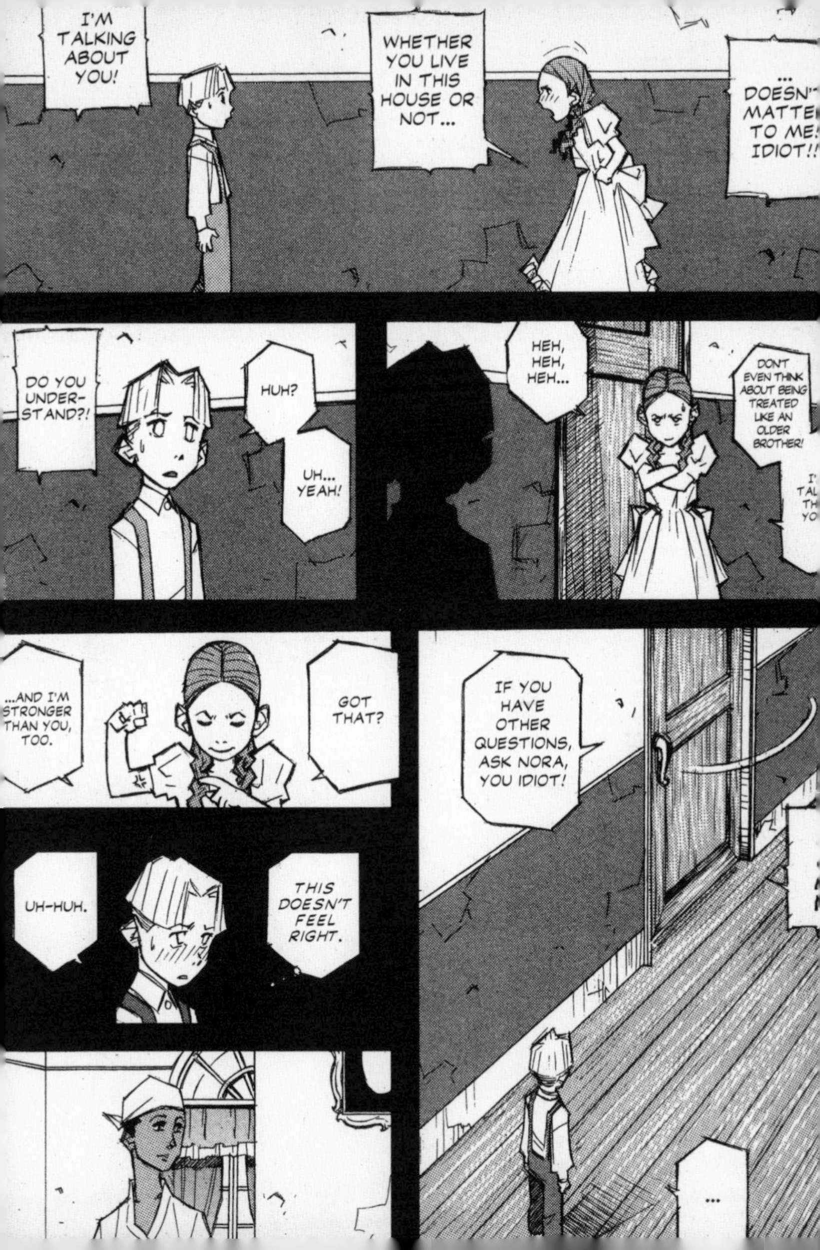
I'M TALKING ABOUT YOU!
WHETHER YOU LIVE IN THIS HOUSE OR NOT...
... DOESN' MATTE TO ME IDIOT!!
DO YOU UNDER-STAND?!
HUH?
UH... YEAH!
HEH, HEH, HEH...
DONT EVEN THINK ABOUT BEING TREATED LIKE AN OLDER BROTHER!
...AND I'M STRONGER THAN YOU, TOO.
GOT THAT?
IF YOU HAVE OTHER QUESTIONS, ASK NORA, YOU IDIOT!
UH-HUH.
THIS DOESN'T FEEL RIGHT.
...

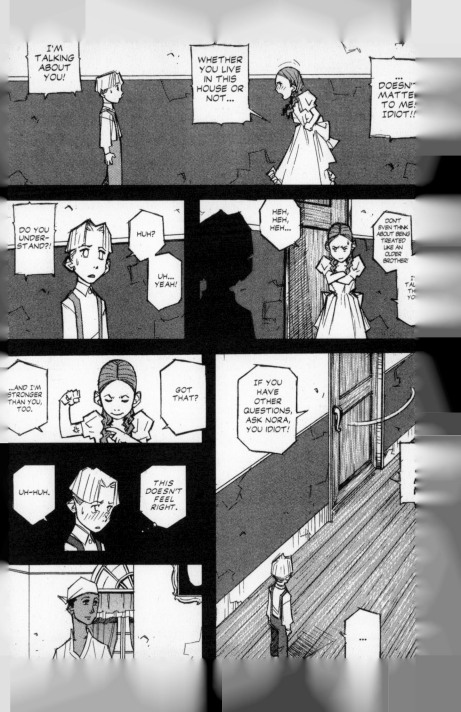

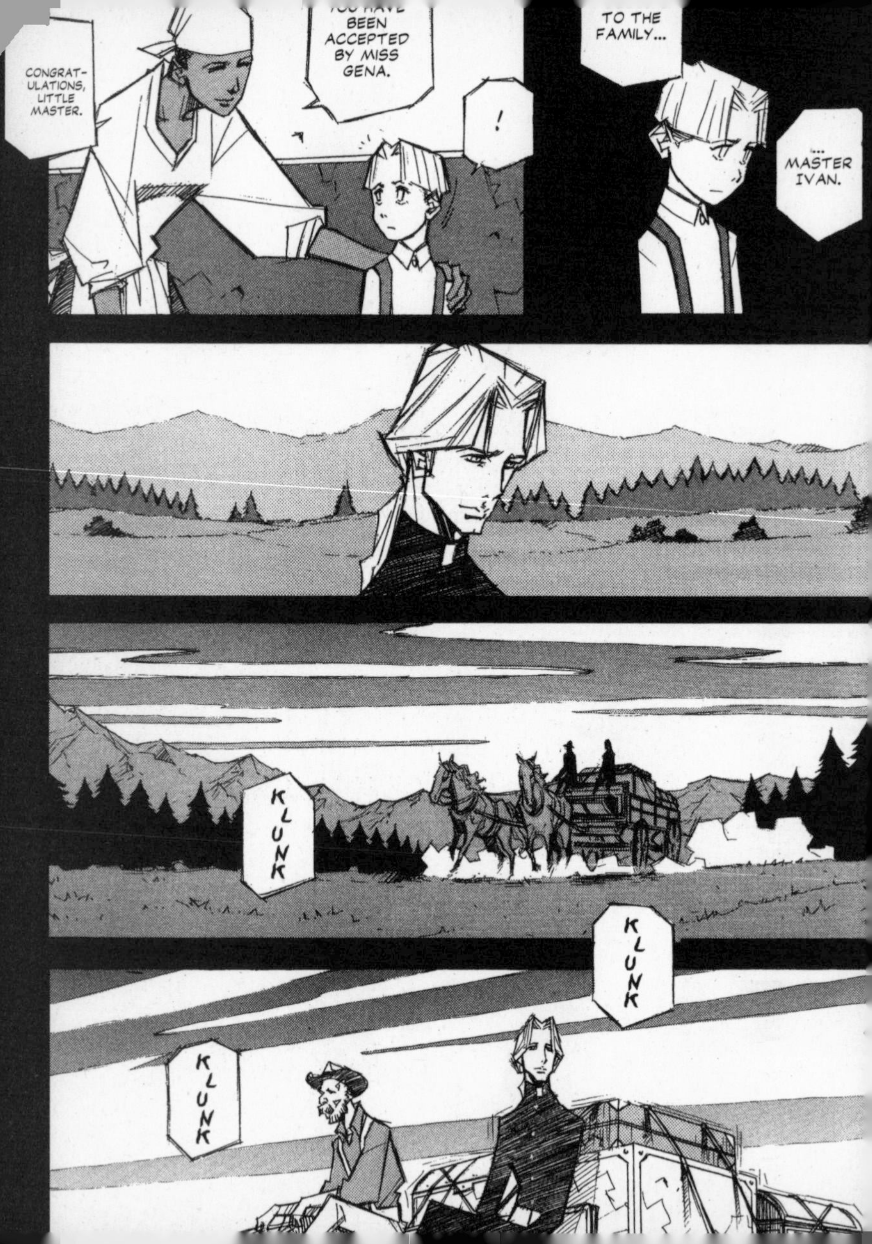

CONGRAT-ULATIONS, LITTLE MASTER.
BEEN ACCEPTED BY MISS GENA.
!
TO THE FAMILY...
...MASTER IVAN.
KLUNK
KLUNK
KLUNK

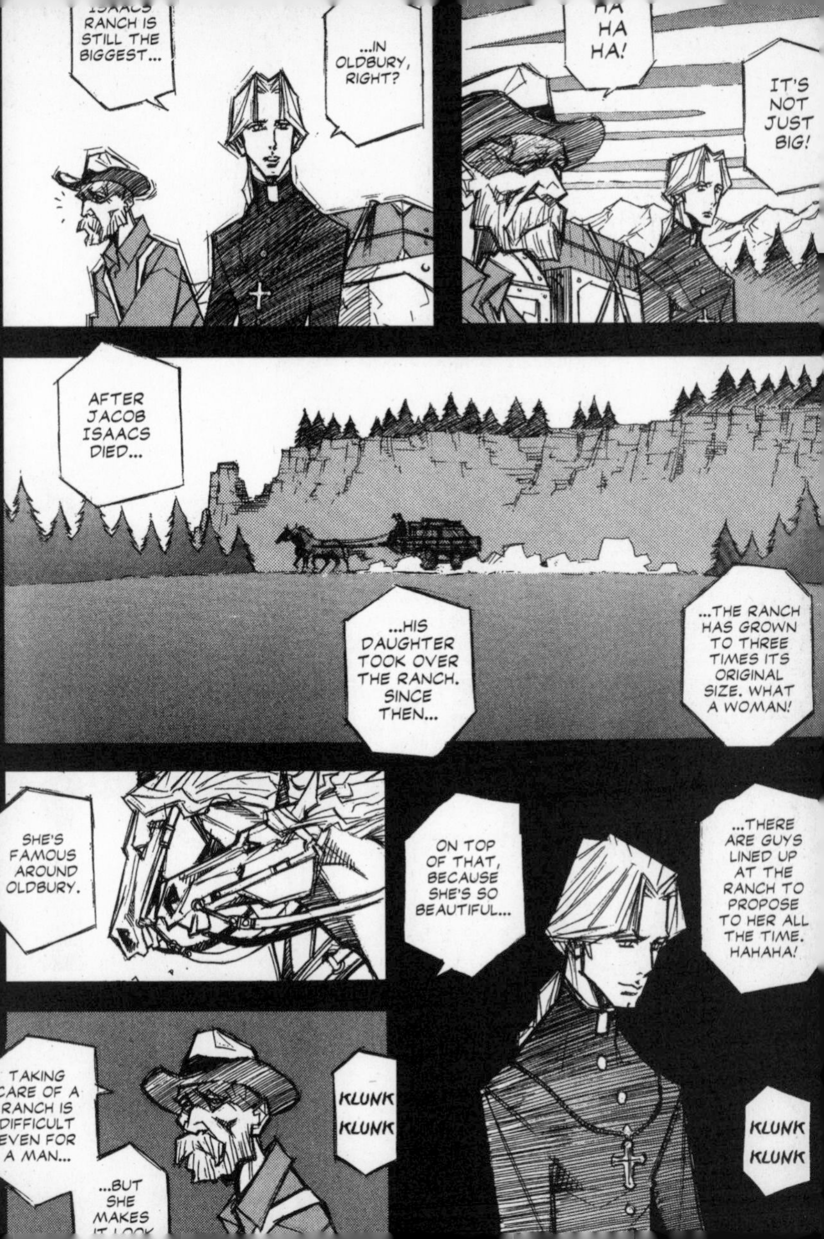
ISAACS RANCH IS STILL THE BIGGEST...
...IN OLDBURY, RIGHT?
HA HA!
IT'S NOT JUST BIG!
AFTER JACOB ISAACS DIED...
...HIS DAUGHTER TOOK OVER THE RANCH. SINCE THEN...
...THE RANCH HAS GROWN TO THREE TIMES ITS ORIGINAL SIZE. WHAT A WOMAN!
SHE'S FAMOUS AROUND OLDBURY.
TAKING CARE OF A RANCH IS DIFFICULT EVEN FOR A MAN...
...BUT SHE MAKES
KLUNK KLUNK
ON TOP OF THAT, BECAUSE SHE'S SO BEAUTIFUL...
...THERE ARE GUYS LINED UP AT THE RANCH TO PROPOSE TO HER ALL THE TIME. HAHAHA!
KLUNK KLUNK

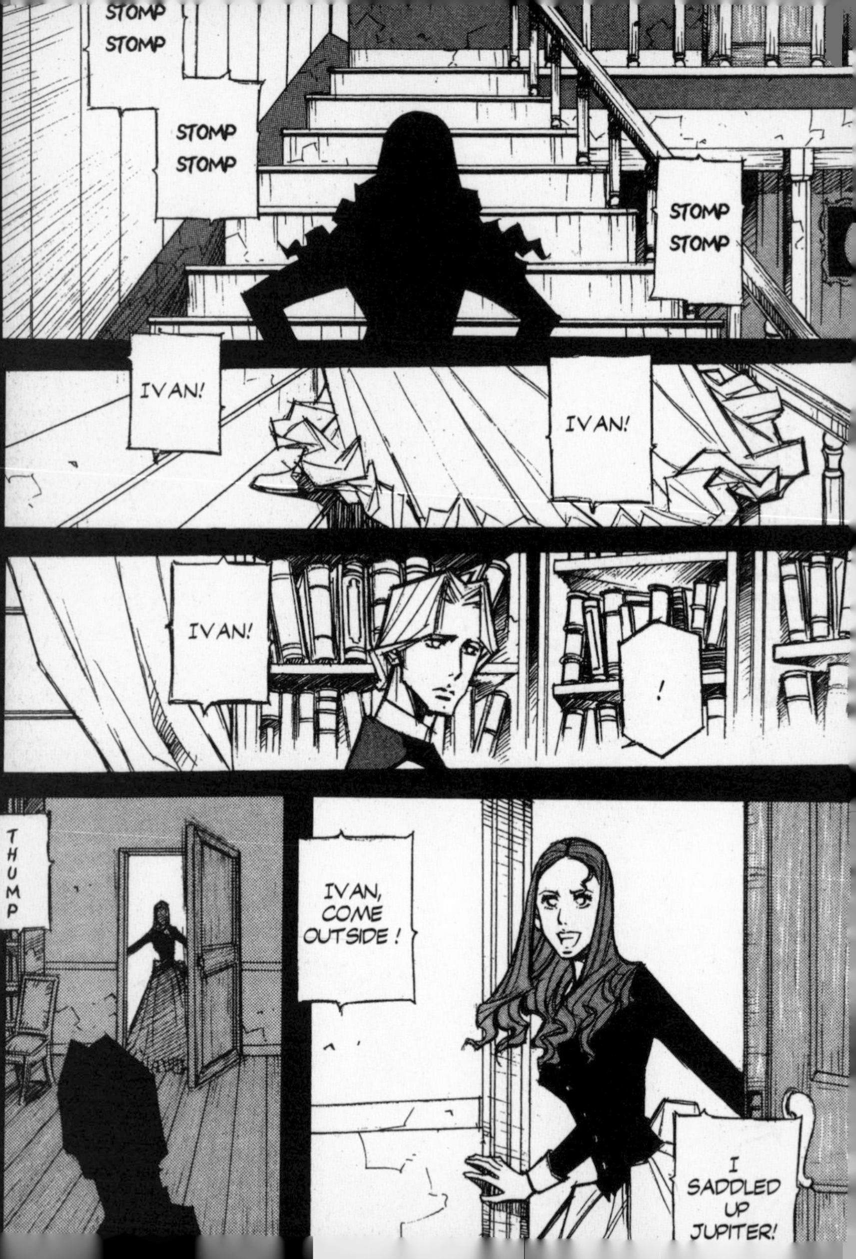
STOMP
STOMP
STOMP
STOMP
STOMP
STOMP
IVAN!
IVAN!
IVAN!
!
THUMP
IVAN, COME OUTSIDE!
I SADDLED UP JUPITER!

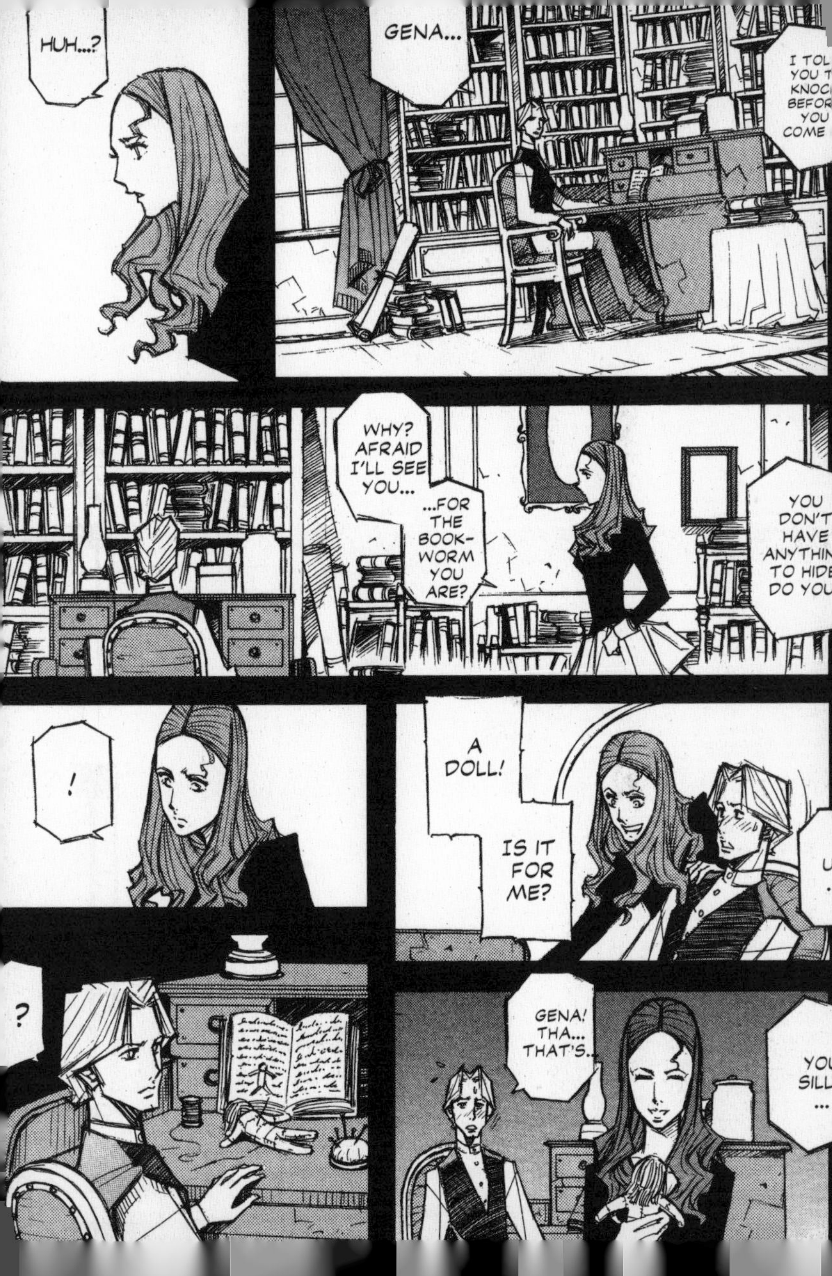
HUH...?
GENA...
I TOL YOU T KNOC BEFOR YOU COME
WHY? AFRAID I'LL SEE YOU...
...FOR THE BOOK-WORM YOU ARE?
YOU DON'T HAVE ANYTHIN TO HIDE DO YOU
!
A DOLL!
IS IT FOR ME?
U ...
?
GENA! THA... THAT'S...
YOU SILL ...

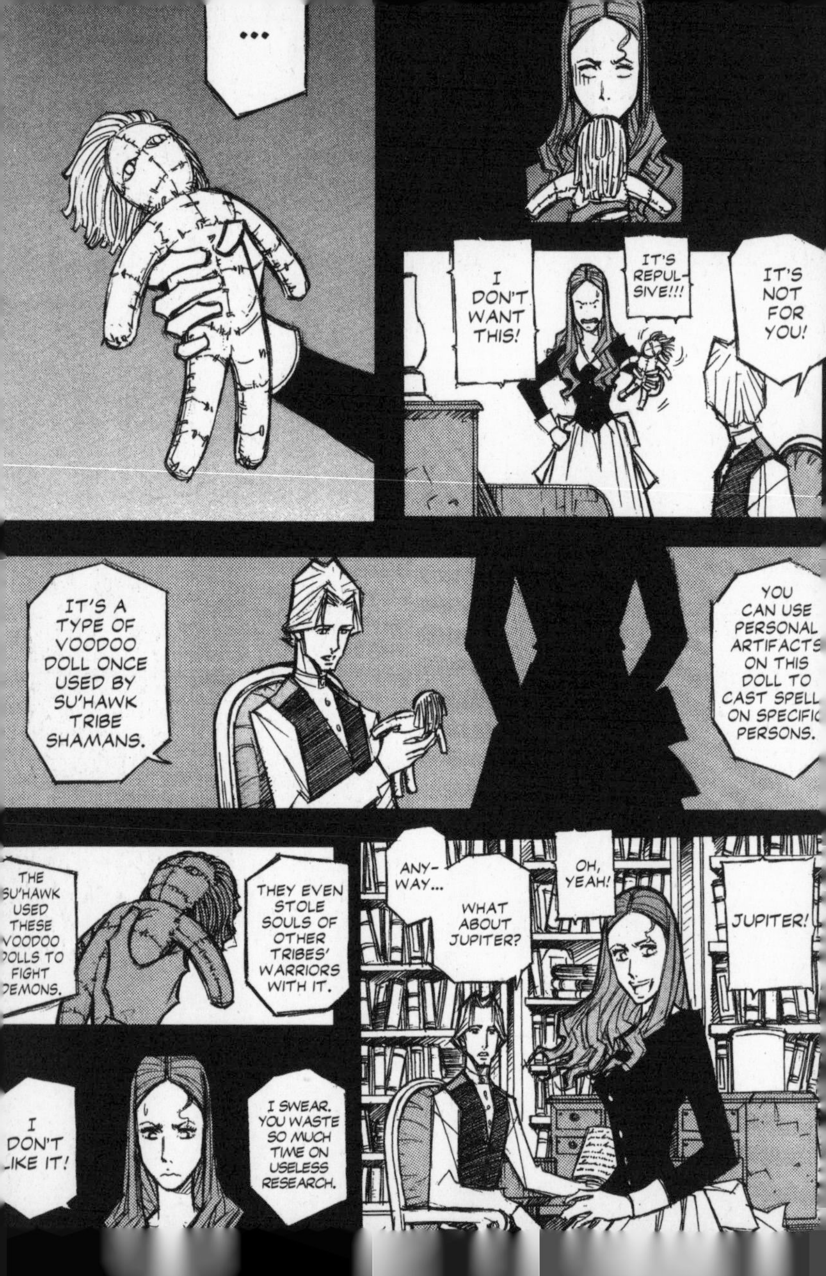
...
I DON'T WANT THIS!
IT'S REPULSIVE!!!
IT'S NOT FOR YOU!
IT'S A TYPE OF VOODOO DOLL ONCE USED BY SU'HAWK TRIBE SHAMANS.
YOU CAN USE PERSONAL ARTIFACTS ON THIS DOLL TO CAST SPELL ON SPECIFIC PERSONS.
THE SU'HAWK USED THESE VOODOO DOLLS TO FIGHT DEMONS.
THEY EVEN STOLE SOULS OF OTHER TRIBES' WARRIORS WITH IT.
I DON'T LIKE IT!
I SWEAR. YOU WASTE SO MUCH TIME ON USELESS RESEARCH.
ANYWAY...
WHAT ABOUT JUPITER?
OH, YEAH!
JUPITER!

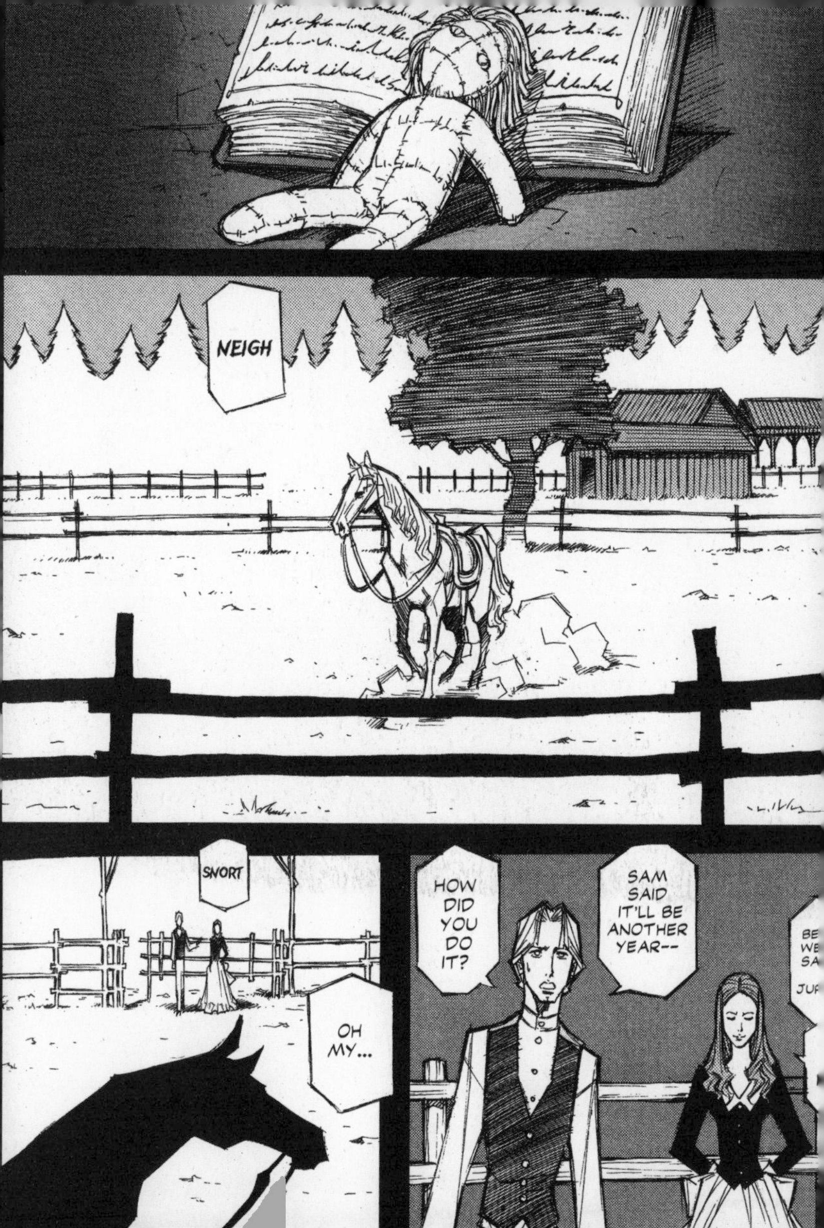
NEIGH
SNORT
OH MY...
HOW DID YOU DO IT?
SAM SAID IT'LL BE ANOTHER YEAR--

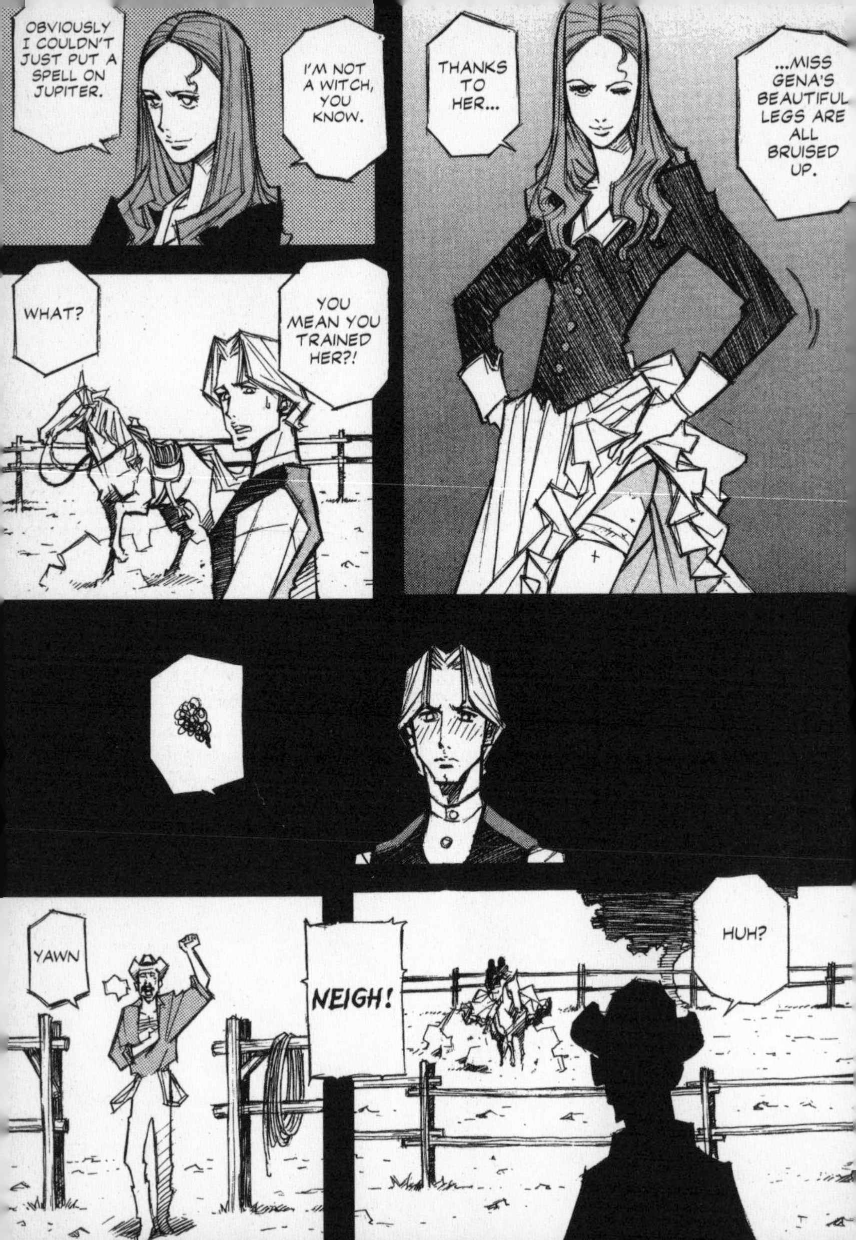
OBVIOUSLY I COULDN'T JUST PUT A SPELL ON JUPITER.
I'M NOT A WITCH, YOU KNOW.
WHAT?
YOU MEAN YOU TRAINED HER?!
THANKS TO HER...
...MISS GENA'S BEAUTIFUL LEGS ARE ALL BRUISED UP.
YAWN
NEIGH!
HUH?

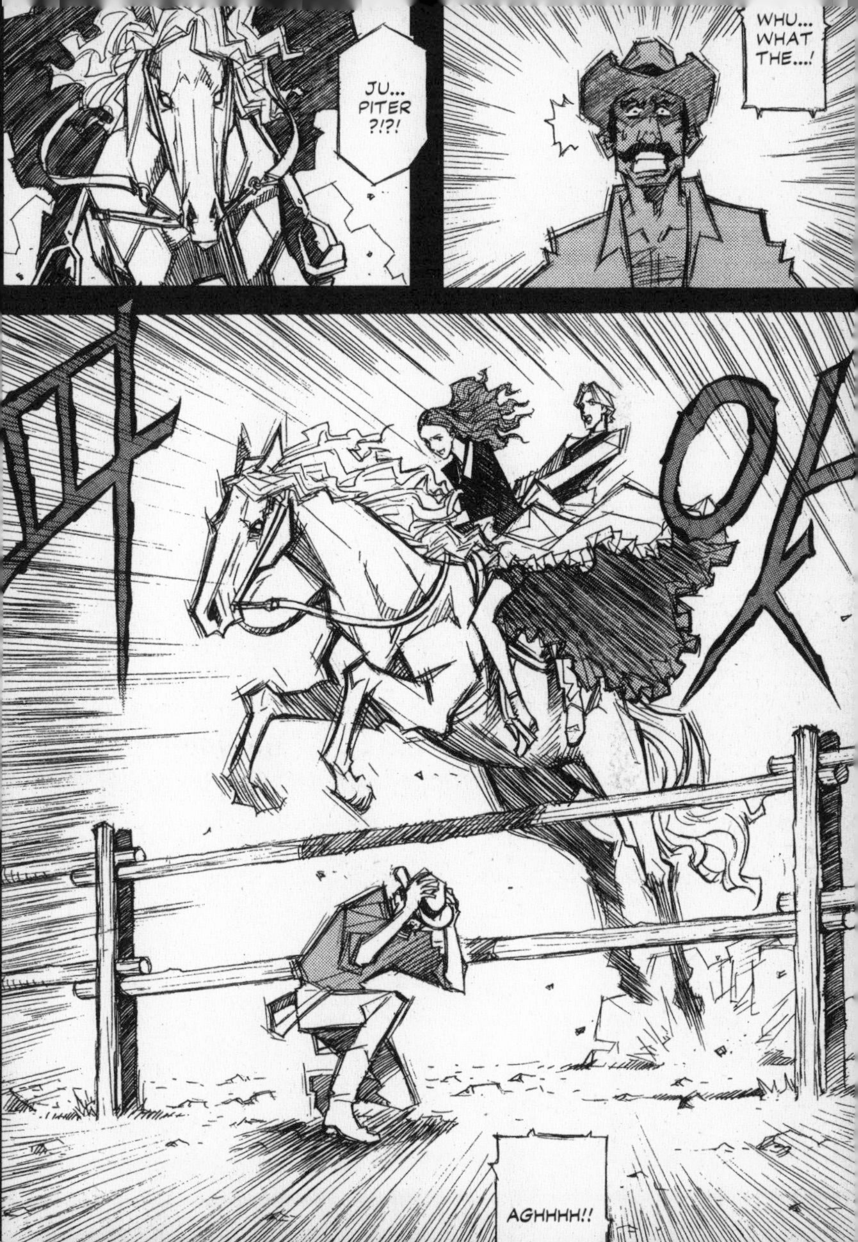
JU... PITER ?!?!
WHU... WHAT THE...!
AGHHHH!!

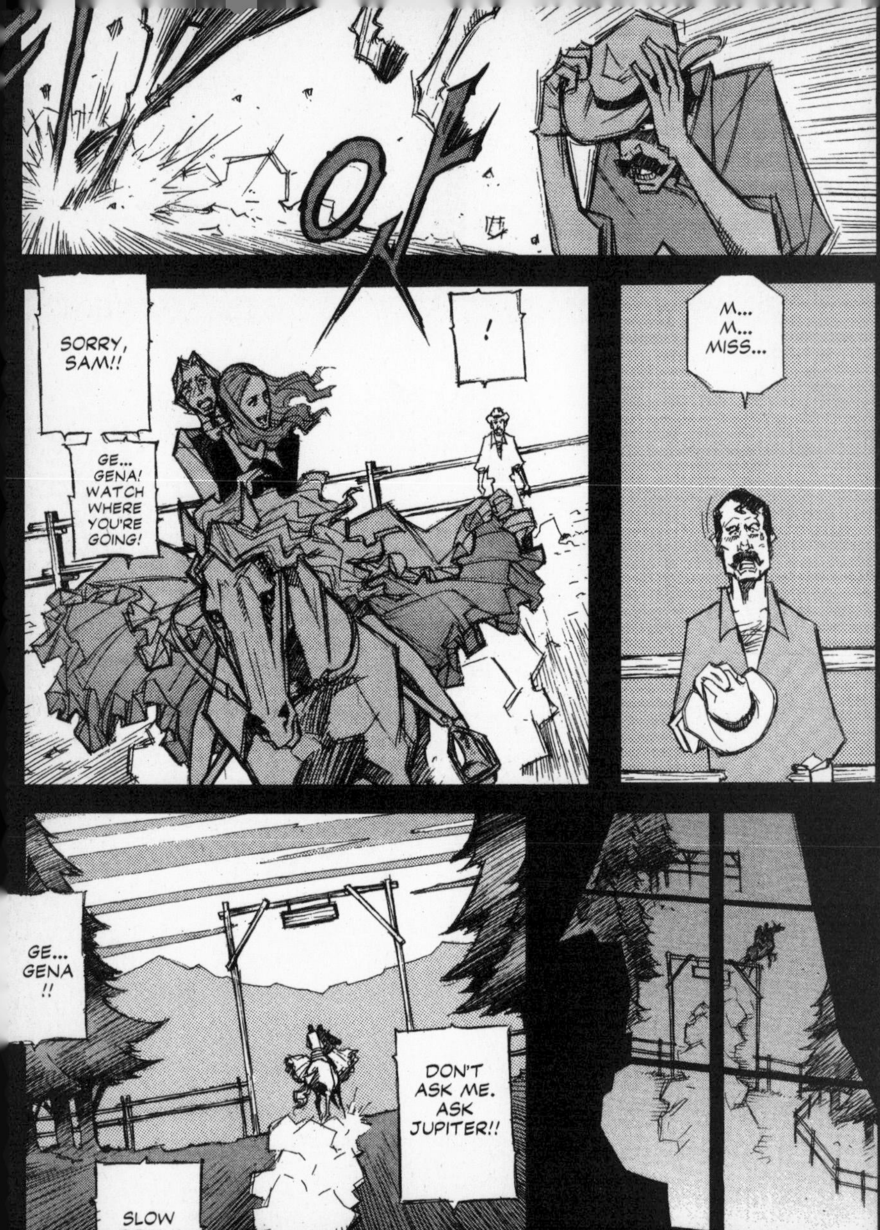

SORRY, SAM!!
GE... GENA! WATCH WHERE YOU'RE GOING!
!
M... M... MISS...
GE... GENA !!
SLOW DOWN!
DON'T ASK ME. ASK JUPITER!!

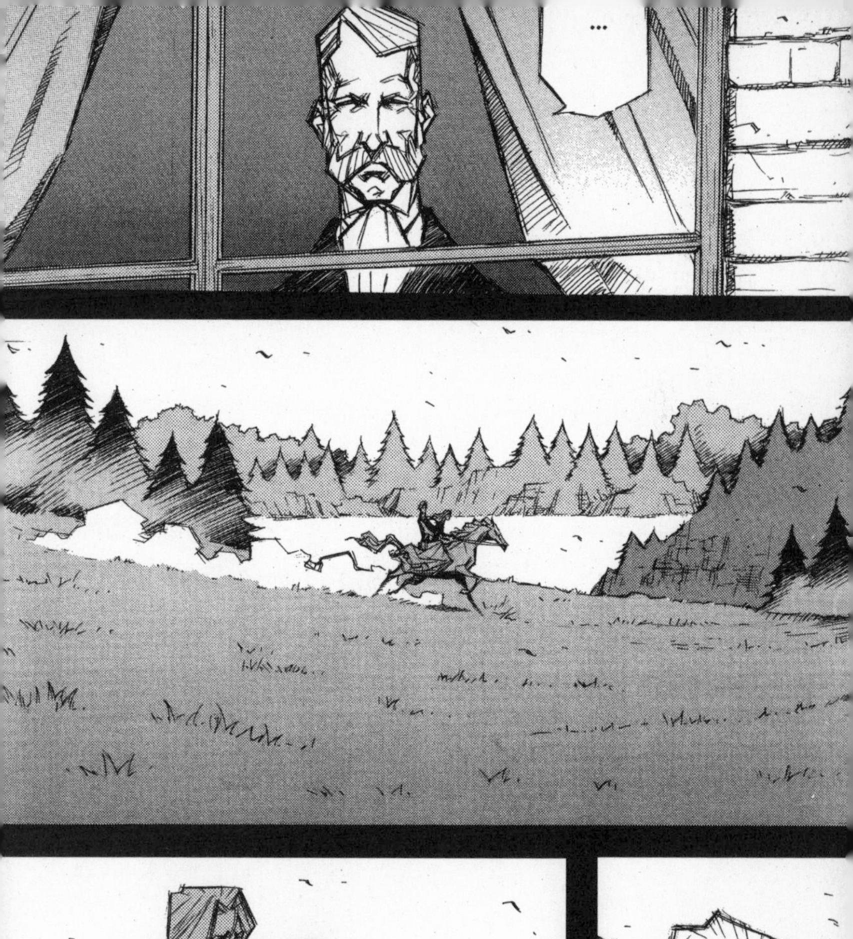
...

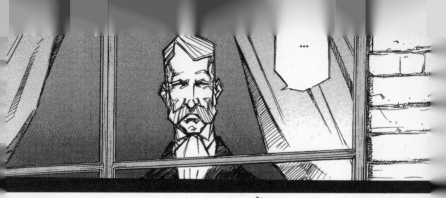

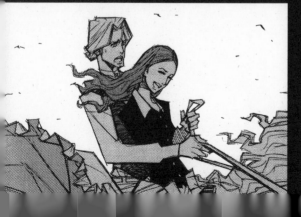

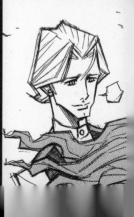

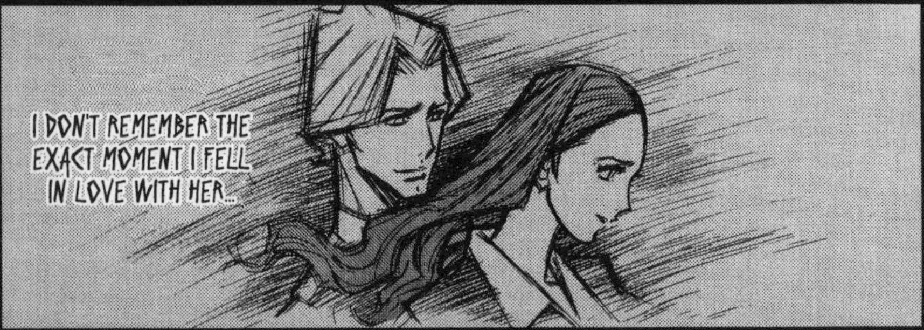
I DON'T REMEMBER THE EXACT MOMENT I FELL IN LOVE WITH HER...

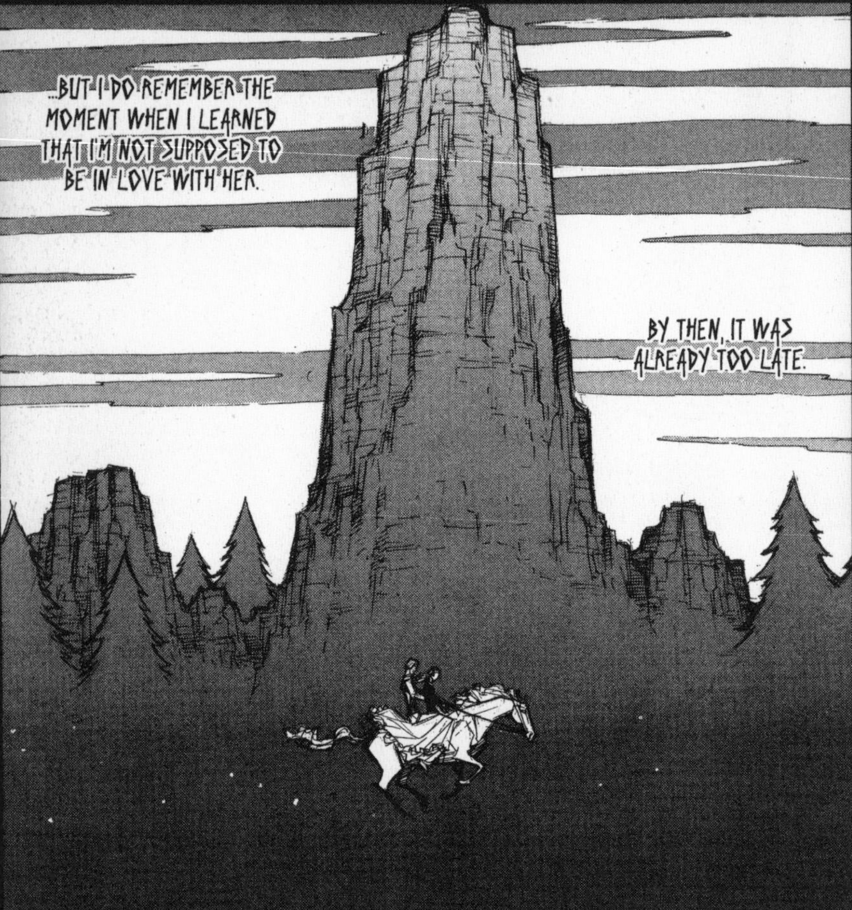
...BUT I DO REMEMBER THE MOMENT WHEN I LEARNED THAT I'M NOT SUPPOSED TO BE IN LOVE WITH HER.
BY THEN, IT WAS ALREADY TOO LATE.

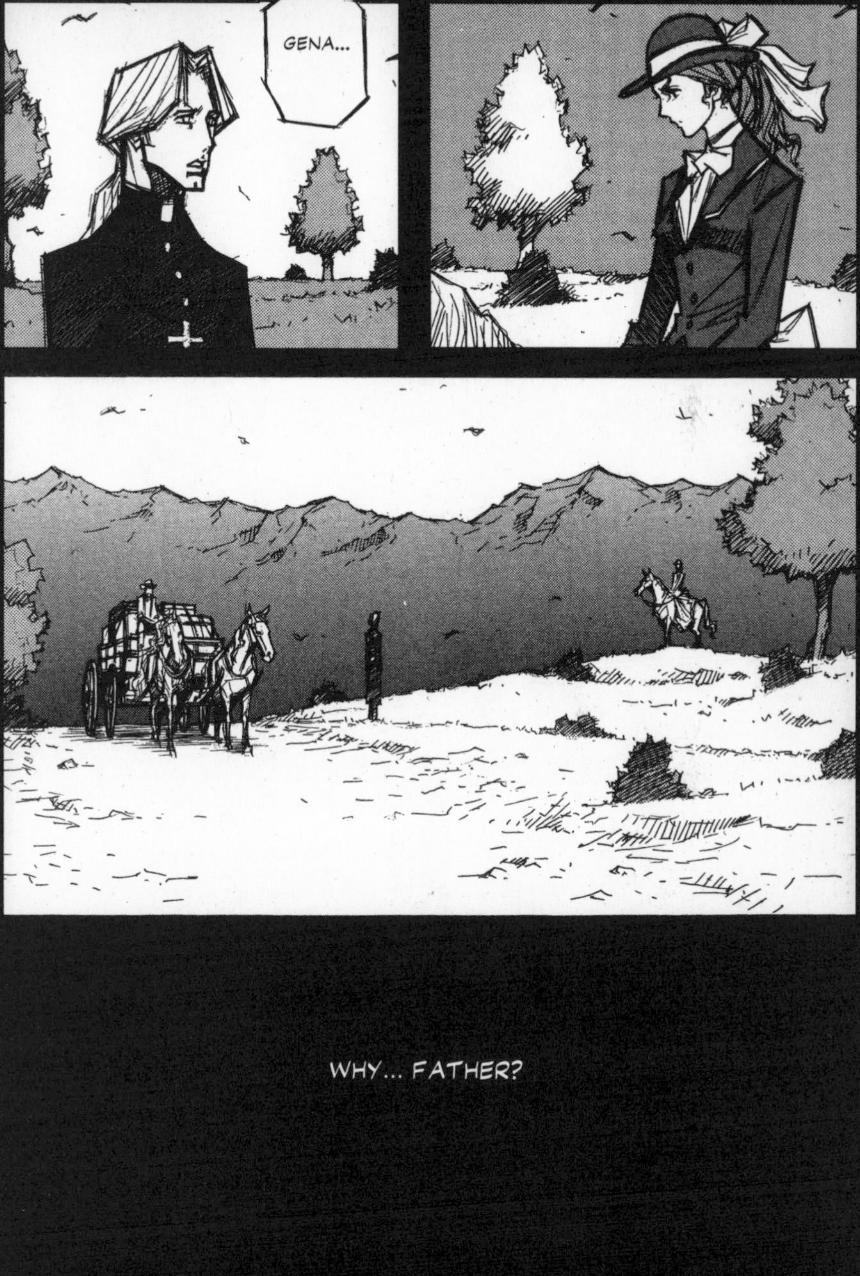
GENA...
WHY... FATHER?

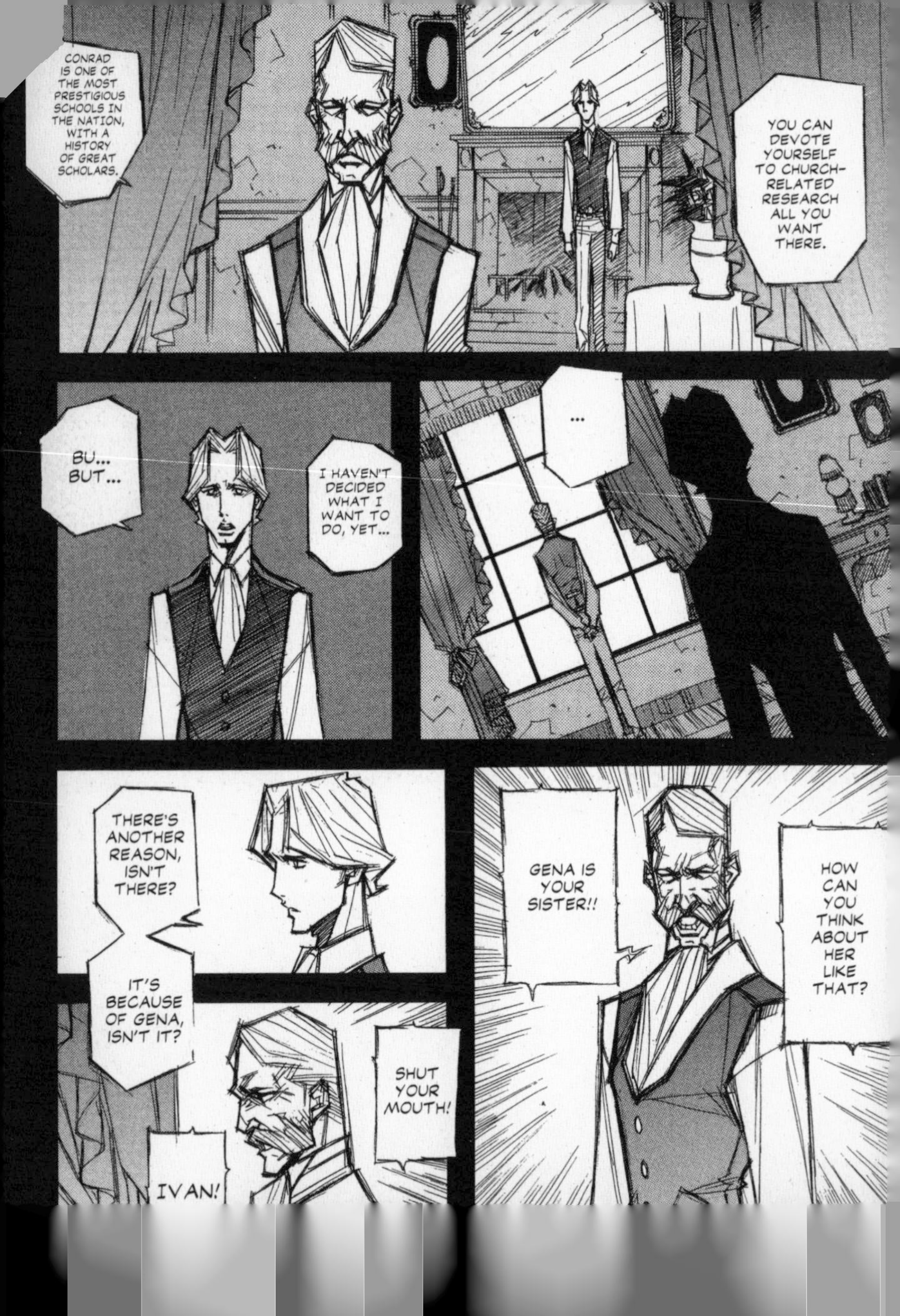
CONRAD IS ONE OF THE MOST PRESTIGIOUS SCHOOLS IN THE NATION, WITH A HISTORY OF GREAT SCHOLARS.
YOU CAN DEVOTE YOURSELF TO CHURCH-RELATED RESEARCH ALL YOU WANT THERE.
BU... BUT...
I HAVEN'T DECIDED WHAT I WANT TO DO, YET...
...
THERE'S ANOTHER REASON, ISN'T THERE?
IT'S BECAUSE OF GENA, ISN'T IT?
IVAN!
SHUT YOUR MOUTH!
GENA IS YOUR SISTER!!
HOW CAN YOU THINK ABOUT HER LIKE THAT?

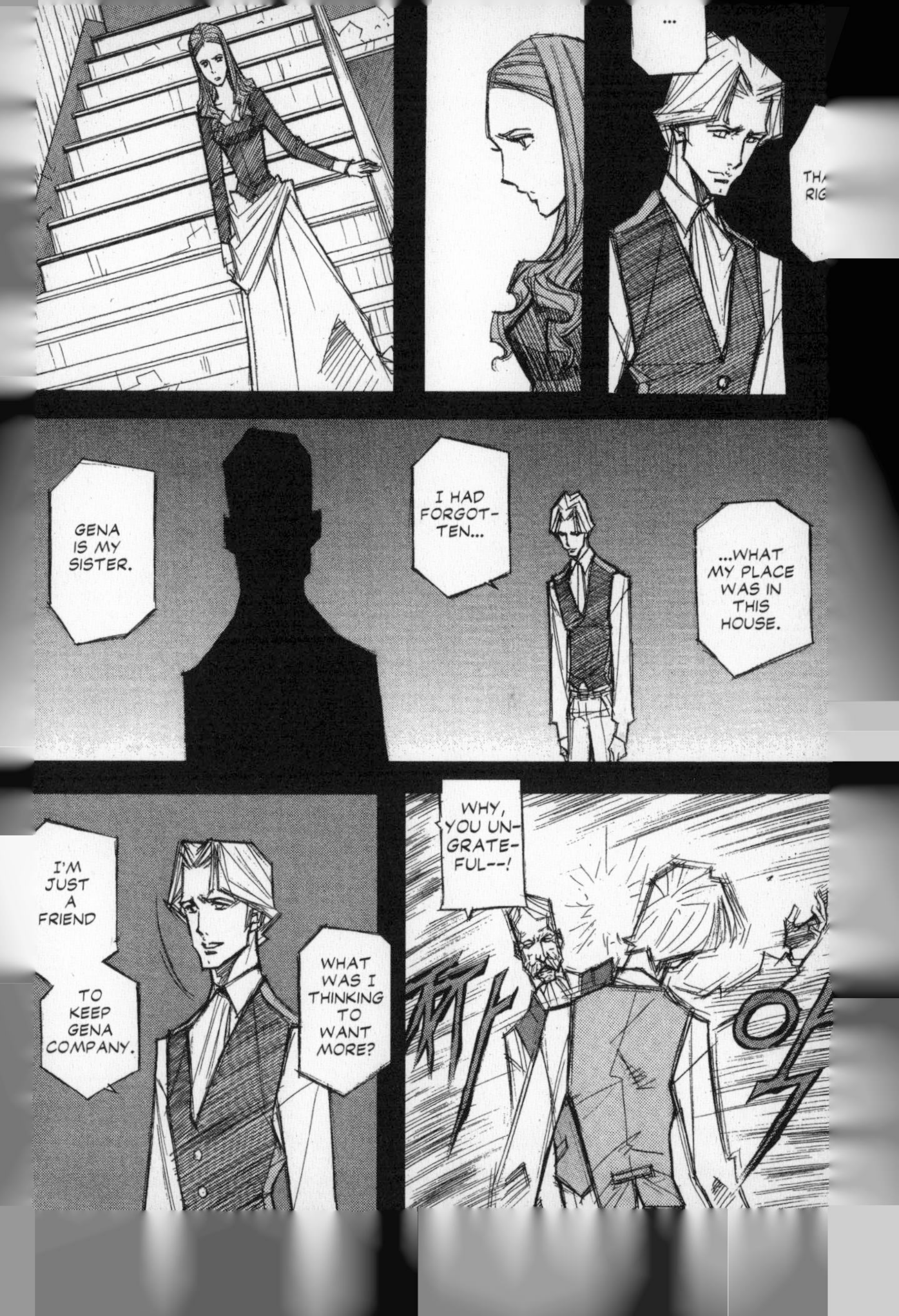
...
THA RIG
GENA IS MY SISTER.
I HAD FORGOT-TEN...
...WHAT MY PLACE WAS IN THIS HOUSE.
I'M JUST A FRIEND
TO KEEP GENA COMPANY.
WHAT WAS I THINKING TO WANT MORE?
WHY, YOU UN-GRATE-FUL--!

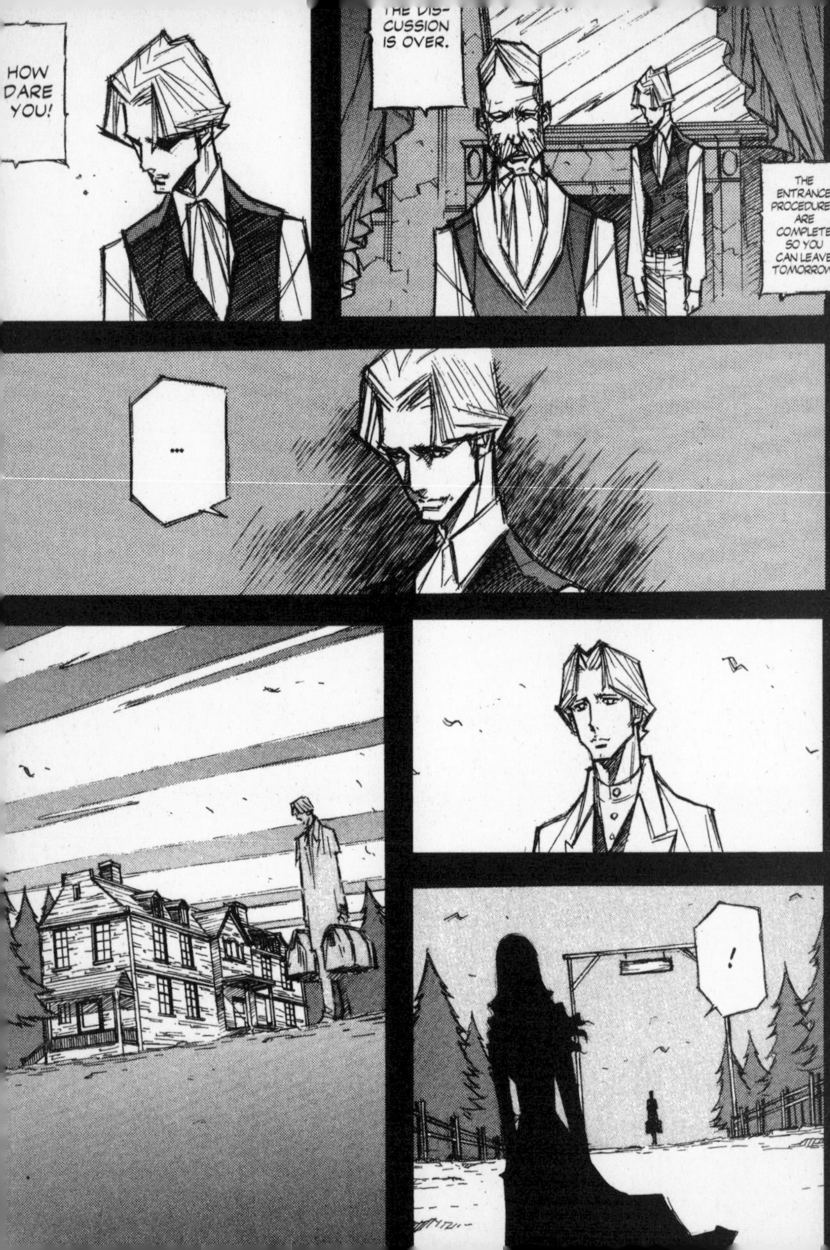
HOW DARE YOU!
THE DIS-CUSSION IS OVER.
THE ENTRANCE PROCEDURES ARE COMPLETE SO YOU CAN LEAVE TOMORROW.
...
!

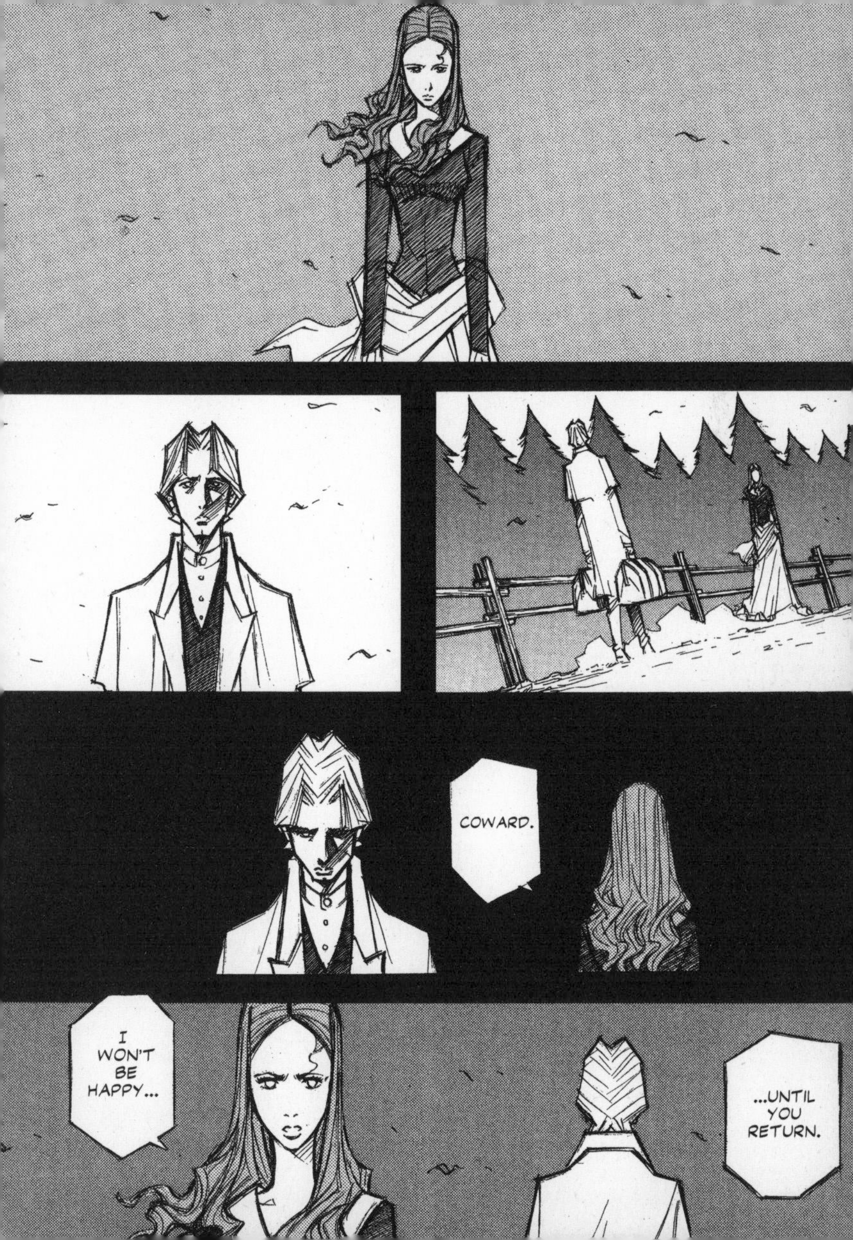

COWARD.
I WON'T BE HAPPY...
...UNTIL YOU RETURN.

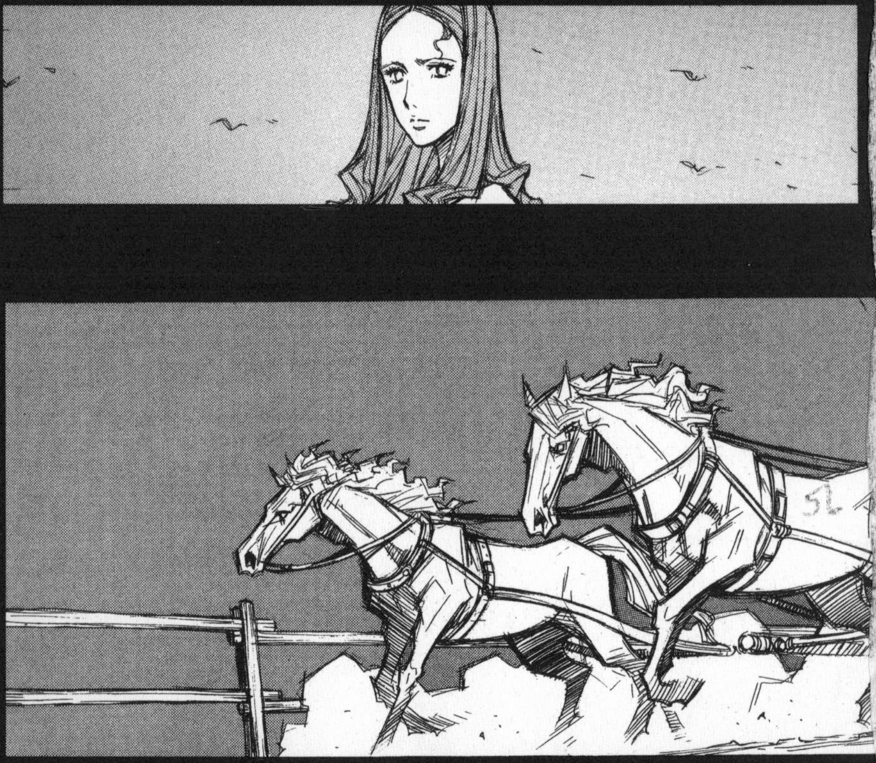

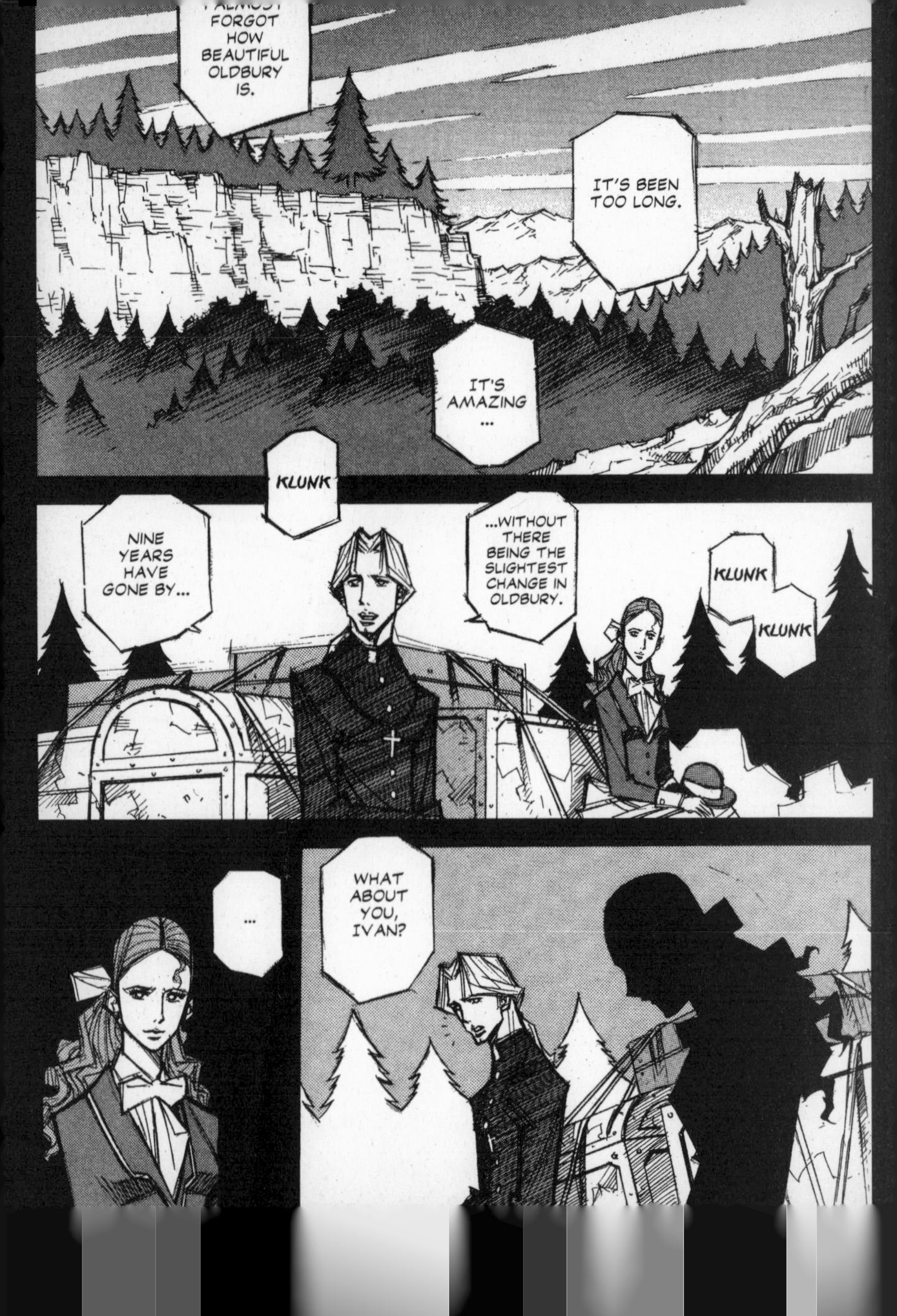

FORGOT HOW BEAUTIFUL OLDBURY IS.
IT'S BEEN TOO LONG.
IT'S AMAZING ...
KLUNK
NINE YEARS HAVE GONE BY...
...WITHOUT THERE BEING THE SLIGHTEST CHANGE IN OLDBURY.
KLUNK
KLUNK
...
WHAT ABOUT YOU, IVAN?

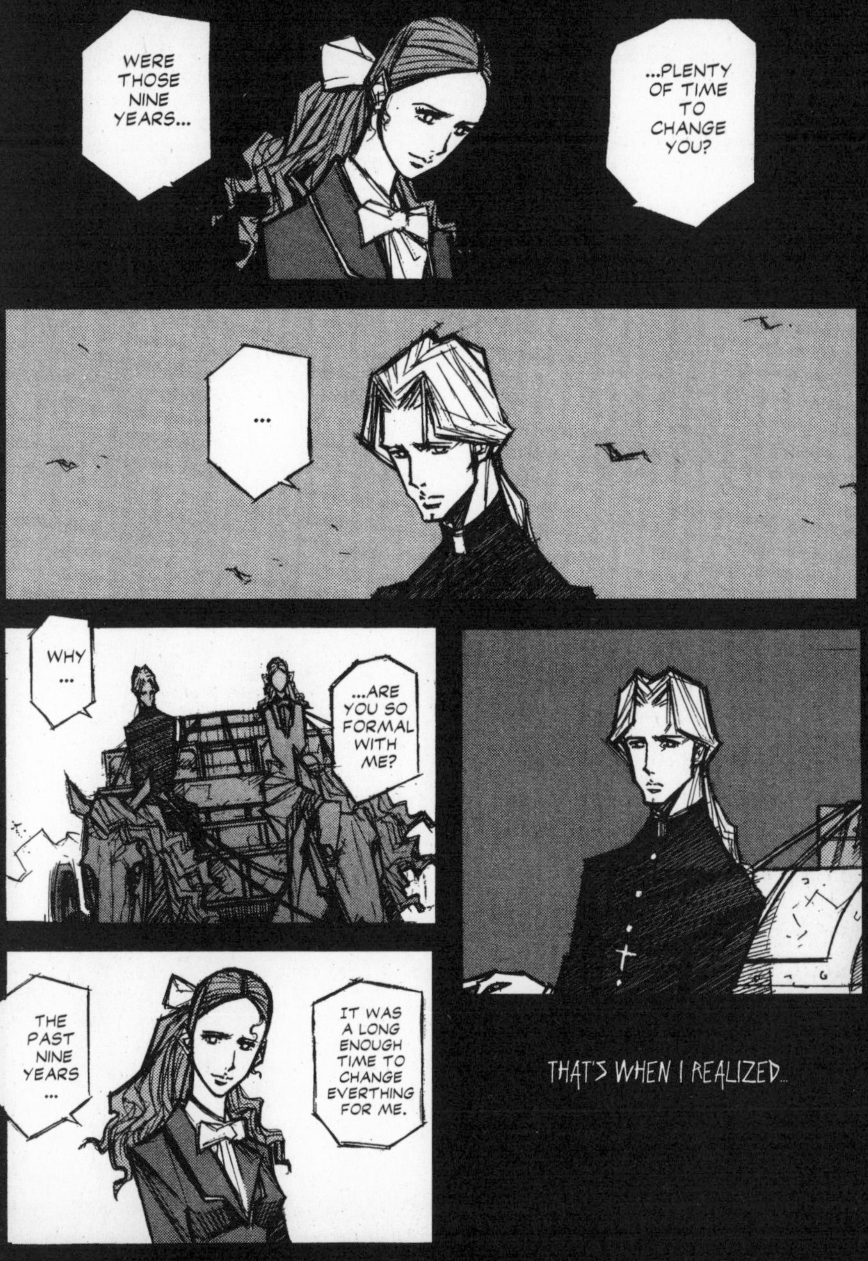
WERE THOSE NINE YEARS...
...PLENTY OF TIME TO CHANGE YOU?
...
WHY ...
...ARE YOU SO FORMAL WITH ME?
THE PAST NINE YEARS ...
IT WAS A LONG ENOUGH TIME TO CHANGE EVERTHING FOR ME.
THAT'S WHEN I REALIZED...

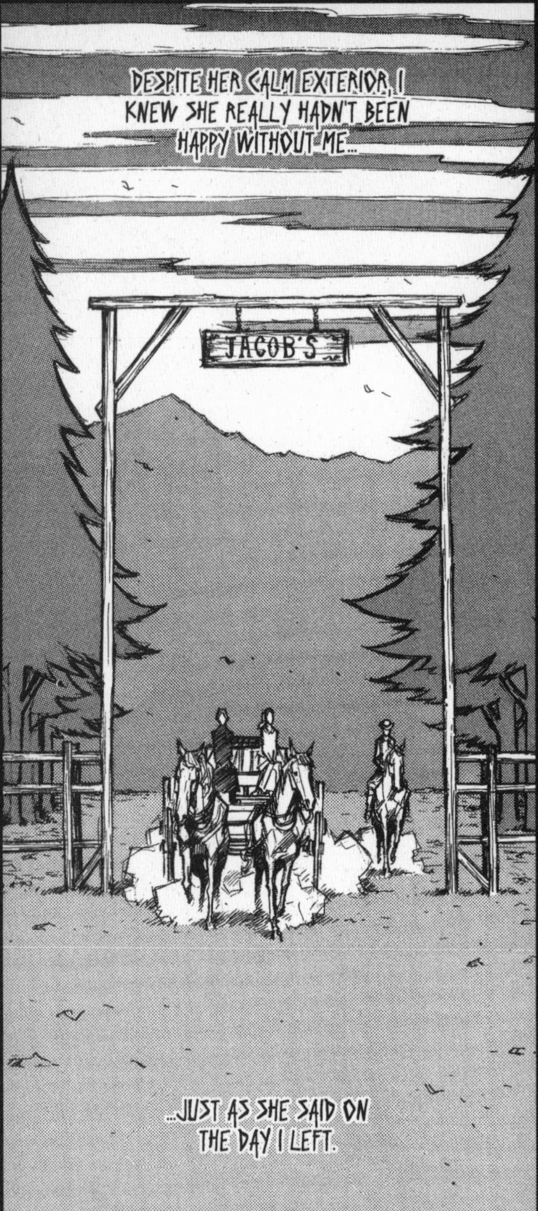
DESPITE HER CALM EXTERIOR, I KNEW SHE REALLY HADN'T BEEN HAPPY WITHOUT ME...
JACOB'S
...JUST AS SHE SAID ON THE DAY I LEFT.

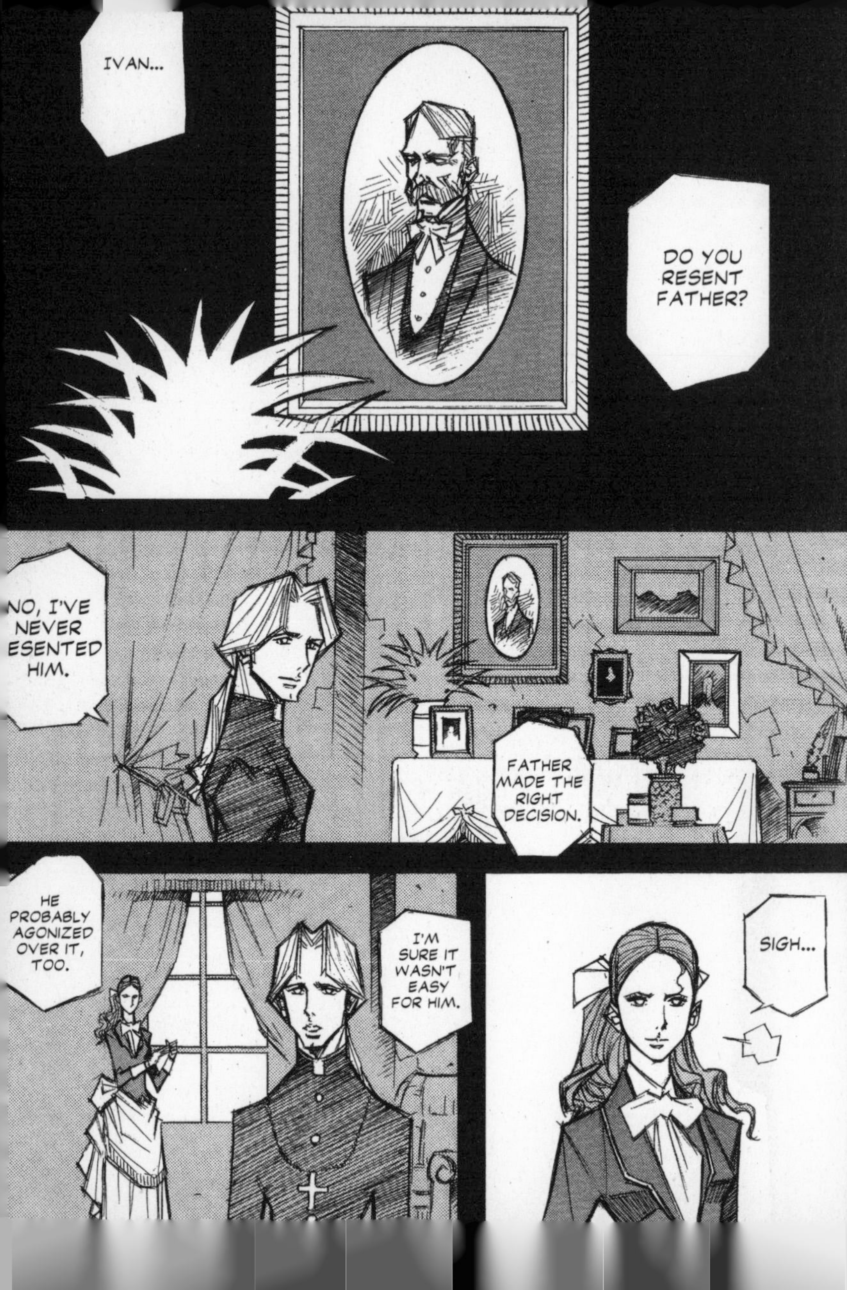
IVAN...
DO YOU RESENT FATHER?
NO, I'VE NEVER ESENTED HIM.
FATHER MADE THE RIGHT DECISION.
HE PROBABLY AGONIZED OVER IT, TOO.
I'M SURE IT WASN'T EASY FOR HIM.
SIGH...

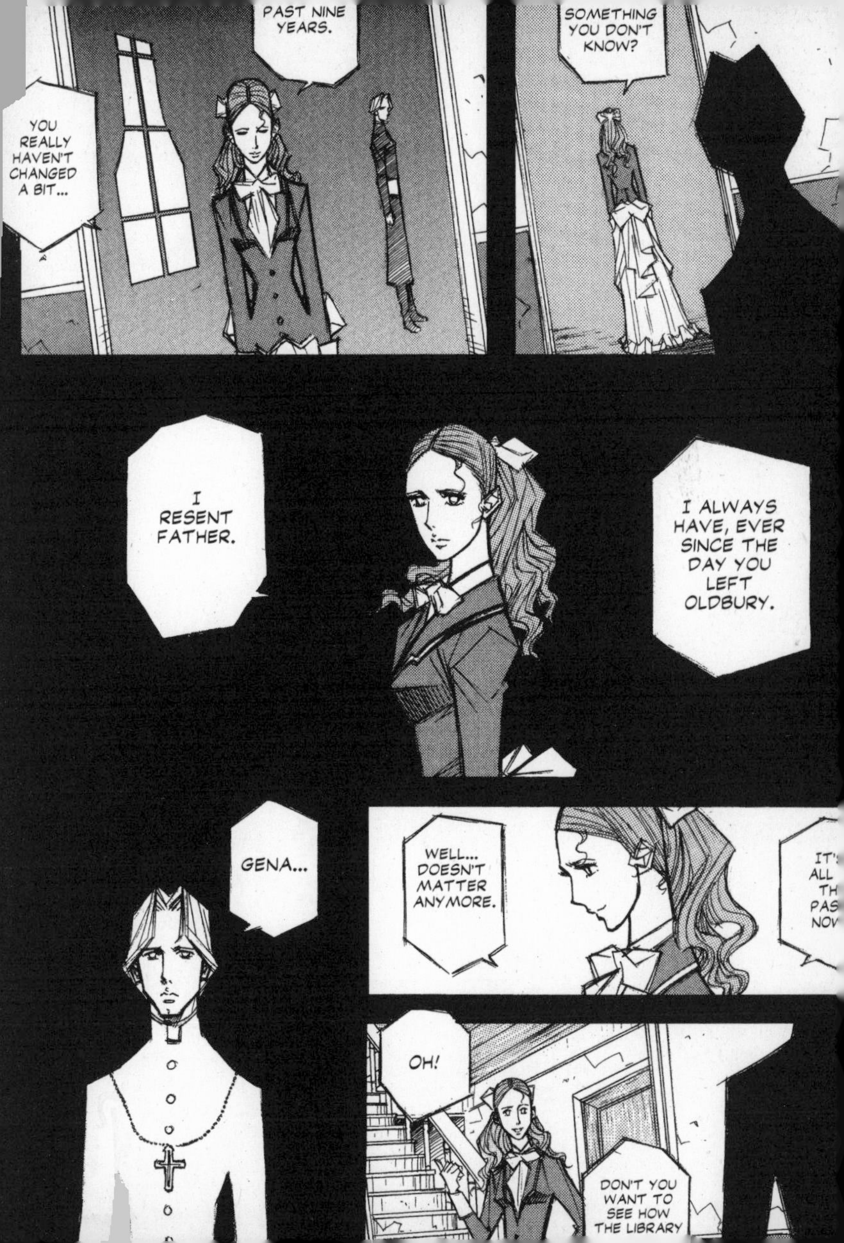

PAST NINE YEARS.
YOU REALLY HAVEN'T CHANGED A BIT...
SOMETHING YOU DON'T KNOW?
I RESENT FATHER.
I ALWAYS HAVE, EVER SINCE THE DAY YOU LEFT OLDBURY.
GENA...
WELL... DOESN'T MATTER ANYMORE.
IT'S ALL TH PAS NOW
OH!
DON'T YOU WANT TO SEE HOW THE LIBRARY

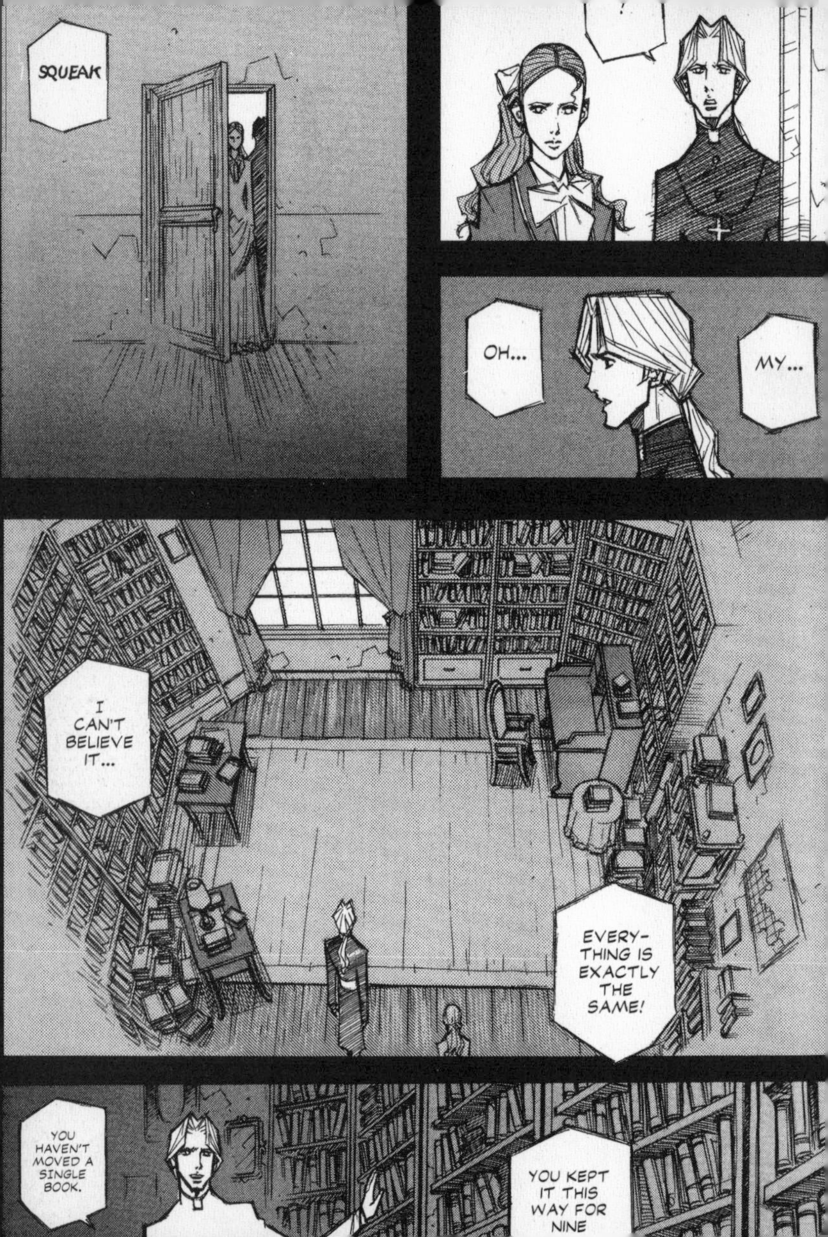
SQUEAK
OH...
MY...
I CAN'T BELIEVE IT...
EVERY-THING IS EXACTLY THE SAME!
YOU HAVEN'T MOVED A SINGLE BOOK.
YOU KEPT IT THIS WAY FOR NINE

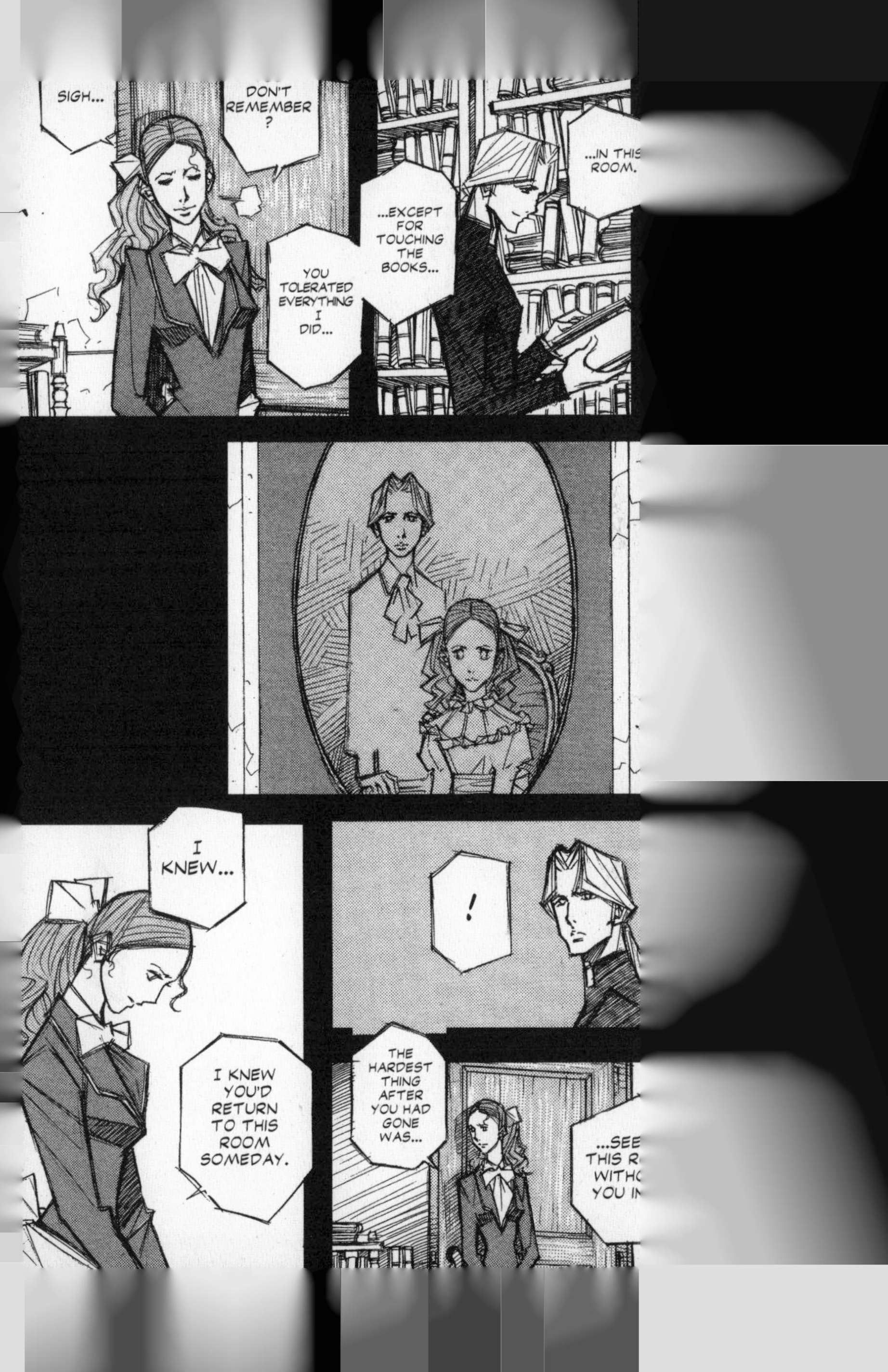

SIGH...
DON'T REMEMBER ?
YOU TOLERATED EVERYTHING I DID...
...EXCEPT FOR TOUCHING THE BOOKS...
...IN THIS ROOM.
I KNEW...
I KNEW YOU'D RETURN TO THIS ROOM SOMEDAY.
!
THE HARDEST THING AFTER YOU HAD GONE WAS...
...SEE THIS R WITHO YOU IN

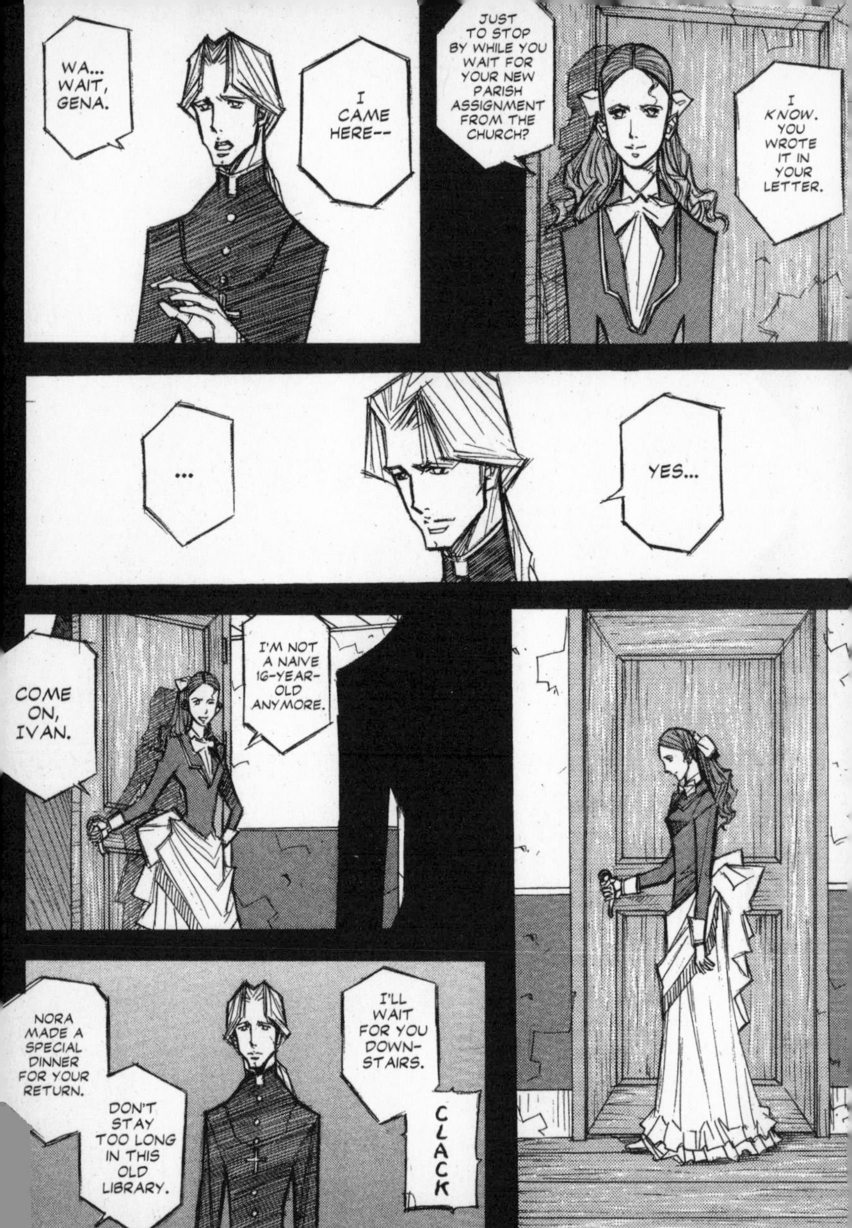
WA... WAIT, GENA.
I CAME HERE--
JUST TO STOP BY WHILE YOU WAIT FOR YOUR NEW PARISH ASSIGNMENT FROM THE CHURCH?
I KNOW. YOU WROTE IT IN YOUR LETTER.
...
YES...
COME ON, IVAN.
I'M NOT A NAIVE 16-YEAR-OLD ANYMORE.
NORA MADE A SPECIAL DINNER FOR YOUR RETURN.
DON'T STAY TOO LONG IN THIS OLD LIBRARY.
I'LL WAIT FOR YOU DOWN-STAIRS.
CLACK

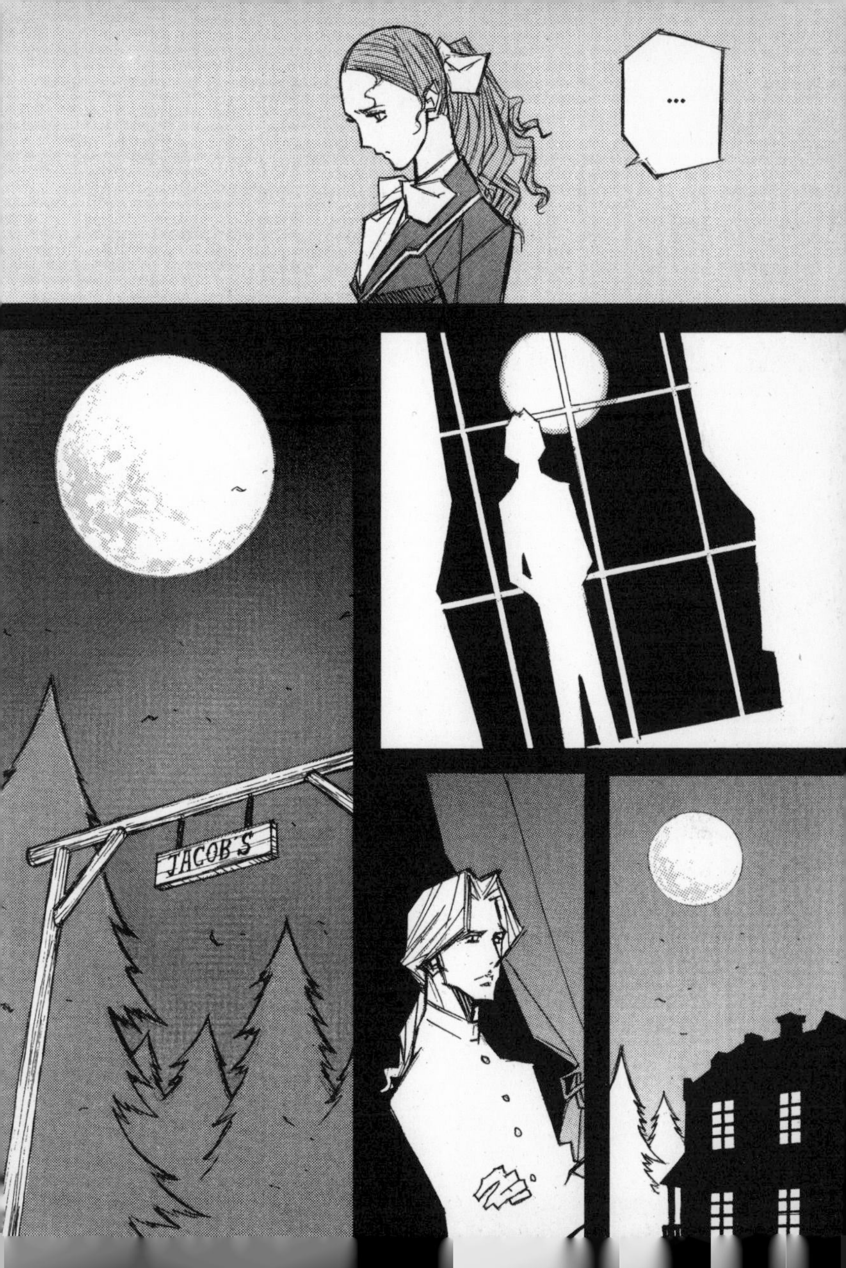
...
JACOB'S

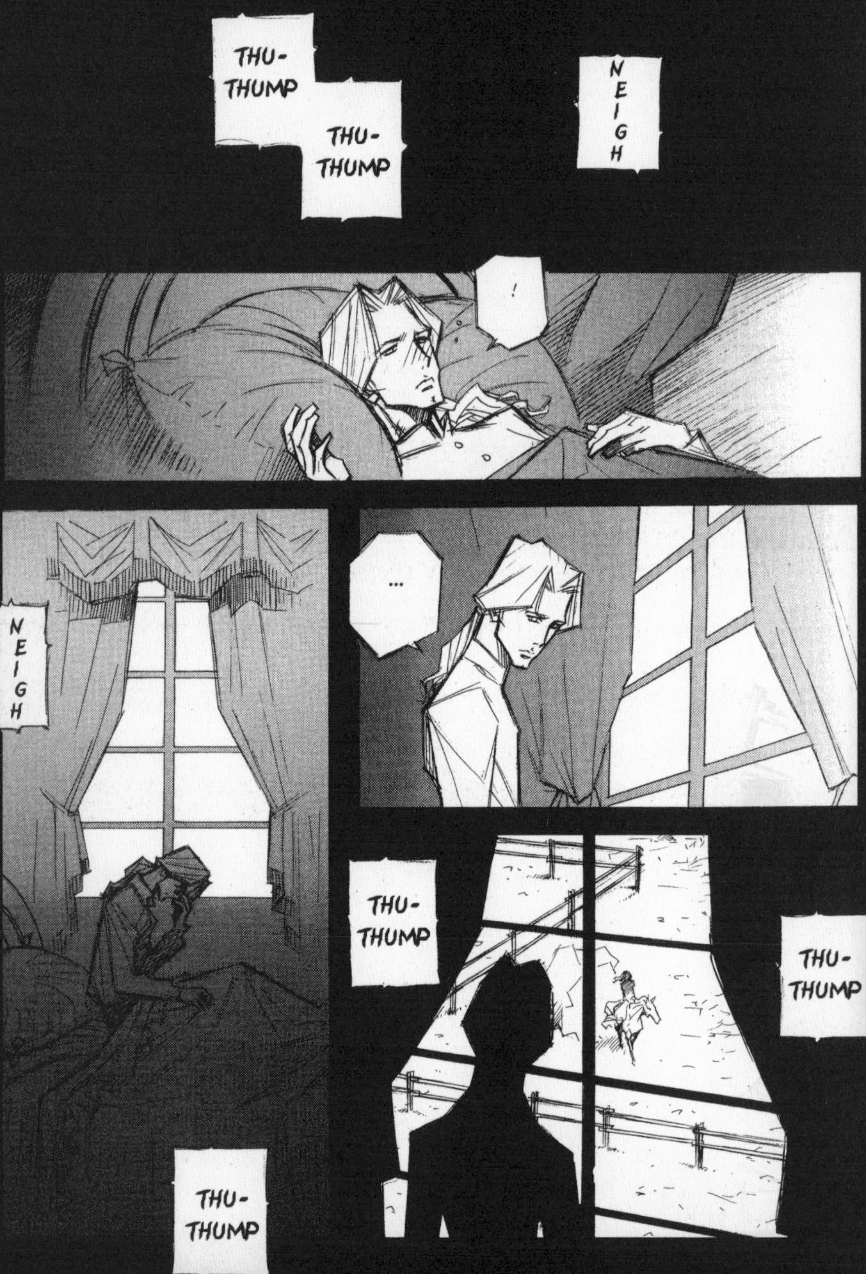
THU-THUMP
THU-THUMP
NEIGH
!
NEIGH
...
THU-THUMP
THU-THUMP
THU-THUMP

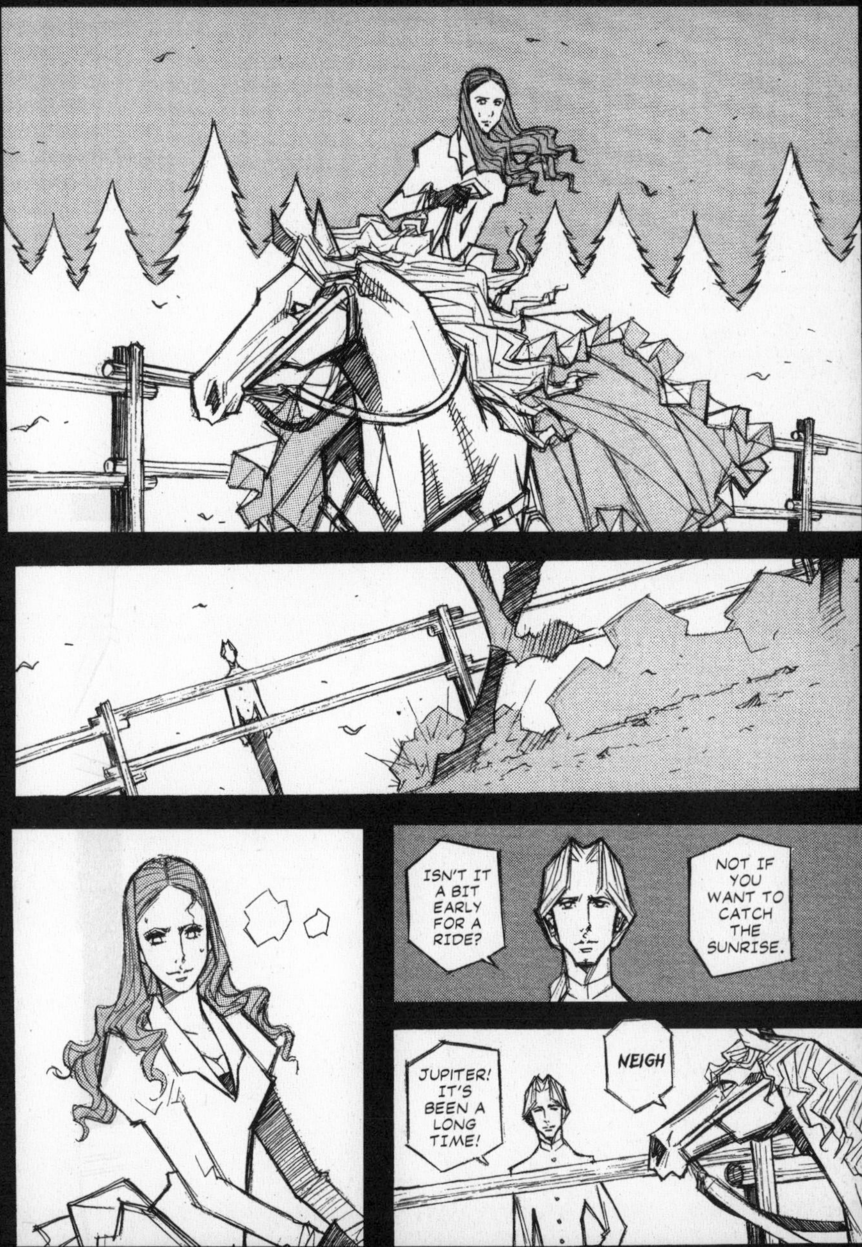

ISN'T IT A BIT EARLY FOR A RIDE?
NOT IF YOU WANT TO CATCH THE SUNRISE.
JUPITER! IT'S BEEN A LONG TIME!
NEIGH

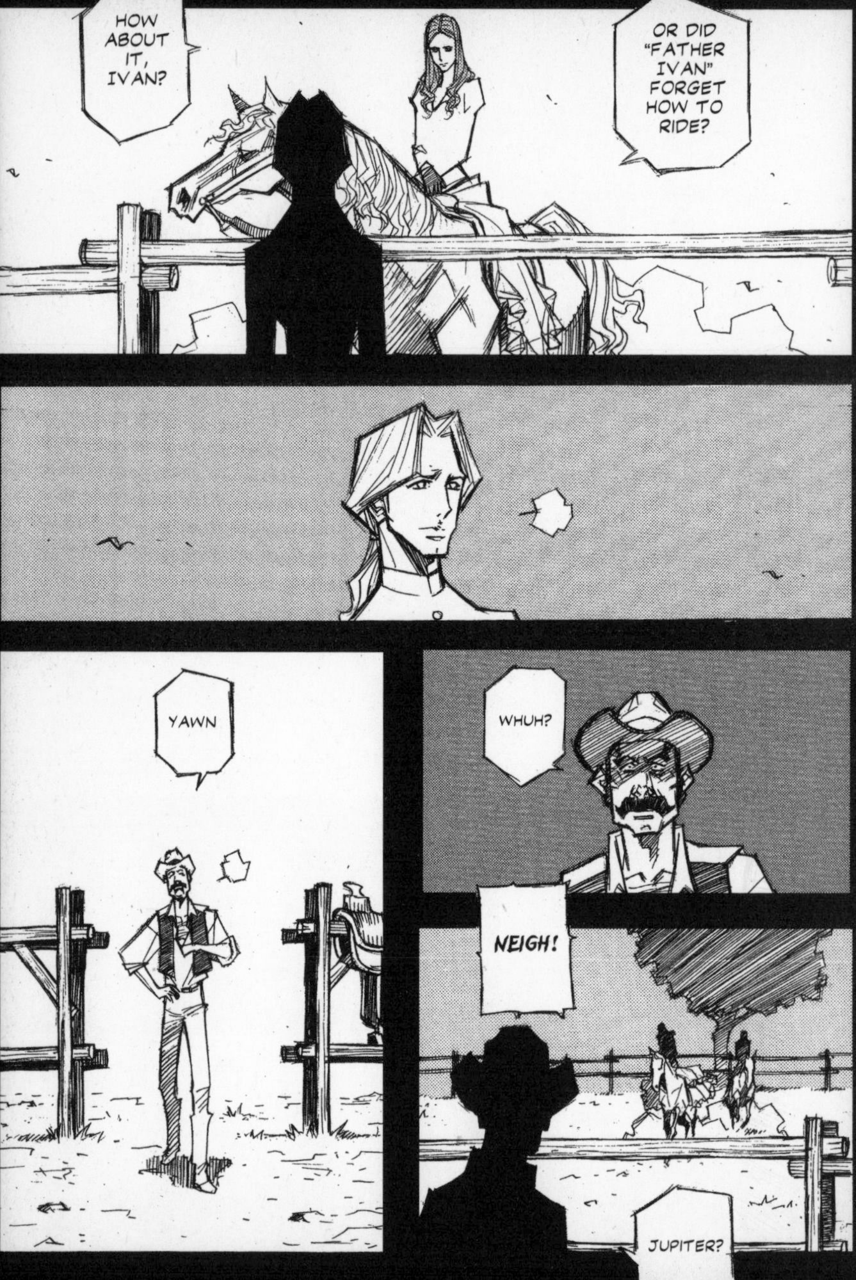
HOW ABOUT IT, IVAN?
OR DID "FATHER IVAN" FORGET HOW TO RIDE?
YAWN
WHUH?
NEIGH!
JUPITER?

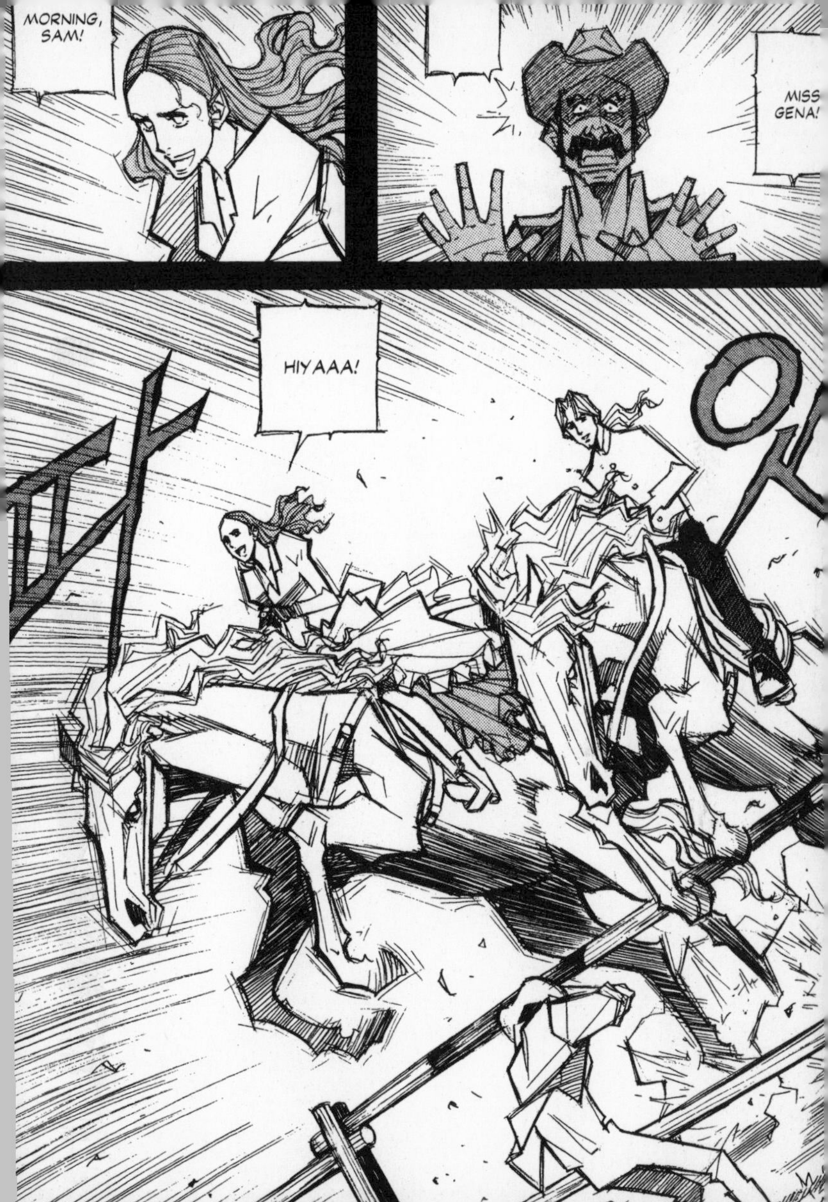
MORNING, SAM!
MISS GENA!
HIYAAA!

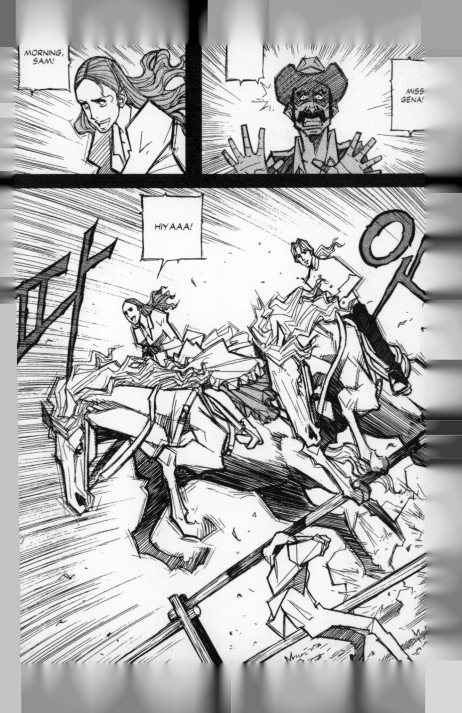

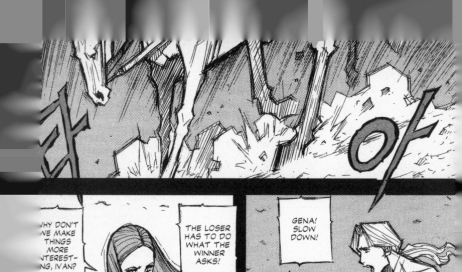

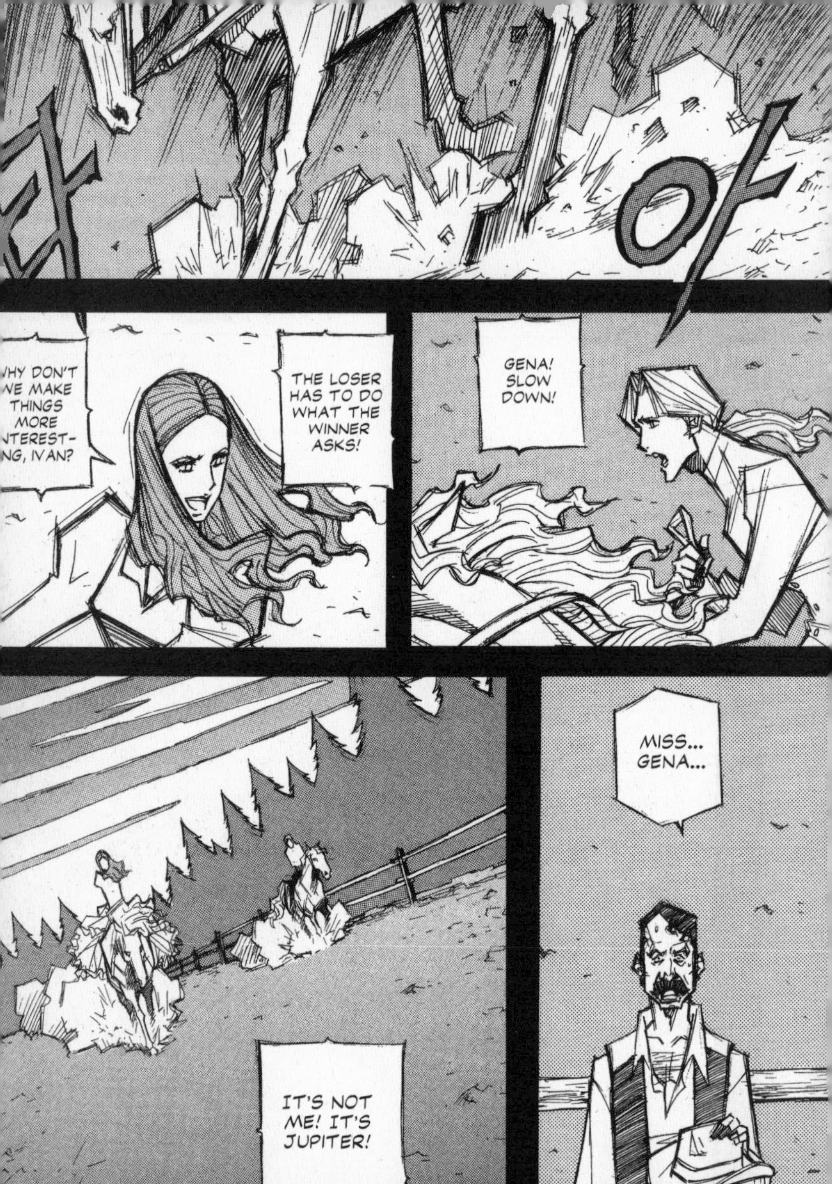
WHY DON'T WE MAKE THINGS MORE INTEREST-ING, IVAN?
THE LOSER HAS TO DO WHAT THE WINNER ASKS!
GENA! SLOW DOWN!
IT'S NOT ME! IT'S JUPITER!
MISS... GENA...

*This figure represents the person convinced of sin, and is endeavouring to flee the wrath to come.*

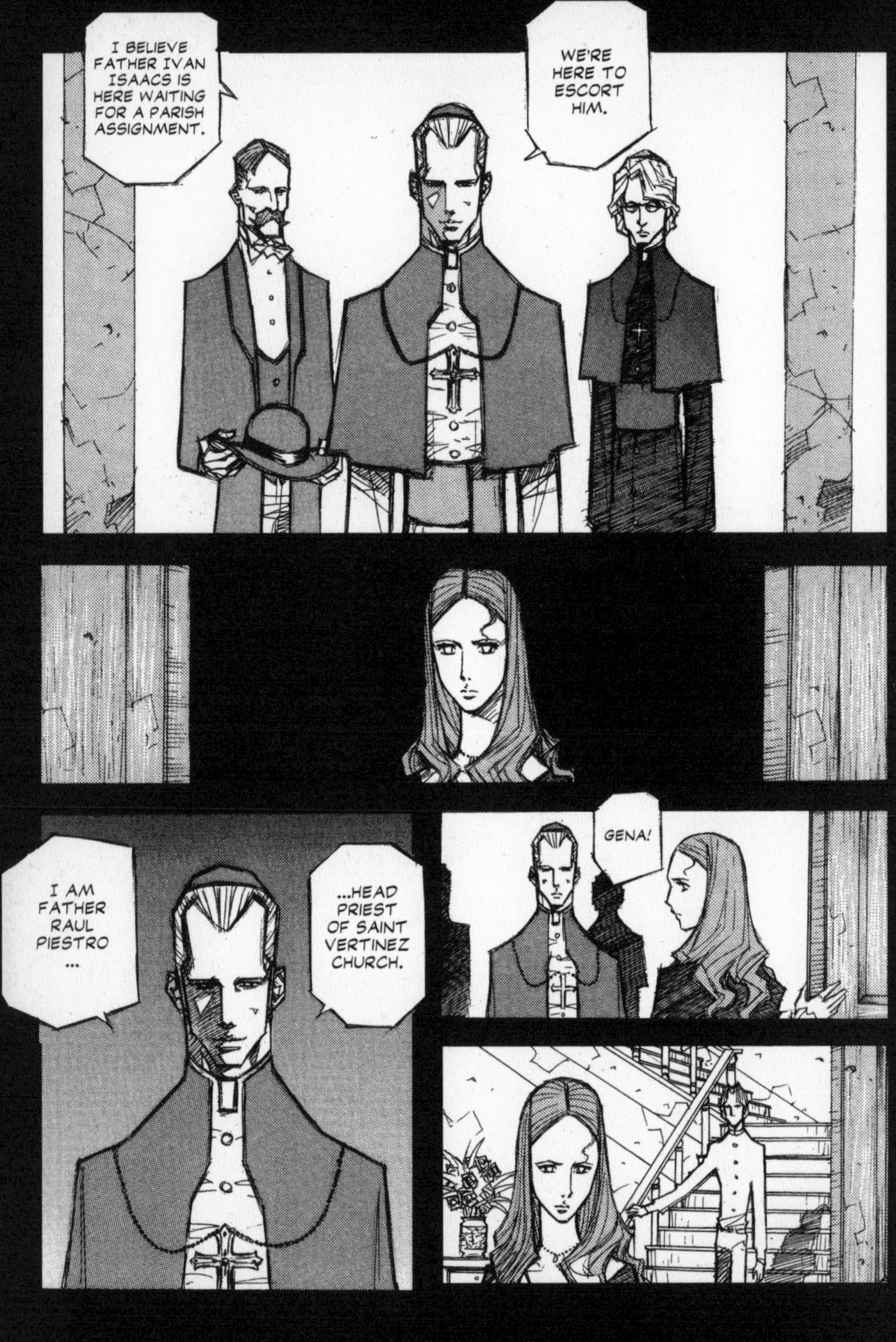
I BELIEVE FATHER IVAN ISAACS IS HERE WAITING FOR A PARISH ASSIGNMENT.
WE'RE HERE TO ESCORT HIM.
I AM FATHER RAUL PIESTRO ...
...HEAD PRIEST OF SAINT VERTINEZ CHURCH.
GENA!

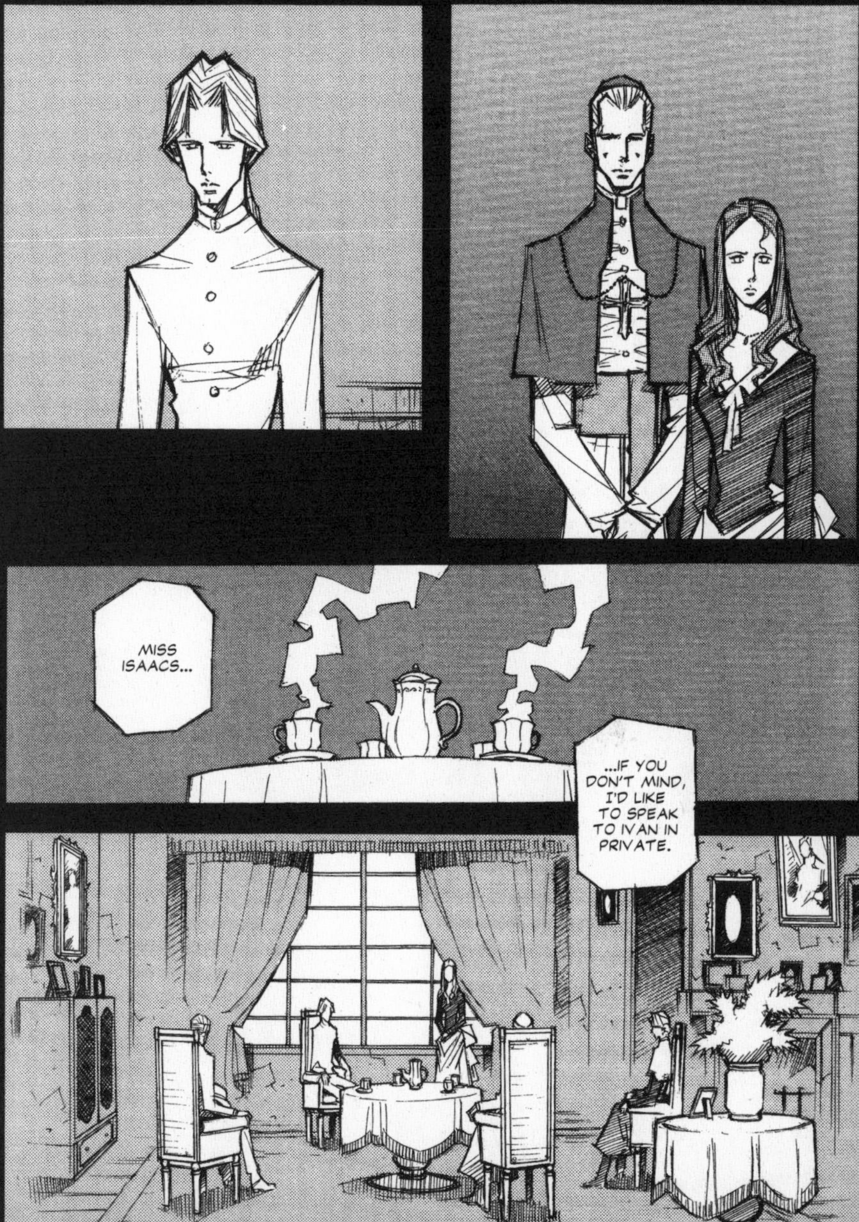
MISS ISAACS...
...IF YOU DON'T MIND, I'D LIKE TO SPEAK TO IVAN IN PRIVATE.

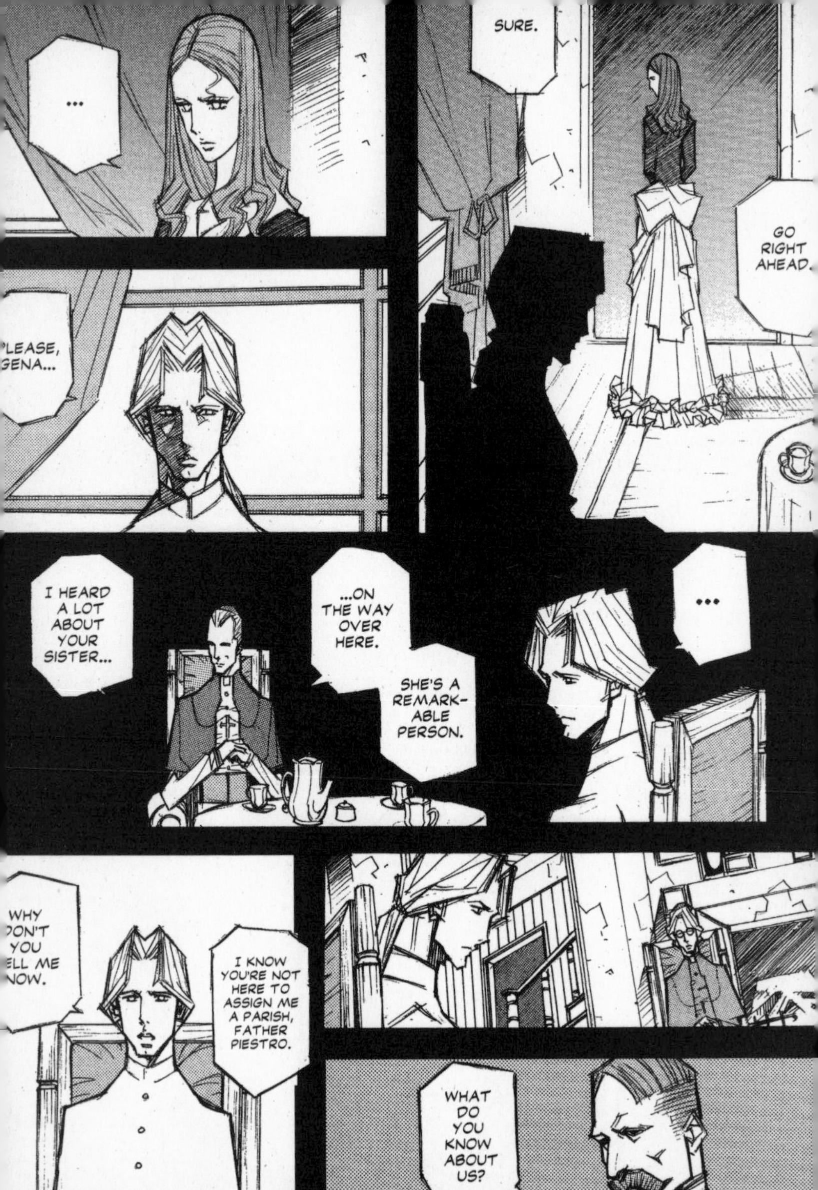
...
PLEASE, GENA...
SURE.
GO RIGHT AHEAD.
I HEARD A LOT ABOUT YOUR SISTER...
...ON THE WAY OVER HERE.
SHE'S A REMARKABLE PERSON.
...
WHY DON'T YOU ELL ME NOW.
I KNOW YOU'RE NOT HERE TO ASSIGN ME A PARISH, FATHER PIESTRO.
WHAT DO YOU KNOW ABOUT US?

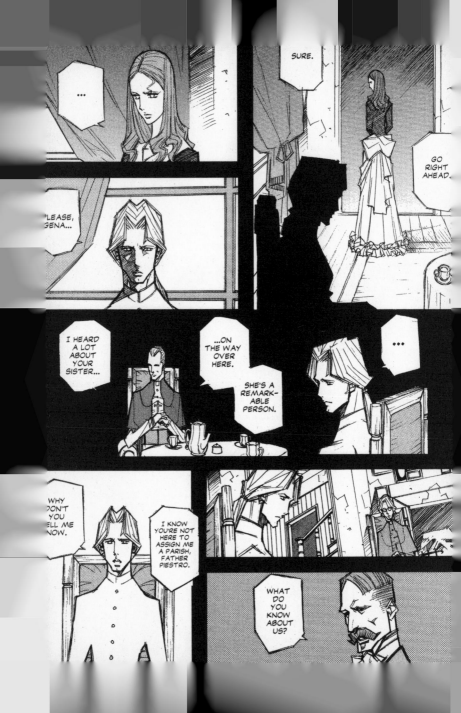

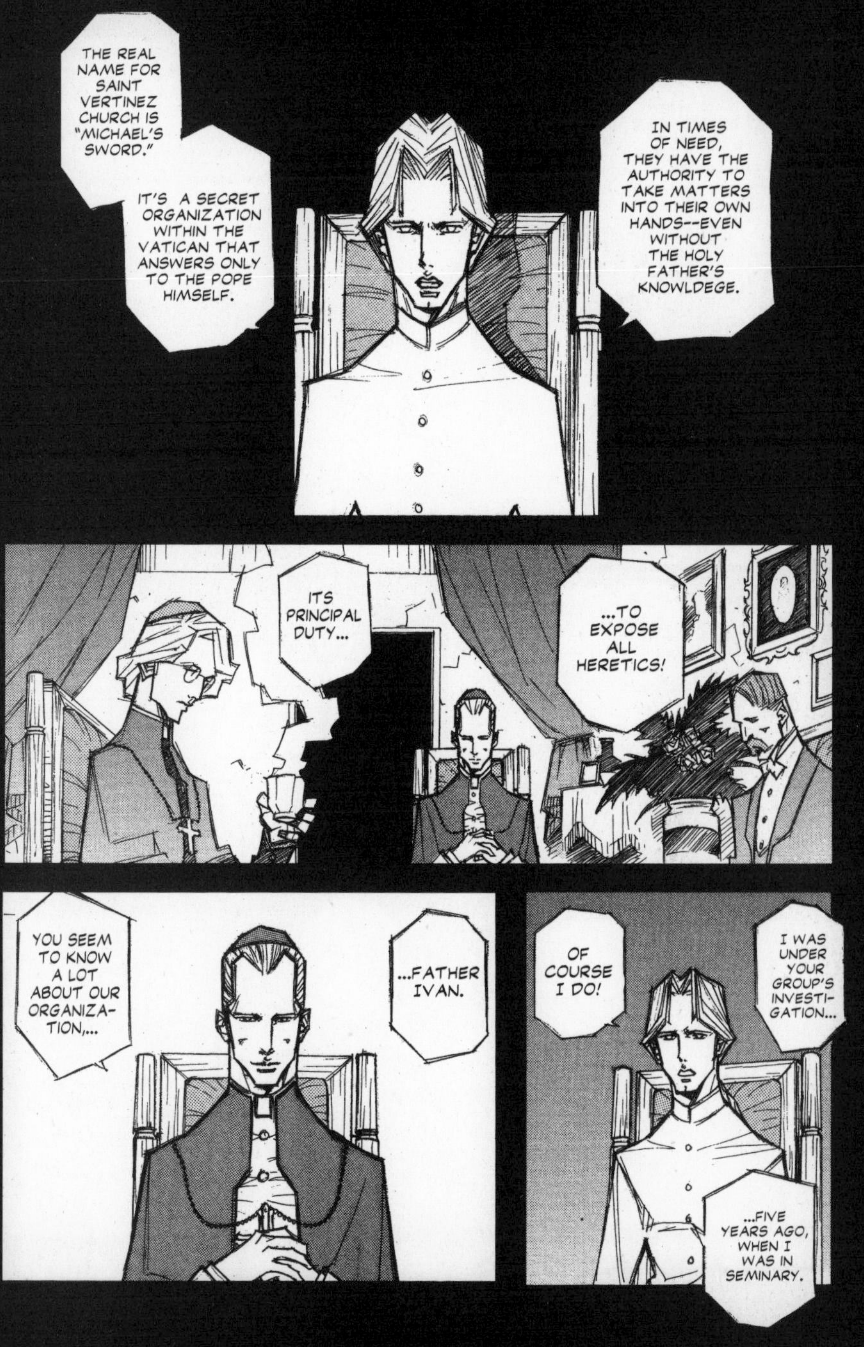
THE REAL NAME FOR SAINT VERTINEZ CHURCH IS "MICHAEL'S SWORD."
IT'S A SECRET ORGANIZATION WITHIN THE VATICAN THAT ANSWERS ONLY TO THE POPE HIMSELF.
IN TIMES OF NEED, THEY HAVE THE AUTHORITY TO TAKE MATTERS INTO THEIR OWN HANDS--EVEN WITHOUT THE HOLY FATHER'S KNOWLDEGE.
ITS PRINCIPAL DUTY...
...TO EXPOSE ALL HERETICS!
YOU SEEM TO KNOW A LOT ABOUT OUR ORGANIZA-TION,...
...FATHER IVAN.
OF COURSE I DO!
I WAS UNDER YOUR GROUP'S INVESTI-GATION...
...FIVE YEARS AGO, WHEN I WAS IN SEMINARY.

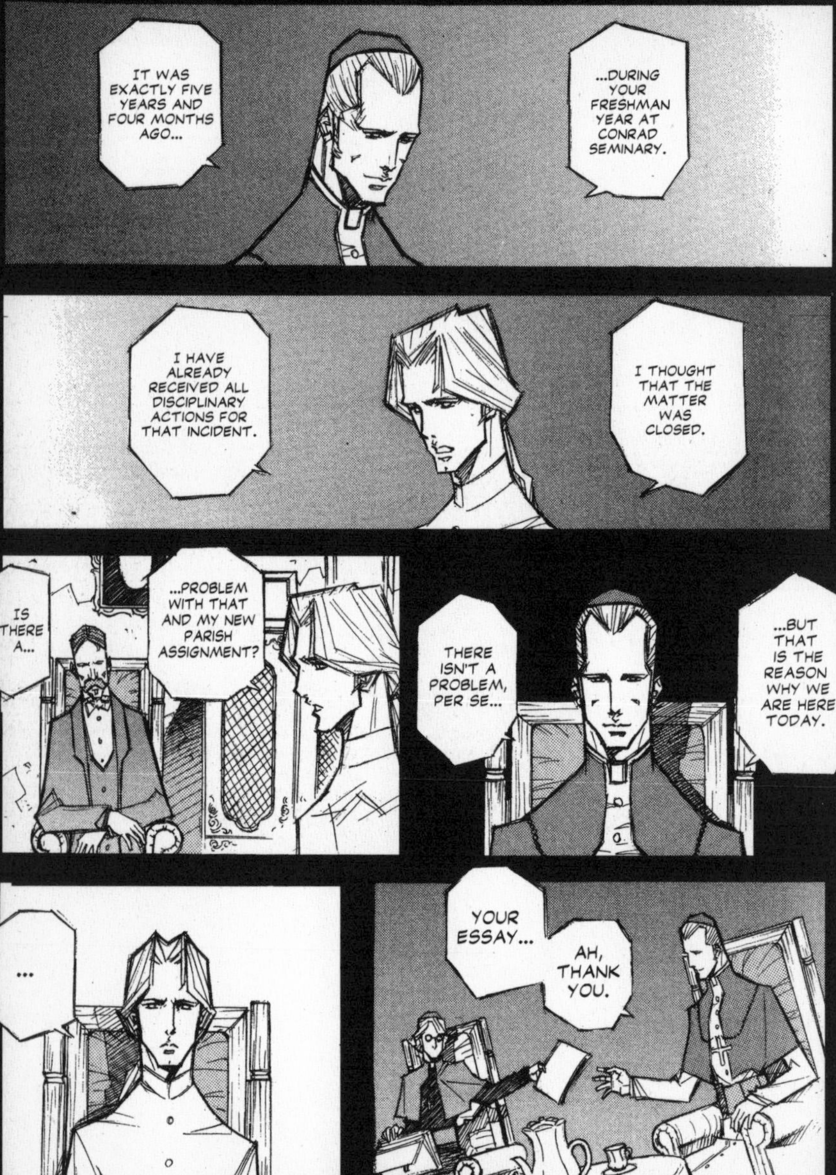
IT WAS EXACTLY FIVE YEARS AND FOUR MONTHS AGO...
...DURING YOUR FRESHMAN YEAR AT CONRAD SEMINARY.
I HAVE ALREADY RECEIVED ALL DISCIPLINARY ACTIONS FOR THAT INCIDENT.
I THOUGHT THAT THE MATTER WAS CLOSED.
IS THERE A...
...PROBLEM WITH THAT AND MY NEW PARISH ASSIGNMENT?
THERE ISN'T A PROBLEM, PER SE...
...BUT THAT IS THE REASON WHY WE ARE HERE TODAY.
...
YOUR ESSAY...
AH, THANK YOU.

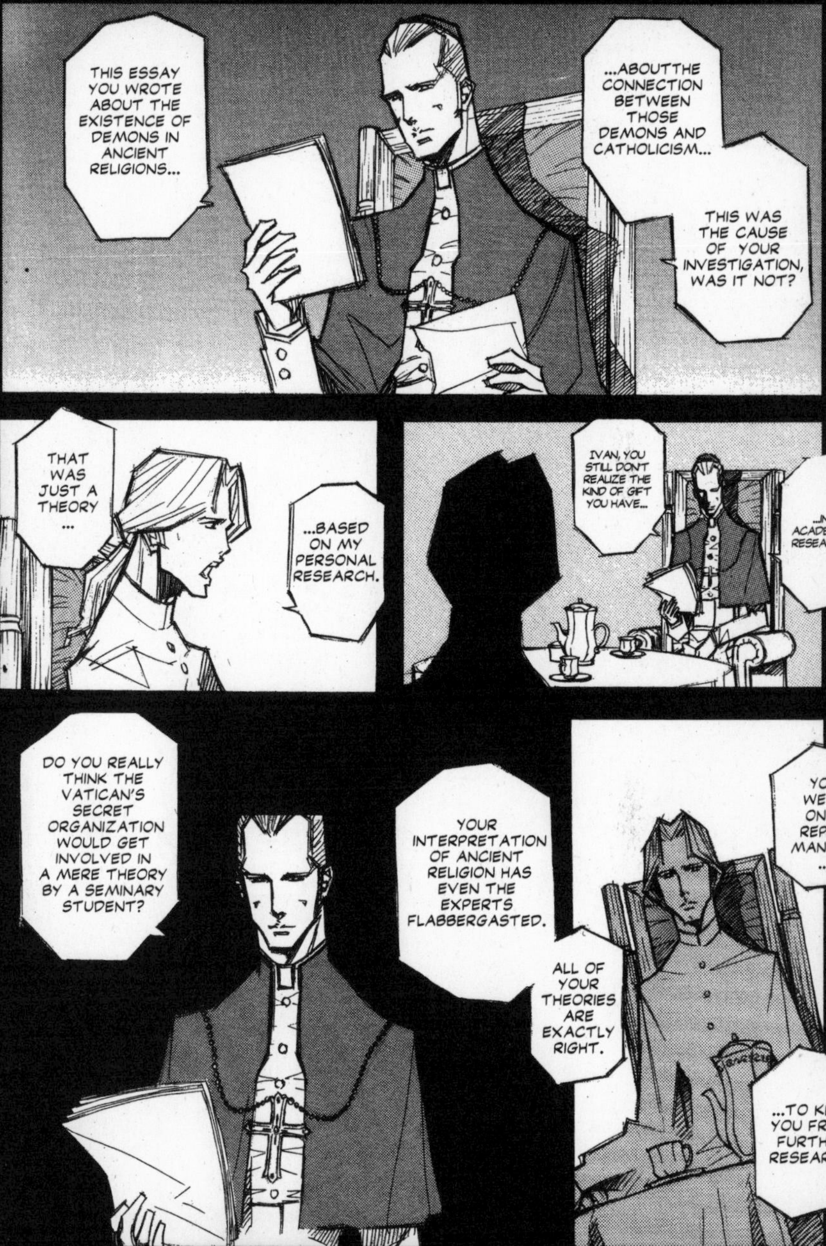
THIS ESSAY YOU WROTE ABOUT THE EXISTENCE OF DEMONS IN ANCIENT RELIGIONS...
...ABOUTTHE CONNECTION BETWEEN THOSE DEMONS AND CATHOLICISM...
THIS WAS THE CAUSE OF YOUR INVESTIGATION, WAS IT NOT?
THAT WAS JUST A THEORY ...
...BASED ON MY PERSONAL RESEARCH.
IVAN, YOU STILL DON'T REALIZE THE KIND OF GIFT YOU HAVE...
...IN ACADEMIC RESEARCH.
DO YOU REALLY THINK THE VATICAN'S SECRET ORGANIZATION WOULD GET INVOLVED IN A MERE THEORY BY A SEMINARY STUDENT?
YOUR INTERPRETATION OF ANCIENT RELIGION HAS EVEN THE EXPERTS FLABBERGASTED.
ALL OF YOUR THEORIES ARE EXACTLY RIGHT.
YOU WERE ONLY REPRI-MANDED ...
...TO KEEP YOU FROM FURTHER RESEARCH.

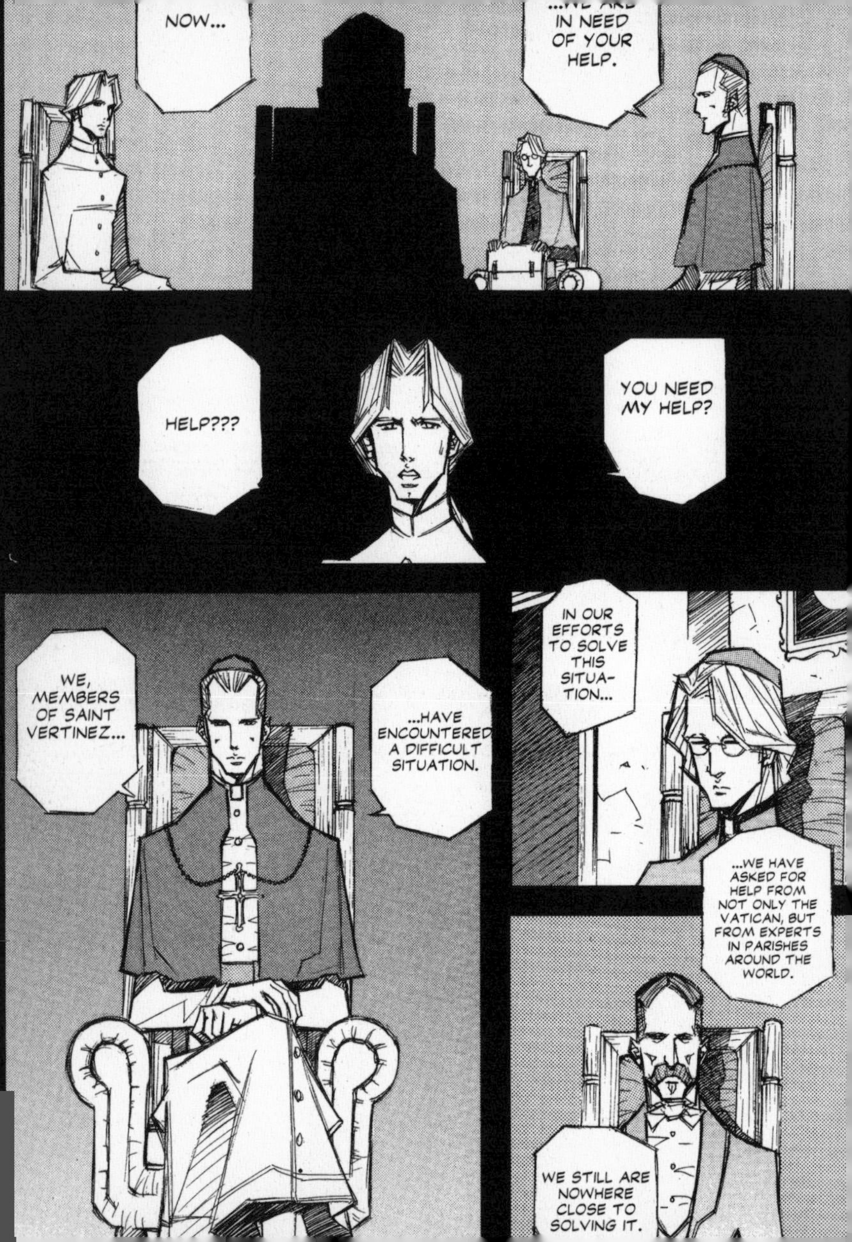
NOW...
IN NEED OF YOUR HELP.
HELP???
YOU NEED MY HELP?
WE, MEMBERS OF SAINT VERTINEZ...
...HAVE ENCOUNTERED A DIFFICULT SITUATION.
IN OUR EFFORTS TO SOLVE THIS SITUA- TION...
...WE HAVE ASKED FOR HELP FROM NOT ONLY THE VATICAN, BUT FROM EXPERTS IN PARISHES AROUND THE WORLD.
WE STILL ARE NOWHERE CLOSE TO SOLVING IT.

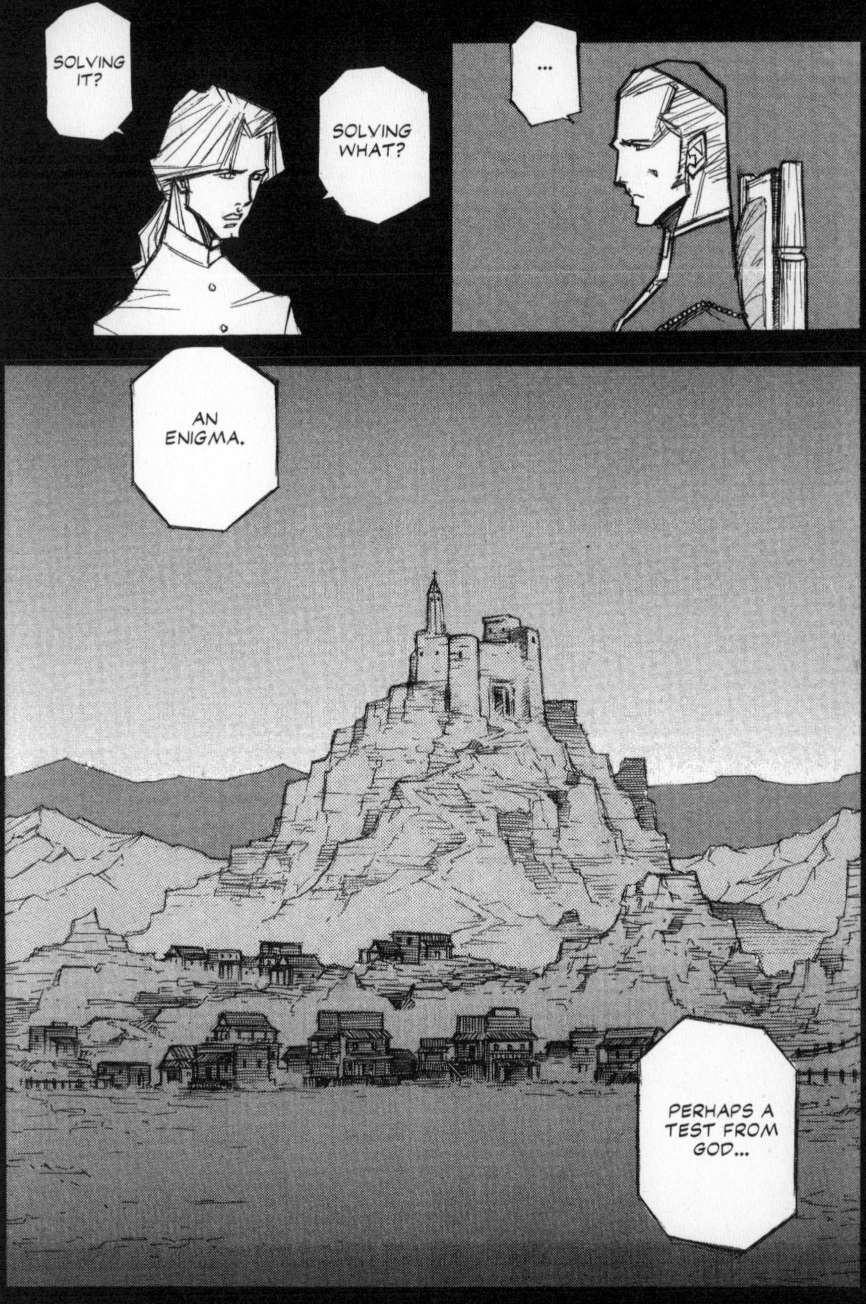
SOLVING IT?
SOLVING WHAT?
...
AN ENIGMA.
PERHAPS A TEST FROM GOD...

...OR PERHAPS SOME
CRUEL JOKE OF THE
DEVIL HIMSELF.

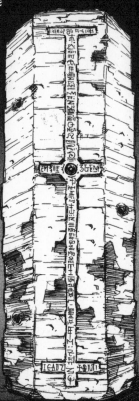

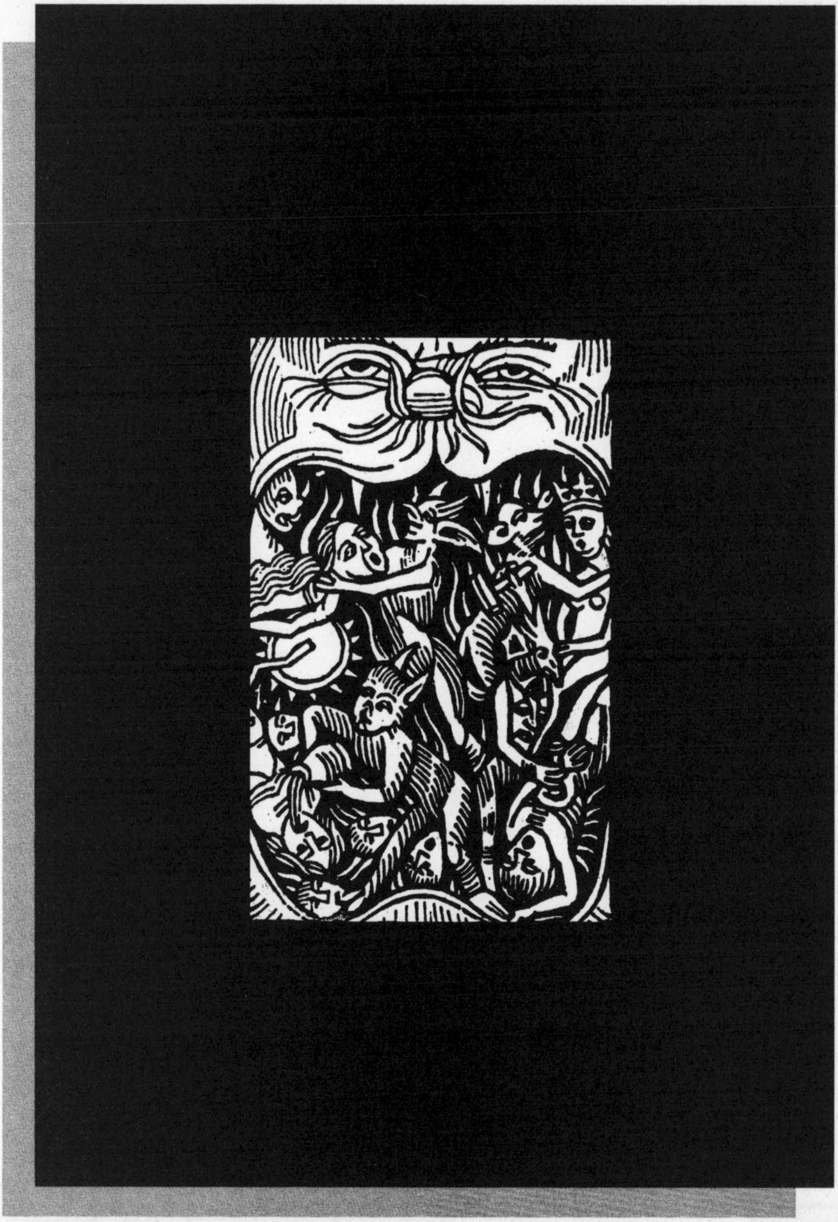

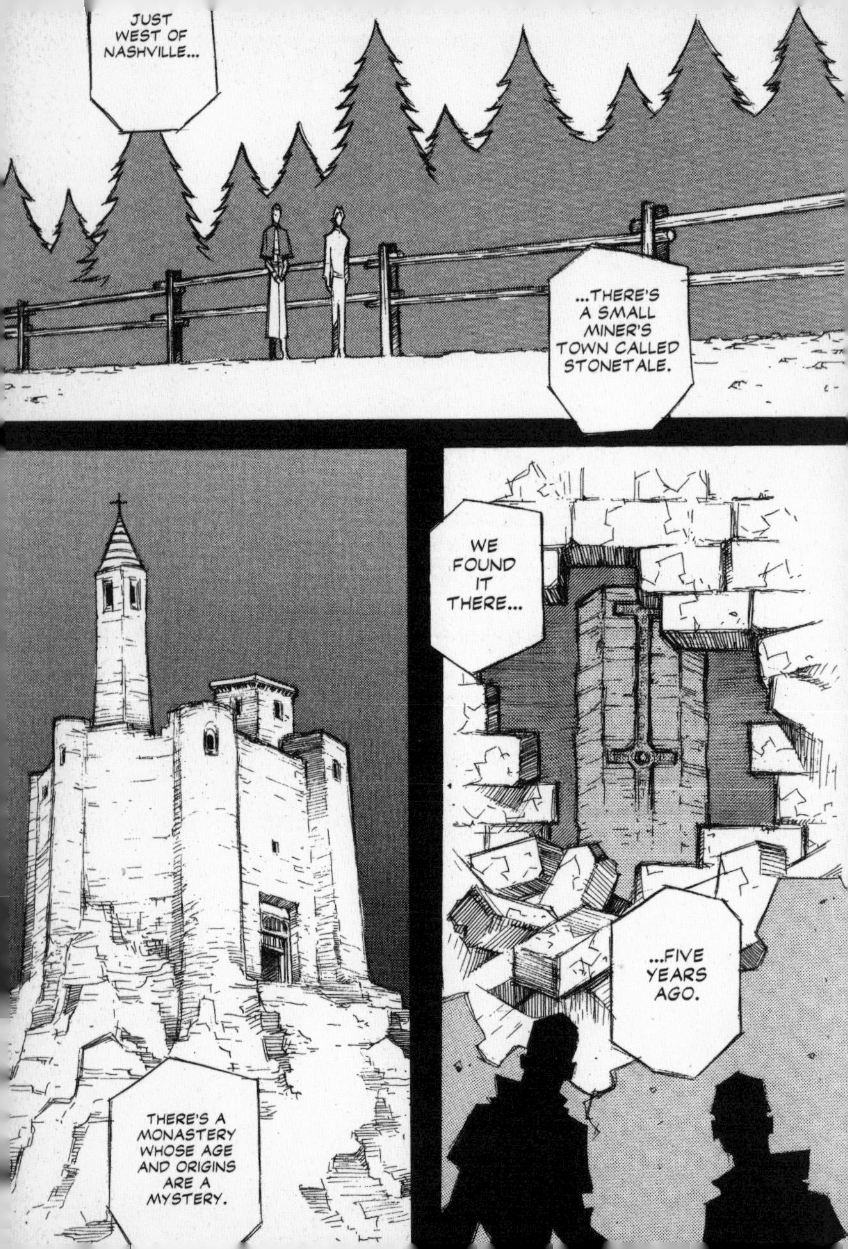
JUST WEST OF NASHVILLE...
...THERE'S A SMALL MINER'S TOWN CALLED STONETALE.
THERE'S A MONASTERY WHOSE AGE AND ORIGINS ARE A MYSTERY.
WE FOUND IT THERE...
...FIVE YEARS AGO.

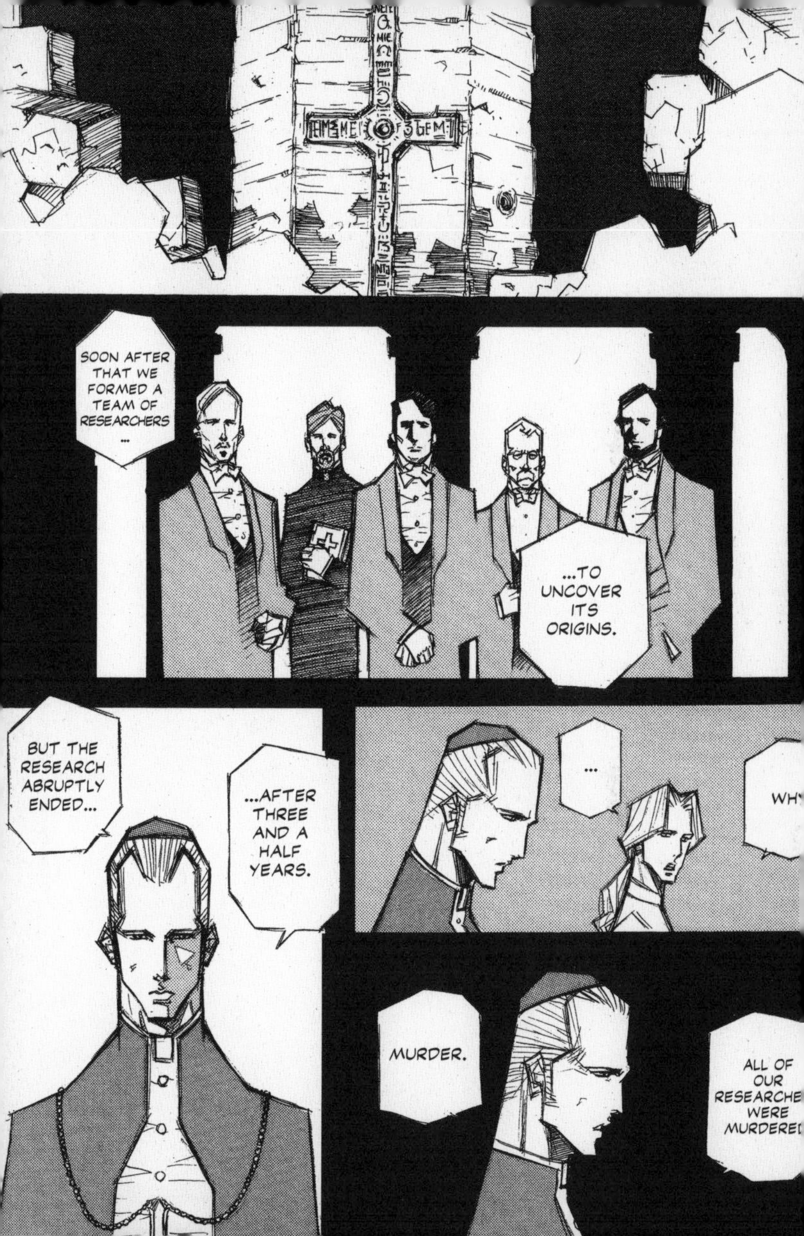

SOON AFTER THAT WE FORMED A TEAM OF RESEARCHERS ...
...TO UNCOVER ITS ORIGINS.
BUT THE RESEARCH ABRUPTLY ENDED...
...AFTER THREE AND A HALF YEARS.
...
WH
MURDER.
ALL OF OUR RESEARCHE WERE MURDERED

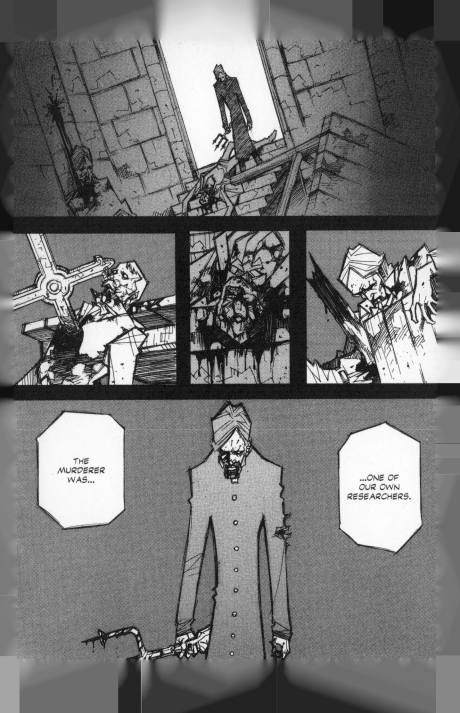

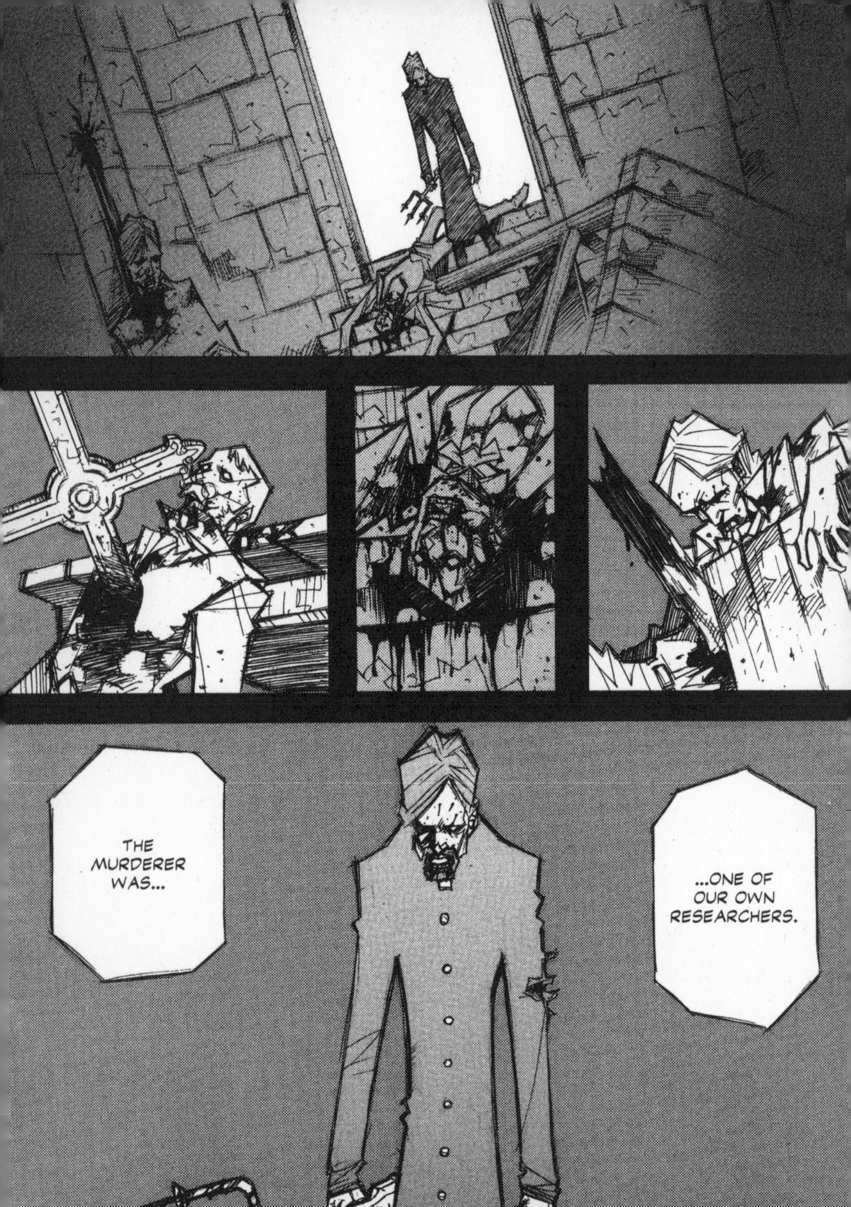
THE MURDERER WAS...
...ONE OF OUR OWN RESEARCHERS.

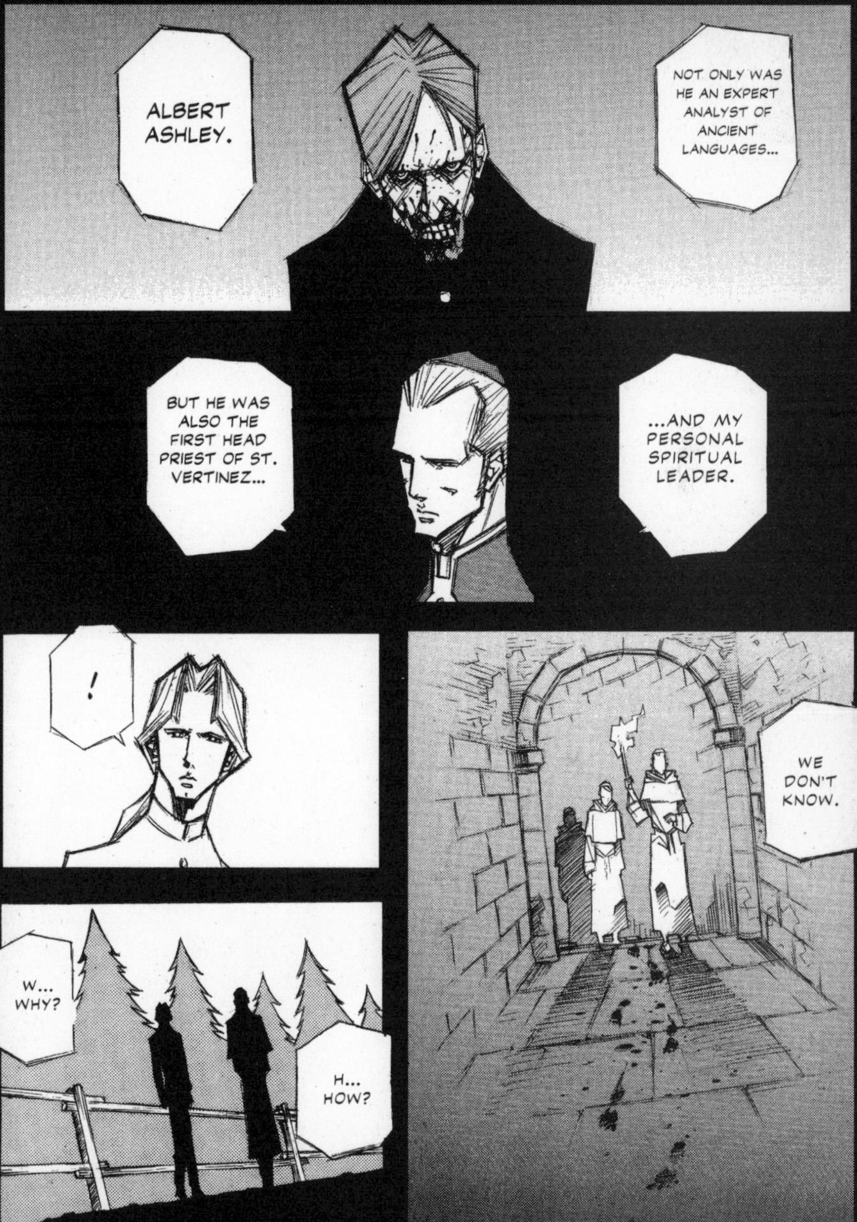
ALBERT ASHLEY.
NOT ONLY WAS HE AN EXPERT ANALYST OF ANCIENT LANGUAGES...
BUT HE WAS ALSO THE FIRST HEAD PRIEST OF ST. VERTINEZ...
...AND MY PERSONAL SPIRITUAL LEADER.
!
WE DON'T KNOW.
W... WHY?
H... HOW?

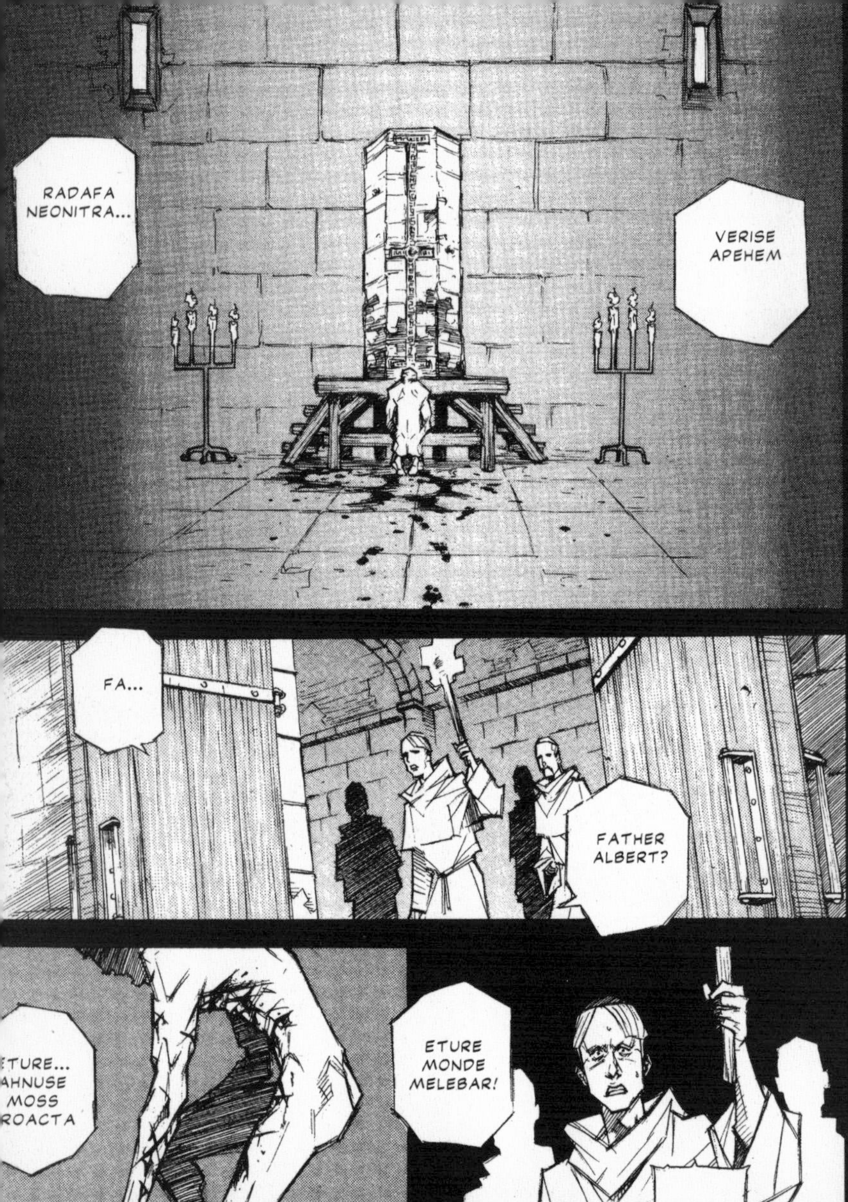
RADAFA NEONITRA...
VERISE APEHEM
FA...
FATHER ALBERT?
ETURE... AHNUSE MOSS ROACTA
ETURE MONDE MELEBAR!
!!

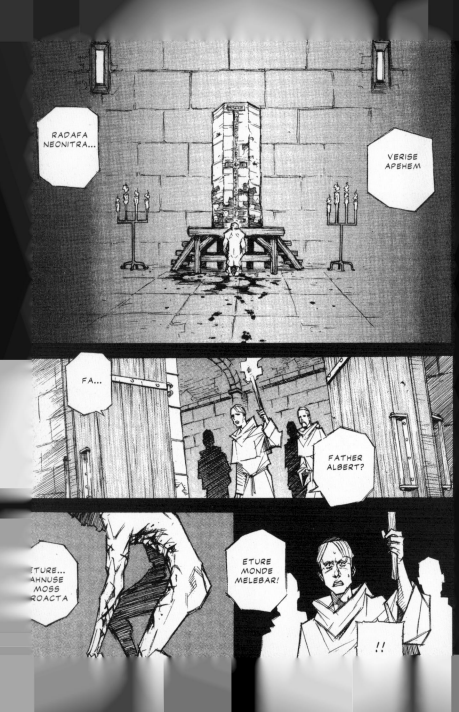

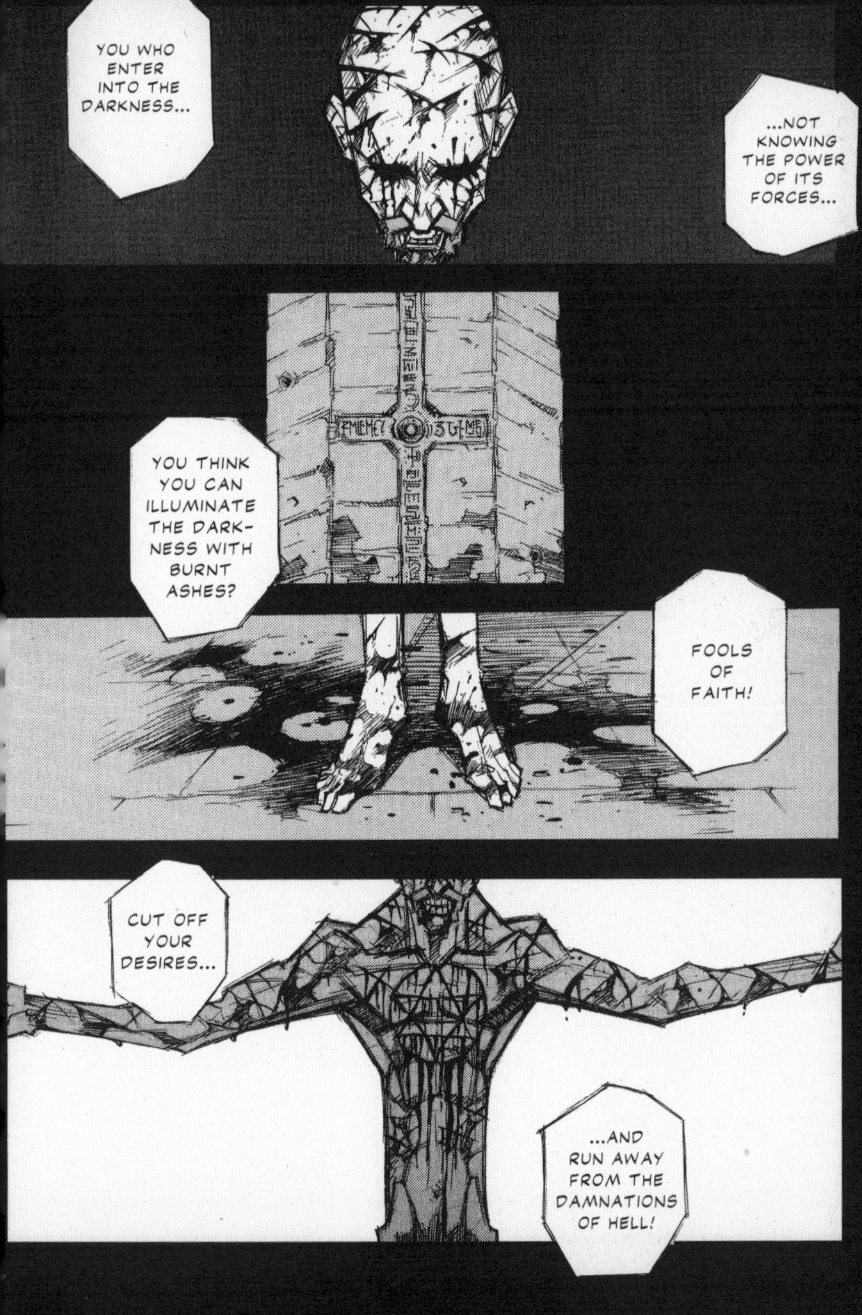
YOU WHO ENTER INTO THE DARKNESS...
...NOT KNOWING THE POWER OF ITS FORCES...
YOU THINK YOU CAN ILLUMINATE THE DARK-NESS WITH BURNT ASHES?
FOOLS OF FAITH!
CUT OFF YOUR DESIRES...
...AND RUN AWAY FROM THE DAMNATIONS OF HELL!

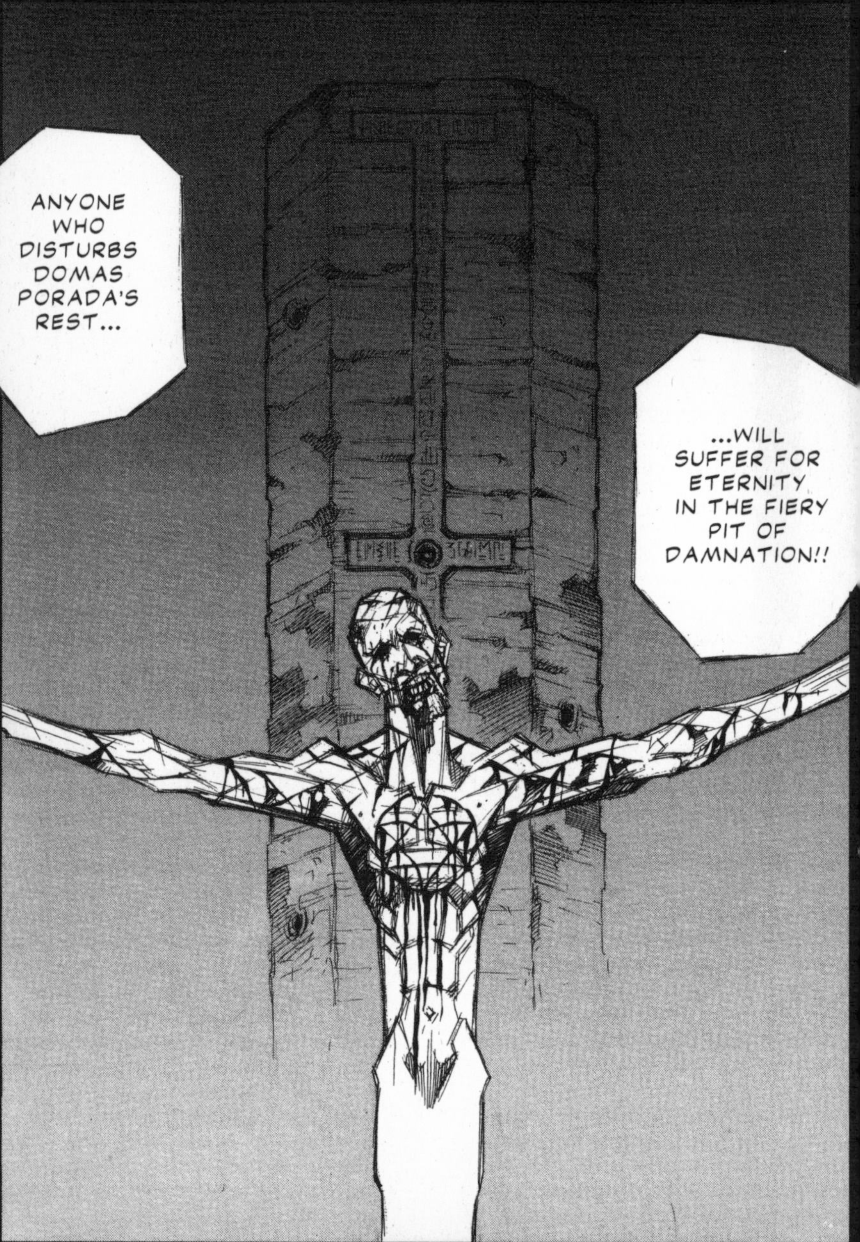
ANYONE WHO DISTURBS DOMAS PORADA'S REST...
...WILL SUFFER FOR ETERNITY IN THE FIERY PIT OF DAMNATION!!

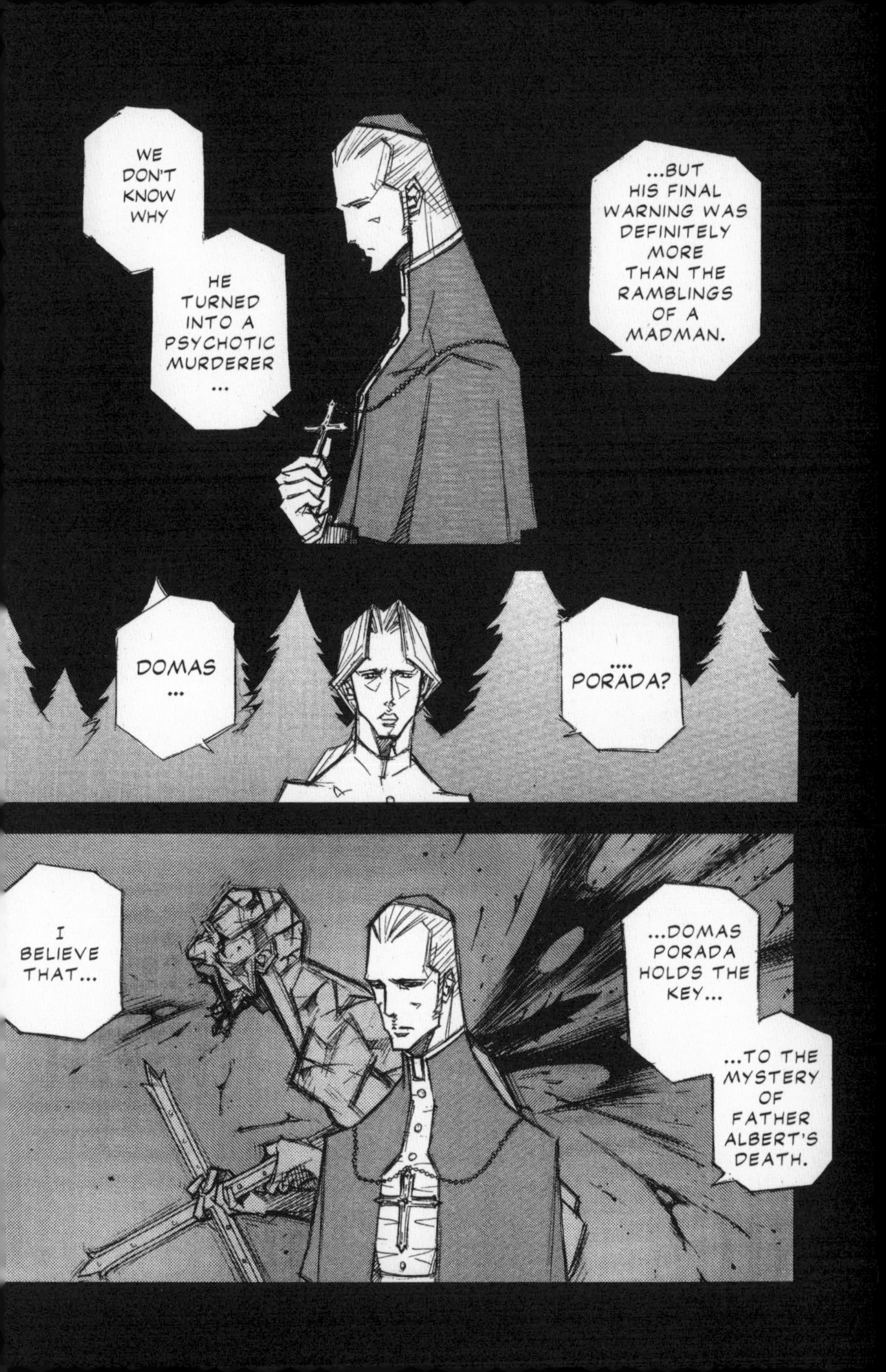
WE DON'T KNOW WHY
HE TURNED INTO A PSYCHOTIC MURDERER ...
...BUT HIS FINAL WARNING WAS DEFINITELY MORE THAN THE RAMBLINGS OF A MADMAN.
DOMAS ...
.... PORADA?
I BELIEVE THAT...
...DOMAS PORADA HOLDS THE KEY...
...TO THE MYSTERY OF FATHER ALBERT'S DEATH.

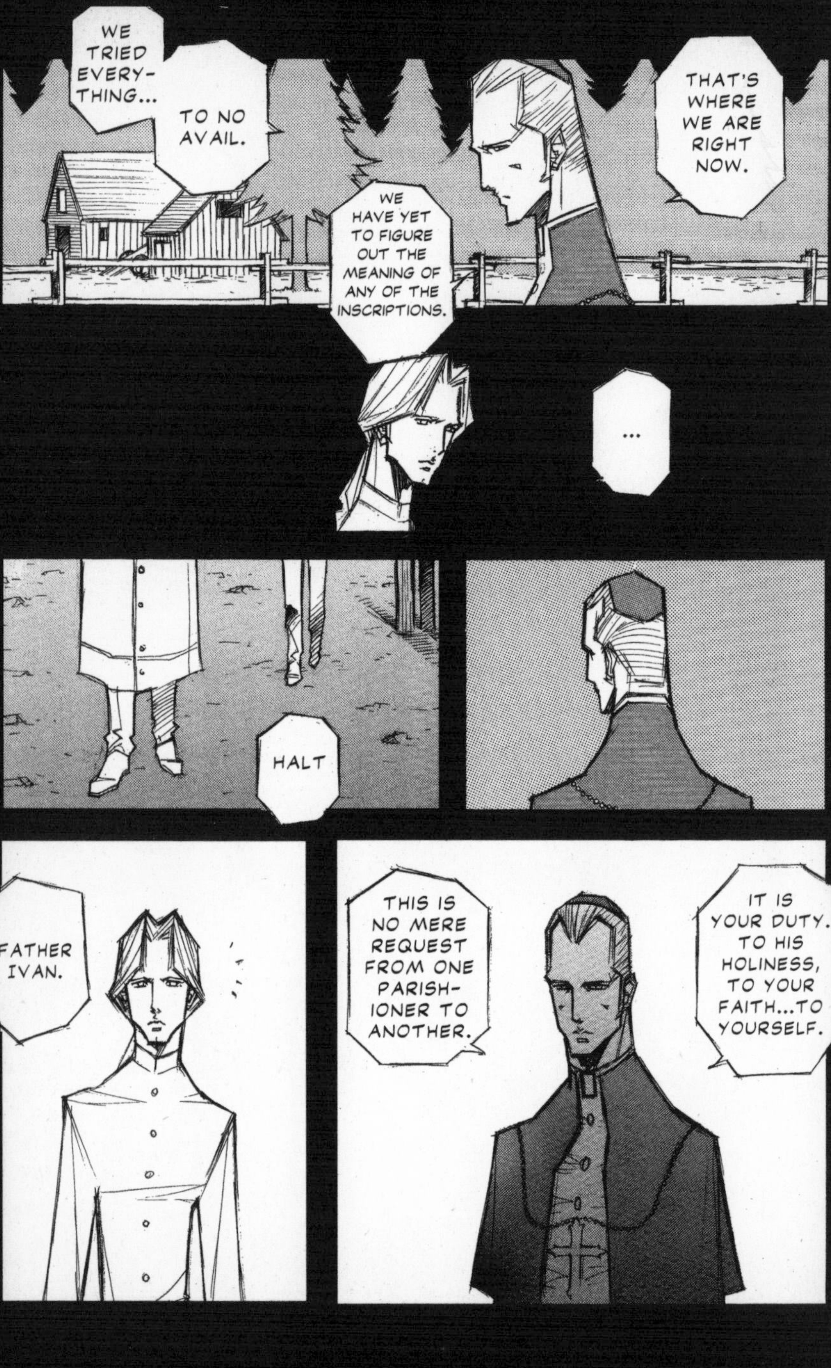

WE TRIED EVERY-THING...
TO NO AVAIL.
WE HAVE YET TO FIGURE OUT THE MEANING OF ANY OF THE INSCRIPTIONS.
THAT'S WHERE WE ARE RIGHT NOW.
...
HALT
FATHER IVAN.
THIS IS NO MERE REQUEST FROM ONE PARISH-IONER TO ANOTHER.
IT IS YOUR DUTY. TO HIS HOLINESS, TO YOUR FAITH...TO YOURSELF.

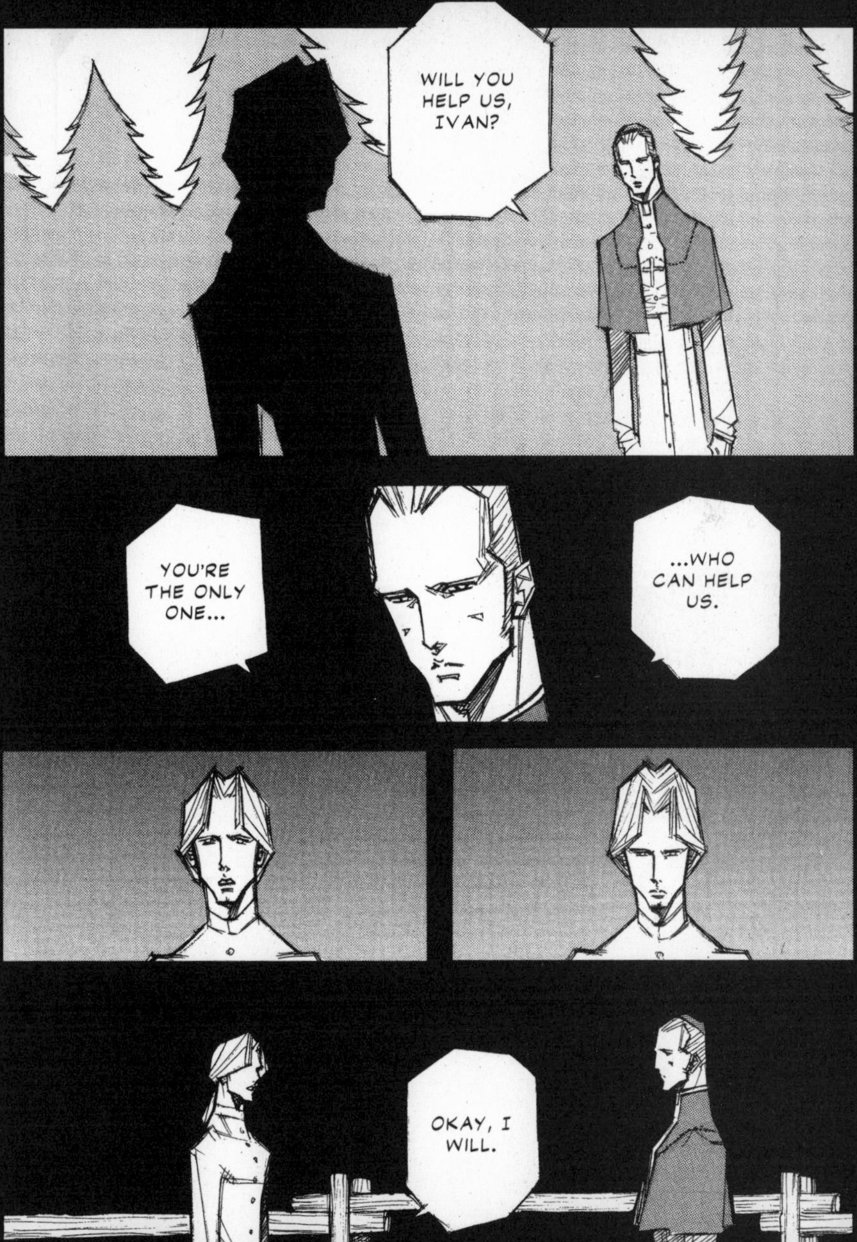
WILL YOU HELP US, IVAN?
YOU'RE THE ONLY ONE...
...WHO CAN HELP US.
OKAY, I WILL.

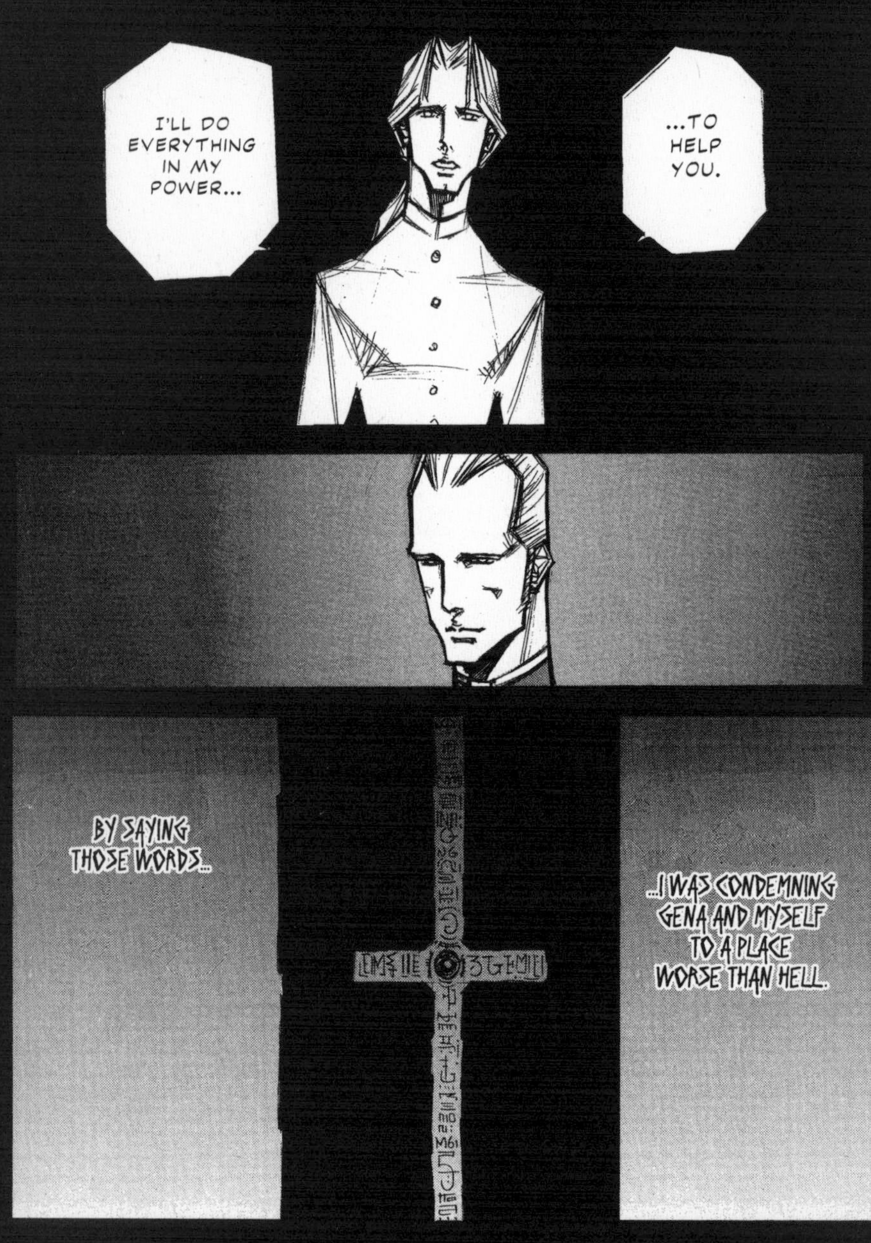
I'LL DO EVERYTHING IN MY POWER...
...TO HELP YOU.
BY SAYING THOSE WORDS...
...I WAS CONDEMNING GENA AND MYSELF TO A PLACE WORSE THAN HELL.

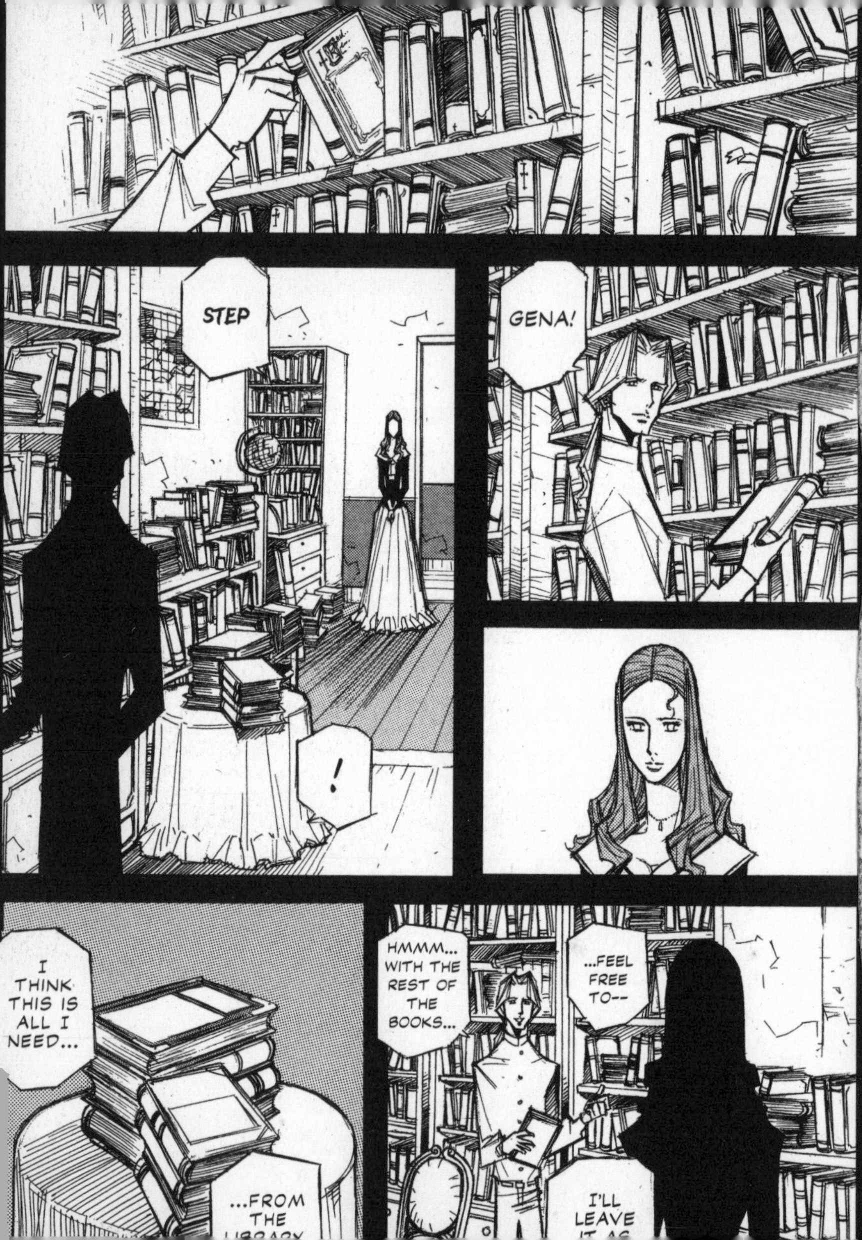
STEP
!
GENA!
I THINK THIS IS ALL I NEED...
...FROM THE
HMMM... WITH THE REST OF THE BOOKS...
...FEEL FREE TO--
I'LL LEAVE

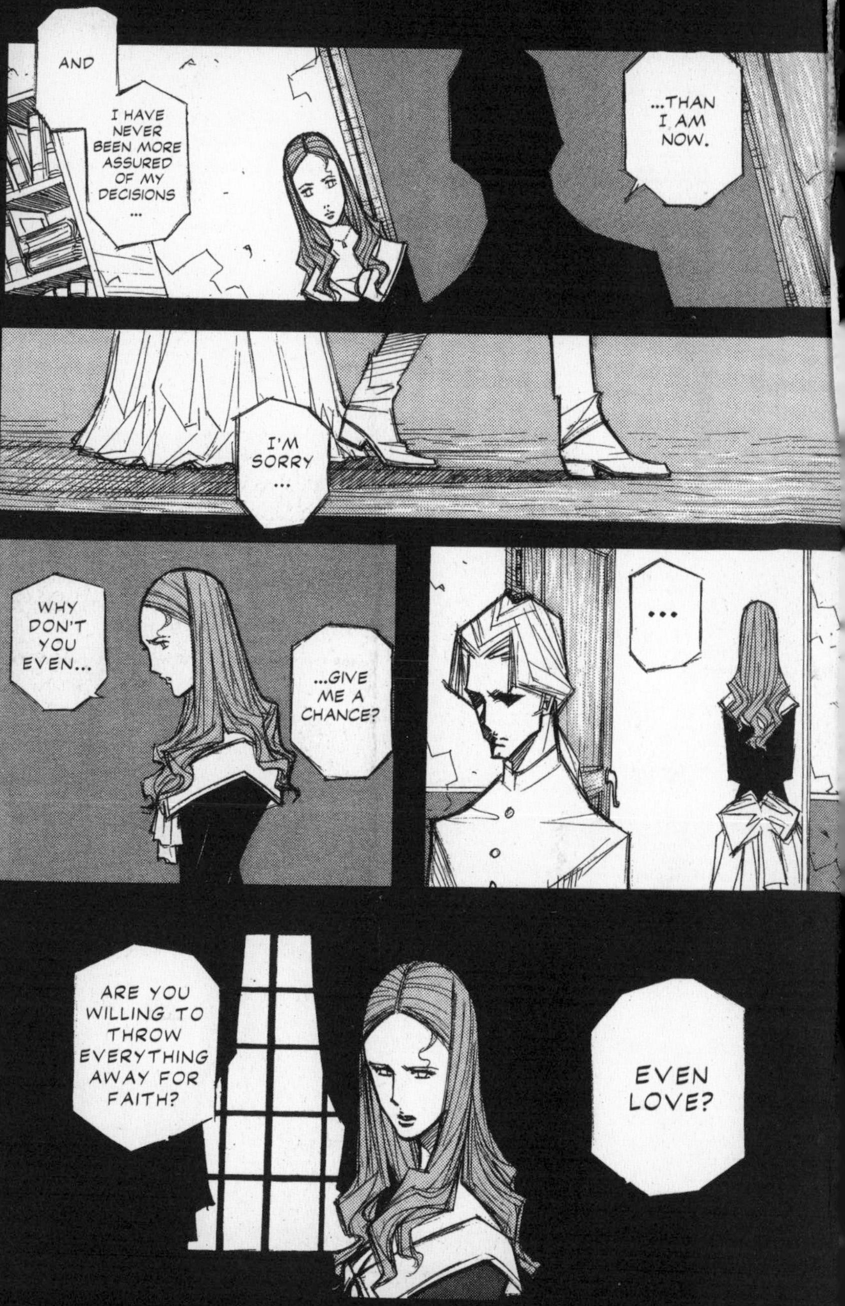
AND
I HAVE NEVER BEEN MORE ASSURED OF MY DECISIONS ...
...THAN I AM NOW.
I'M SORRY ...
WHY DON'T YOU EVEN...
...GIVE ME A CHANCE?
...
ARE YOU WILLING TO THROW EVERYTHING AWAY FOR FAITH?
EVEN LOVE?

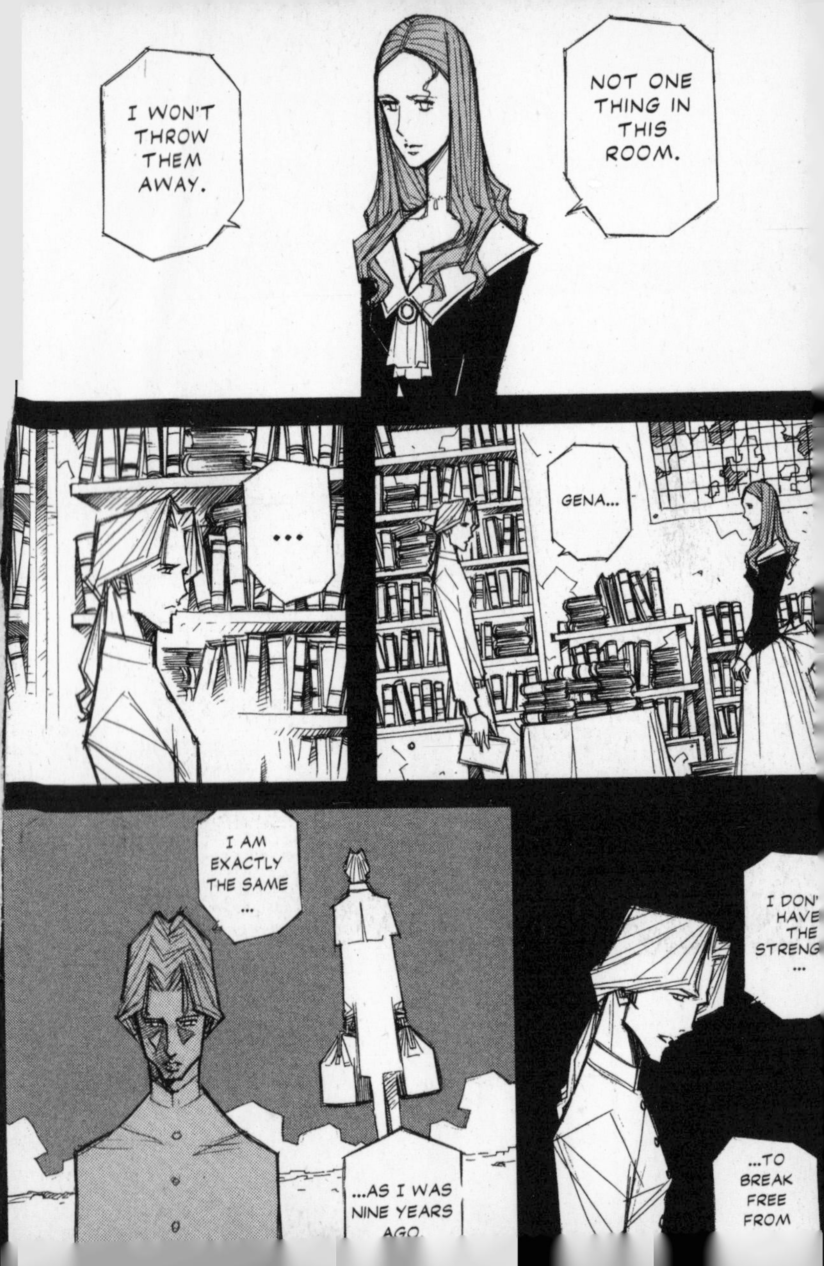
I WON'T THROW THEM AWAY.
NOT ONE THING IN THIS ROOM.
...
GENA...
I AM EXACTLY THE SAME ...
...AS I WAS NINE YEARS AGO.
I DON' HAVE THE STRENG ...
...TO BREAK FREE FROM

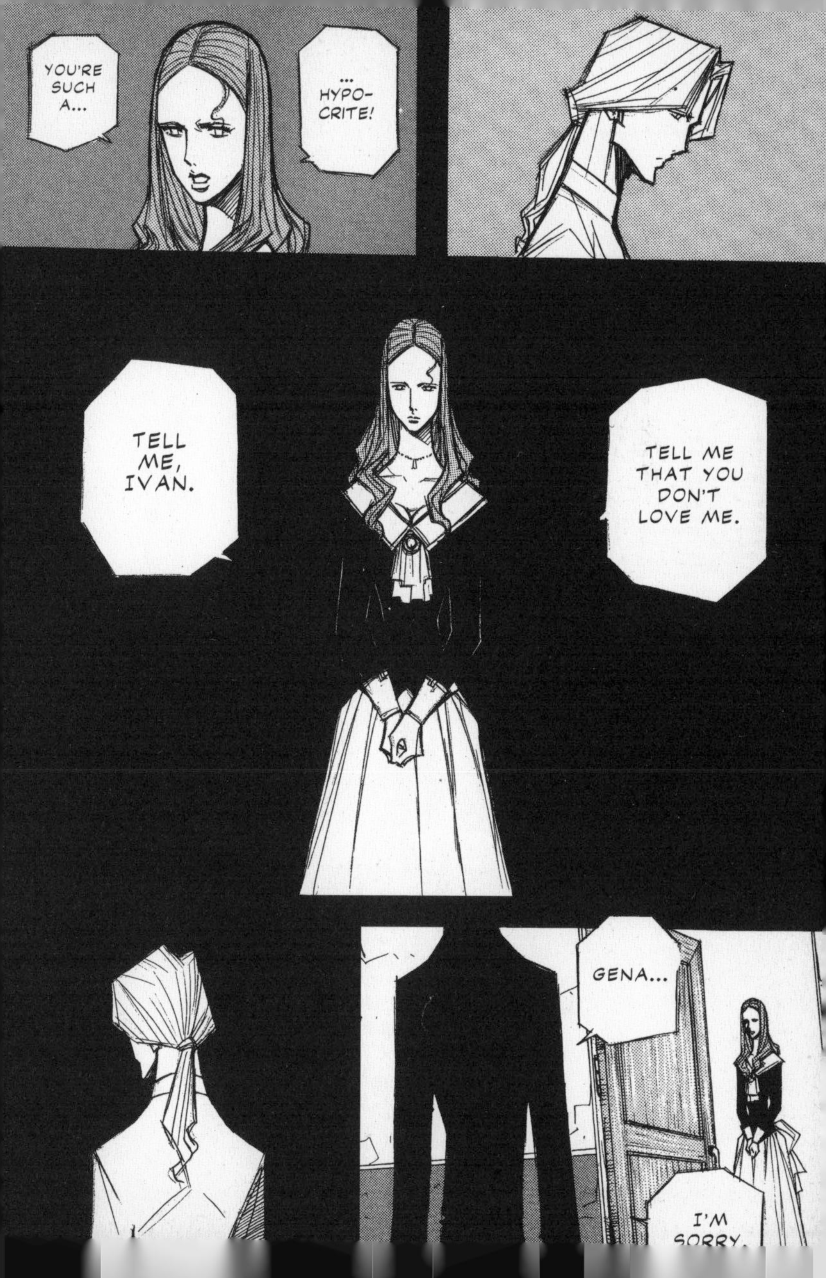
YOU'RE SUCH A...
...HYPO-CRITE!
TELL ME, IVAN.
TELL ME THAT YOU DON'T LOVE ME.
GENA...
I'M SORRY.

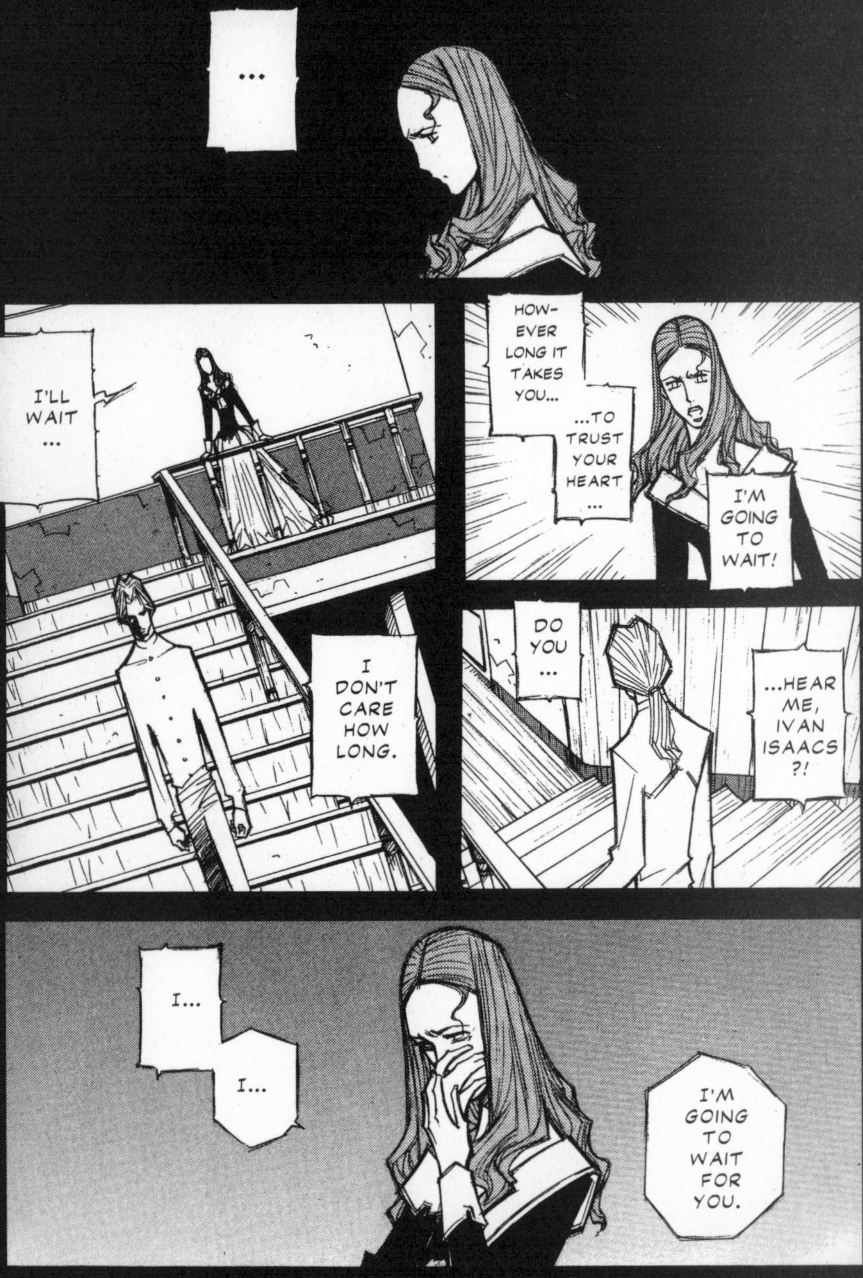
...
I'LL WAIT ...
I DON'T CARE HOW LONG.
HOW-EVER LONG IT TAKES YOU...
...TO TRUST YOUR HEART ...
I'M GOING TO WAIT!
DO YOU ...
...HEAR ME, IVAN ISAACS ?!
I...
I...
I'M GOING TO WAIT FOR YOU.

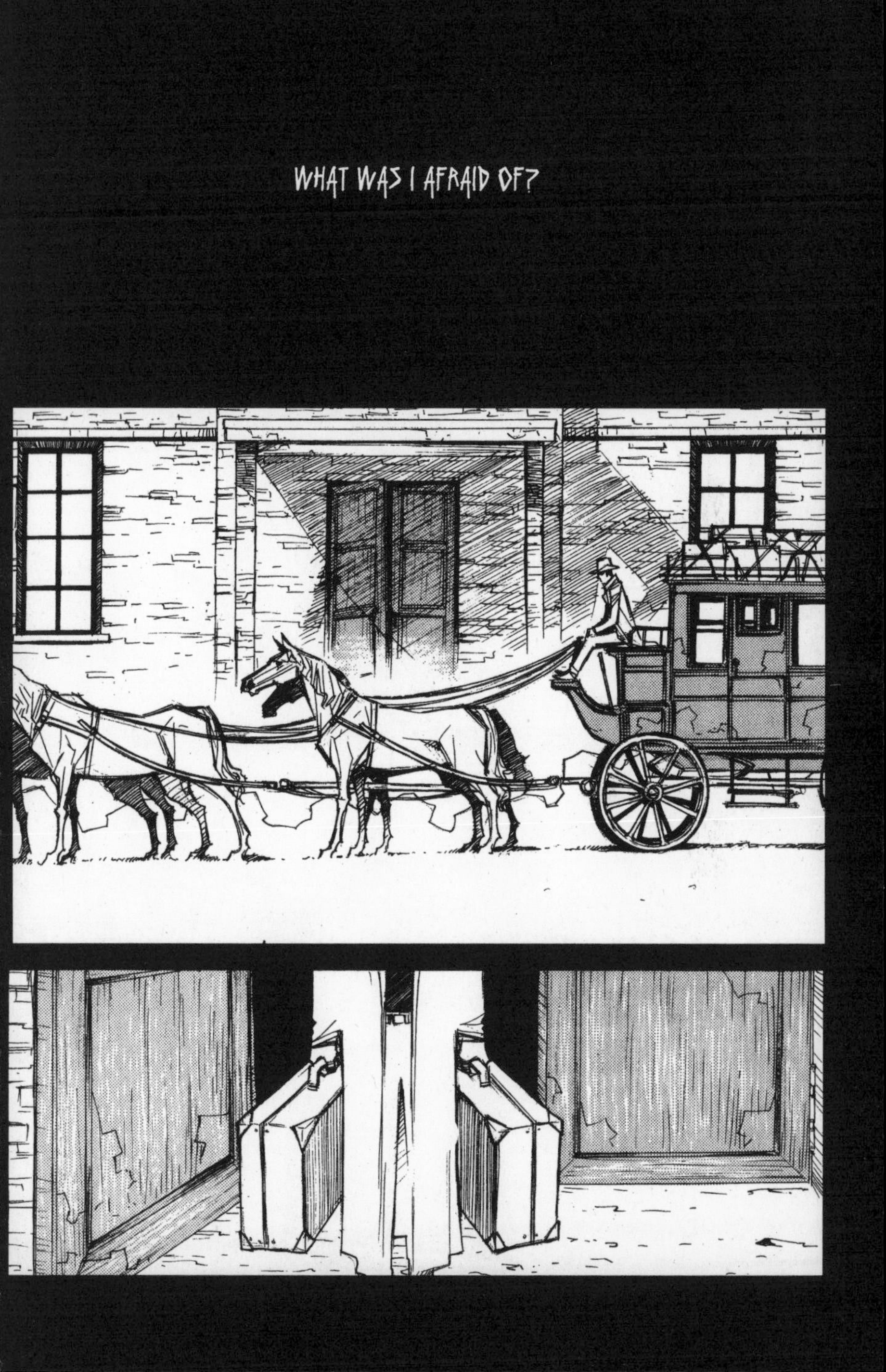
WHAT WAS I AFRAID OF?

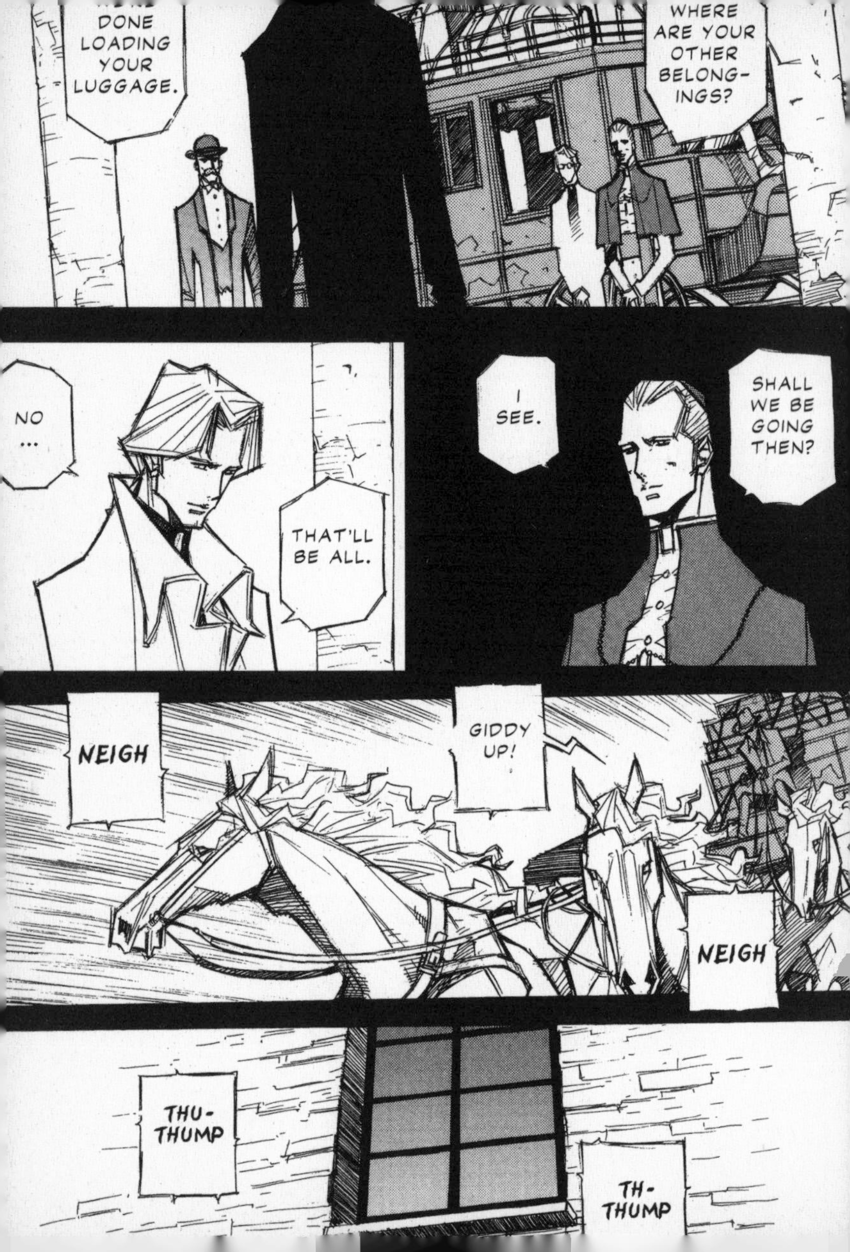
DONE LOADING YOUR LUGGAGE.
WHERE ARE YOUR OTHER BELONG-INGS?
NO ...
THAT'LL BE ALL.
I SEE.
SHALL WE BE GOING THEN?
NEIGH
GIDDY UP!
NEIGH
THU-THUMP
TH-THUMP

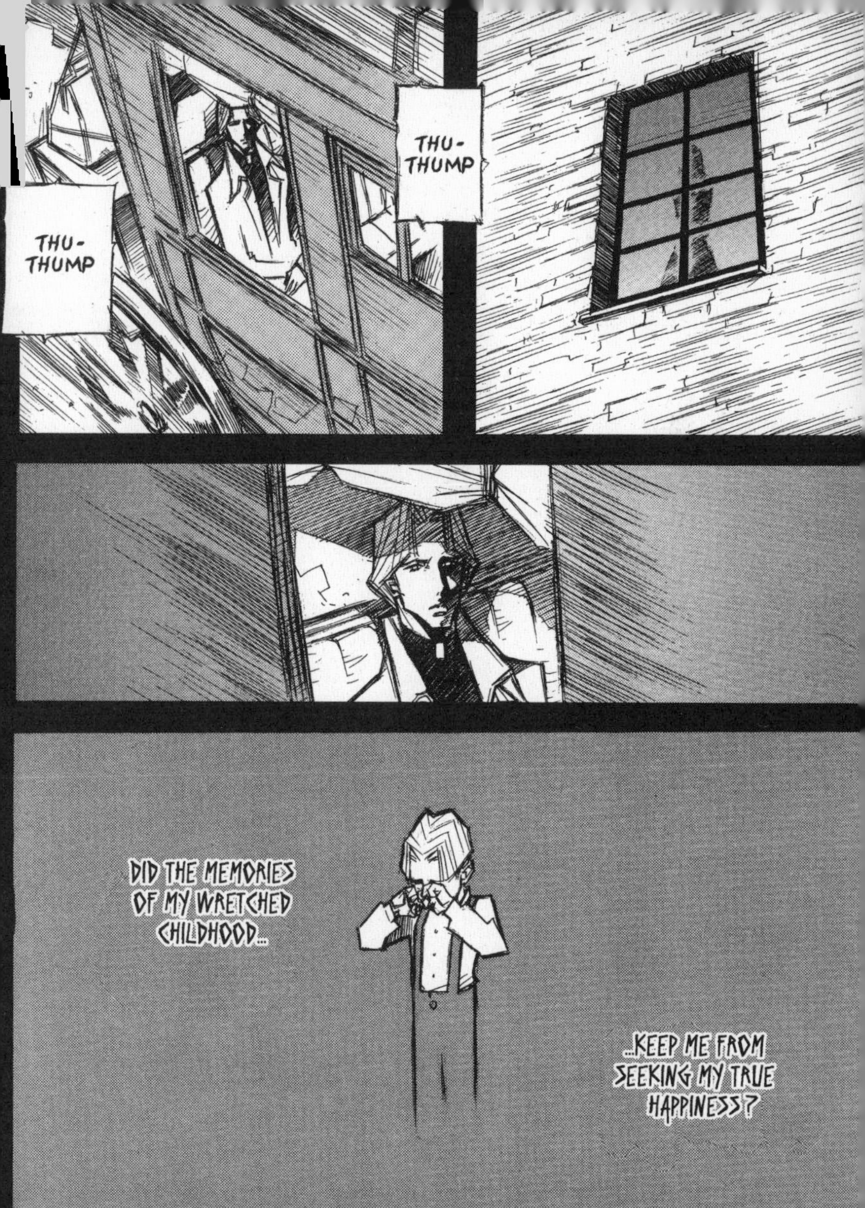
THU-
THUMP
THU-
THUMP
DID THE MEMORIES OF MY WRETCHED CHILDHOOD...
...KEEP ME FROM SEEKING MY TRUE HAPPINESS?

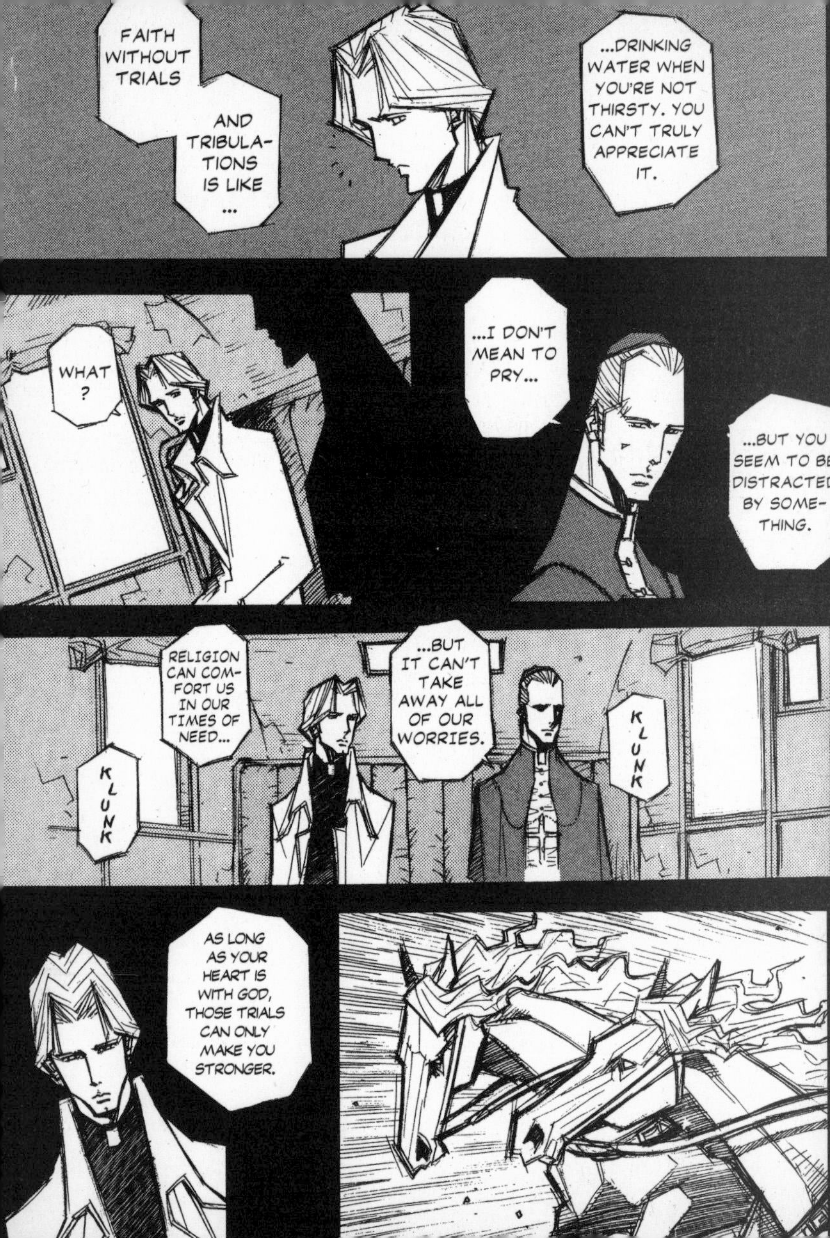
FAITH WITHOUT TRIALS
AND TRIBULATIONS IS LIKE ...
...DRINKING WATER WHEN YOU'RE NOT THIRSTY. YOU CAN'T TRULY APPRECIATE IT.
WHAT?
...I DON'T MEAN TO PRY...
...BUT YOU SEEM TO BE DISTRACTED BY SOMETHING.
KLUNK
RELIGION CAN COMFORT US IN OUR TIMES OF NEED...
...BUT IT CAN'T TAKE AWAY ALL OF OUR WORRIES.
KLUNK
AS LONG AS YOUR HEART IS WITH GOD, THOSE TRIALS CAN ONLY MAKE YOU STRONGER.

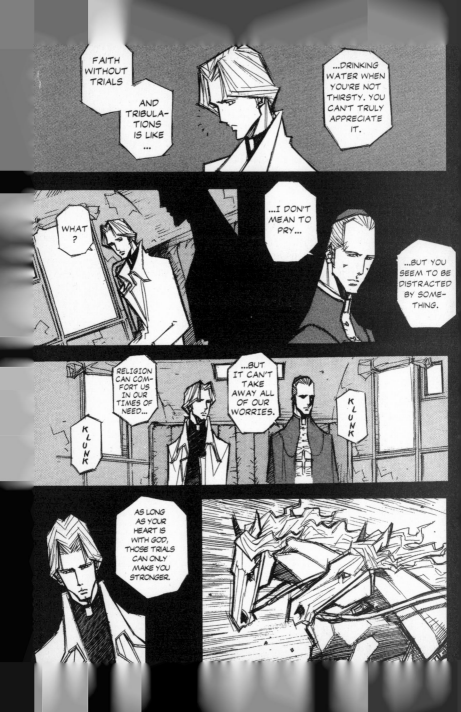

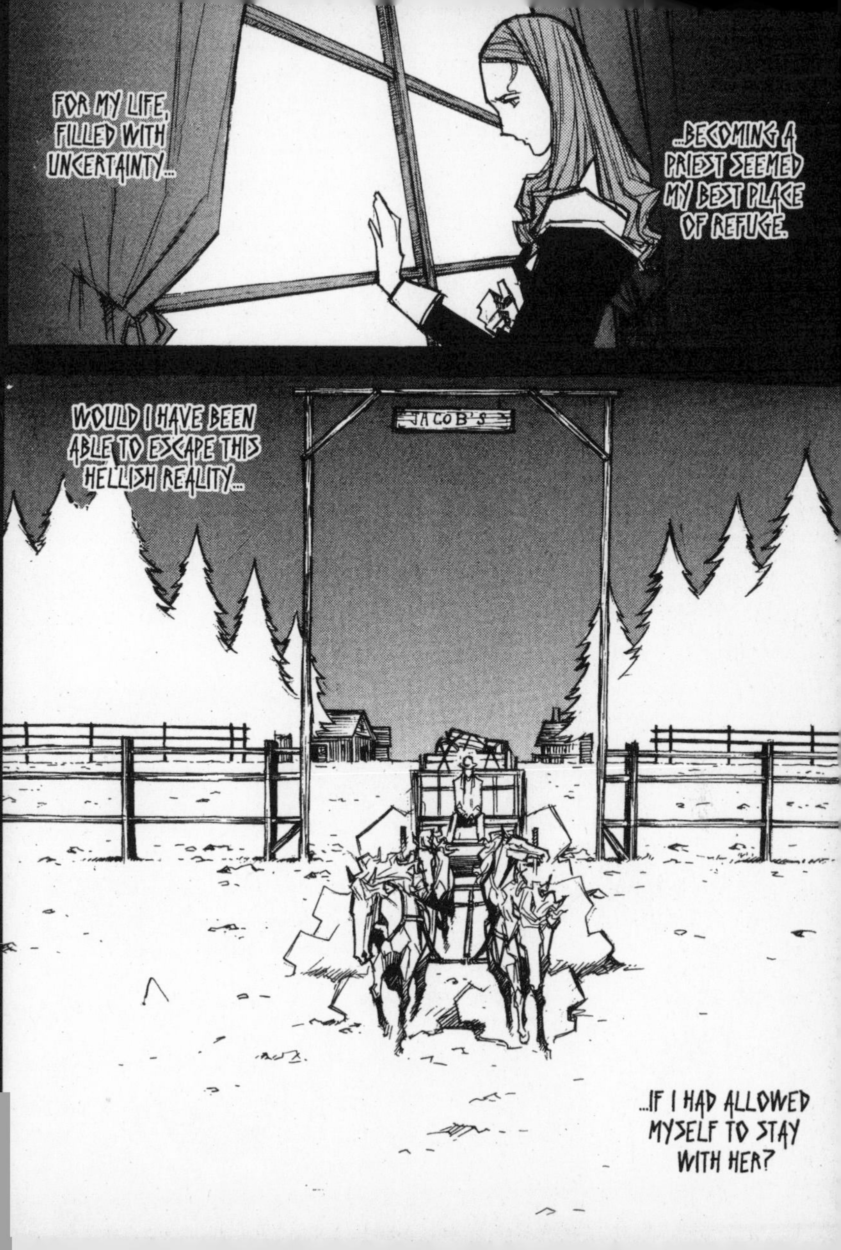
FOR MY LIFE, FILLED WITH UNCERTAINTY...
...BECOMING A PRIEST SEEMED MY BEST PLACE OF REFUGE.
WOULD I HAVE BEEN ABLE TO ESCAPE THIS HELLISH REALITY...
JACOB'S
...IF I HAD ALLOWED MYSELF TO STAY WITH HER?

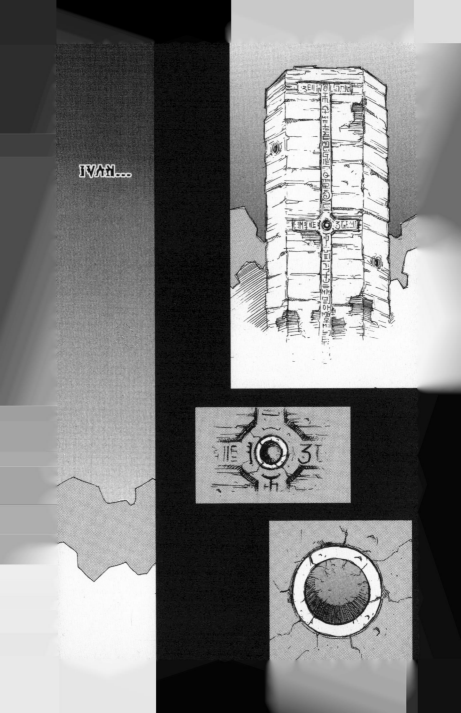

IVAN...

WELCOME...

 ...HE WHO KNOWS THE SECRET OF AWAKENING.

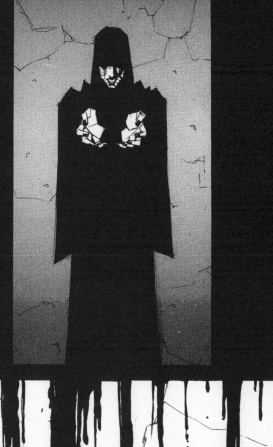

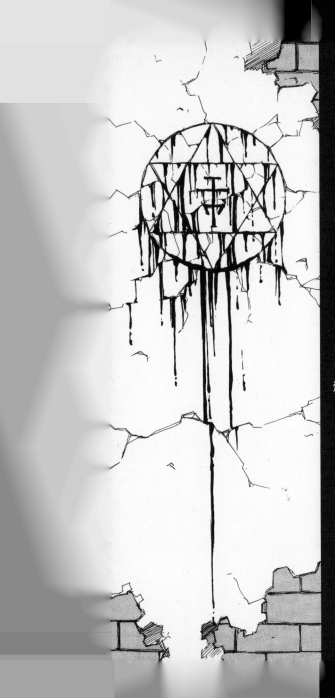

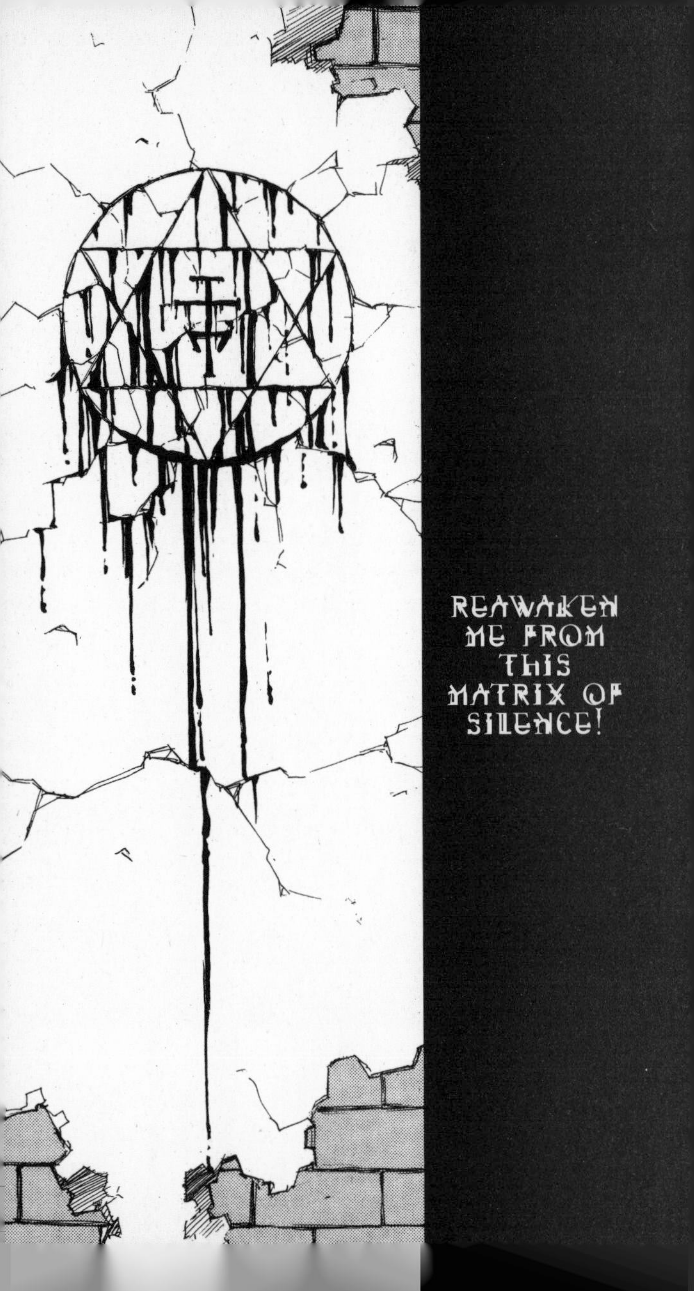
REAWAKEN ME FROM THIS MATRIX OF SILENCE!

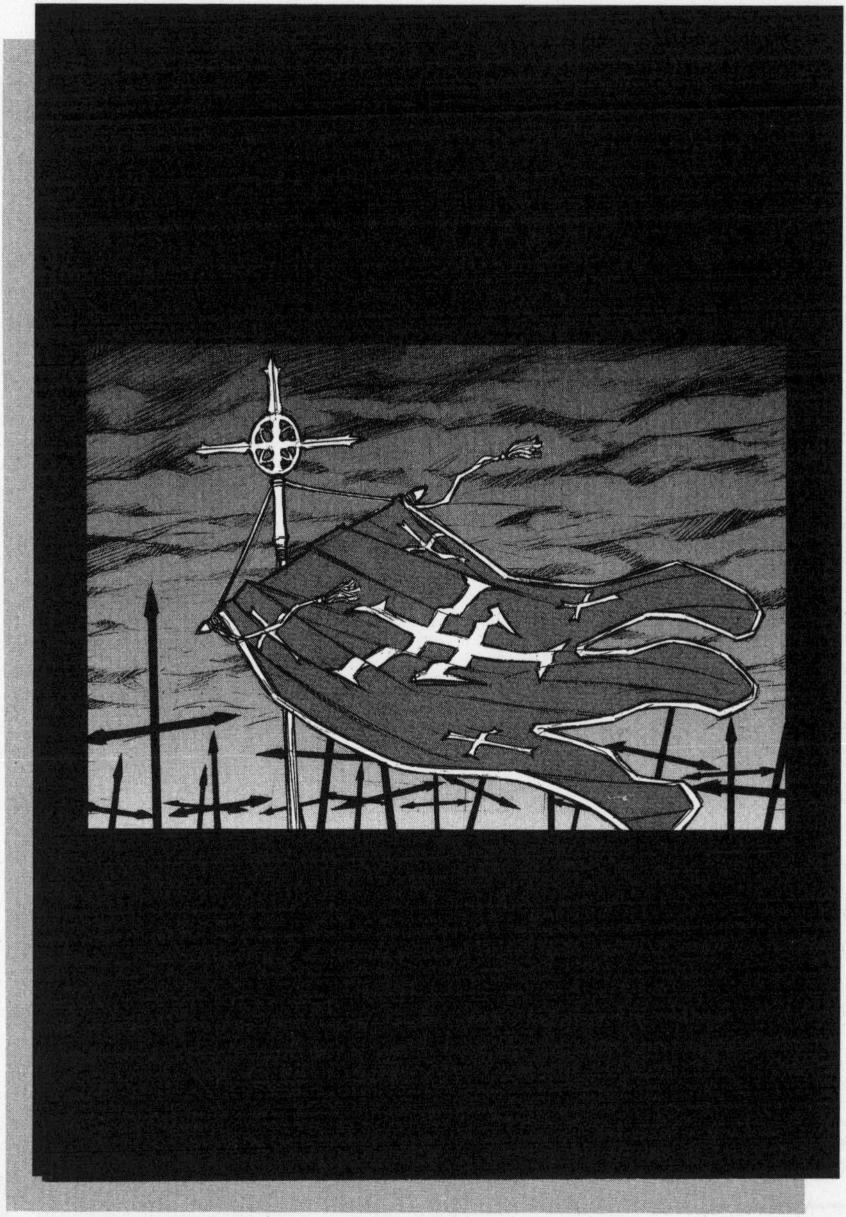

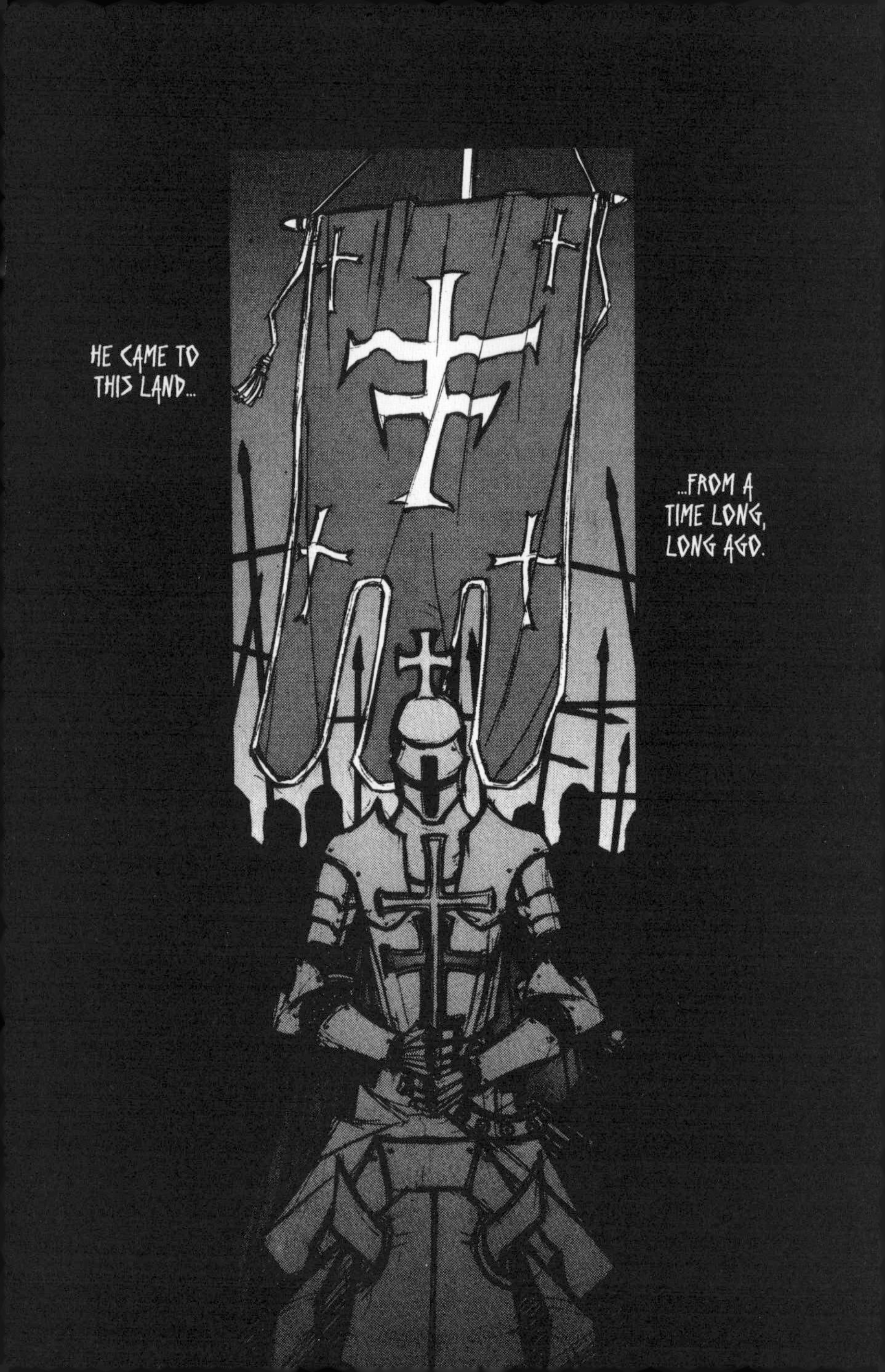
HE CAME TO THIS LAND...
...FROM A TIME LONG, LONG AGO.

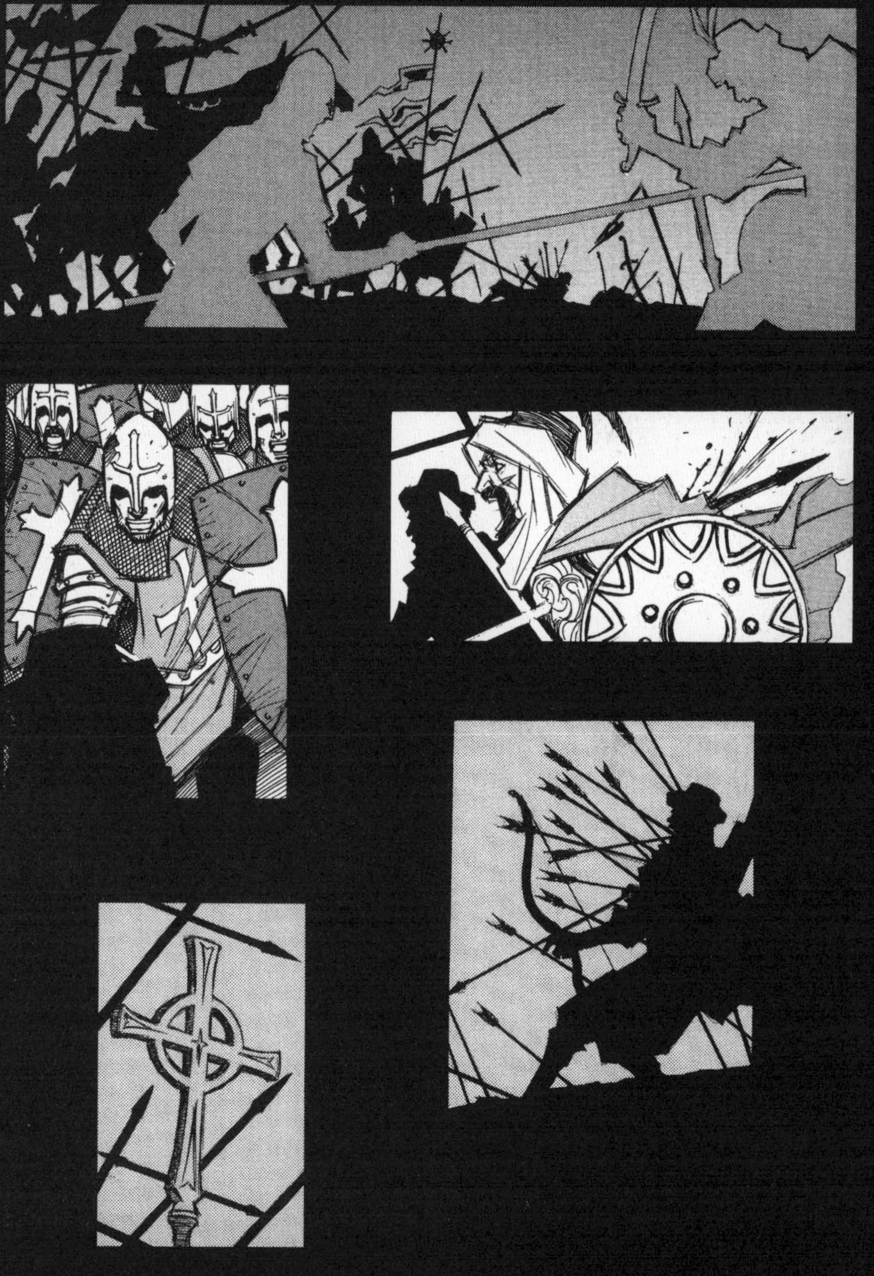

HIS ARMOR WAS MADE OF SILVER...

...HIS MOUTH WAS FULL OF
PRAISE FOR THE LORD...

...AND HIS SWORD...

...HIS SWORD WAS HIS CONDEMNATION
OF THE HERETICS.

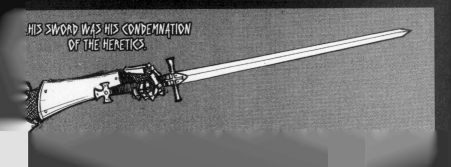

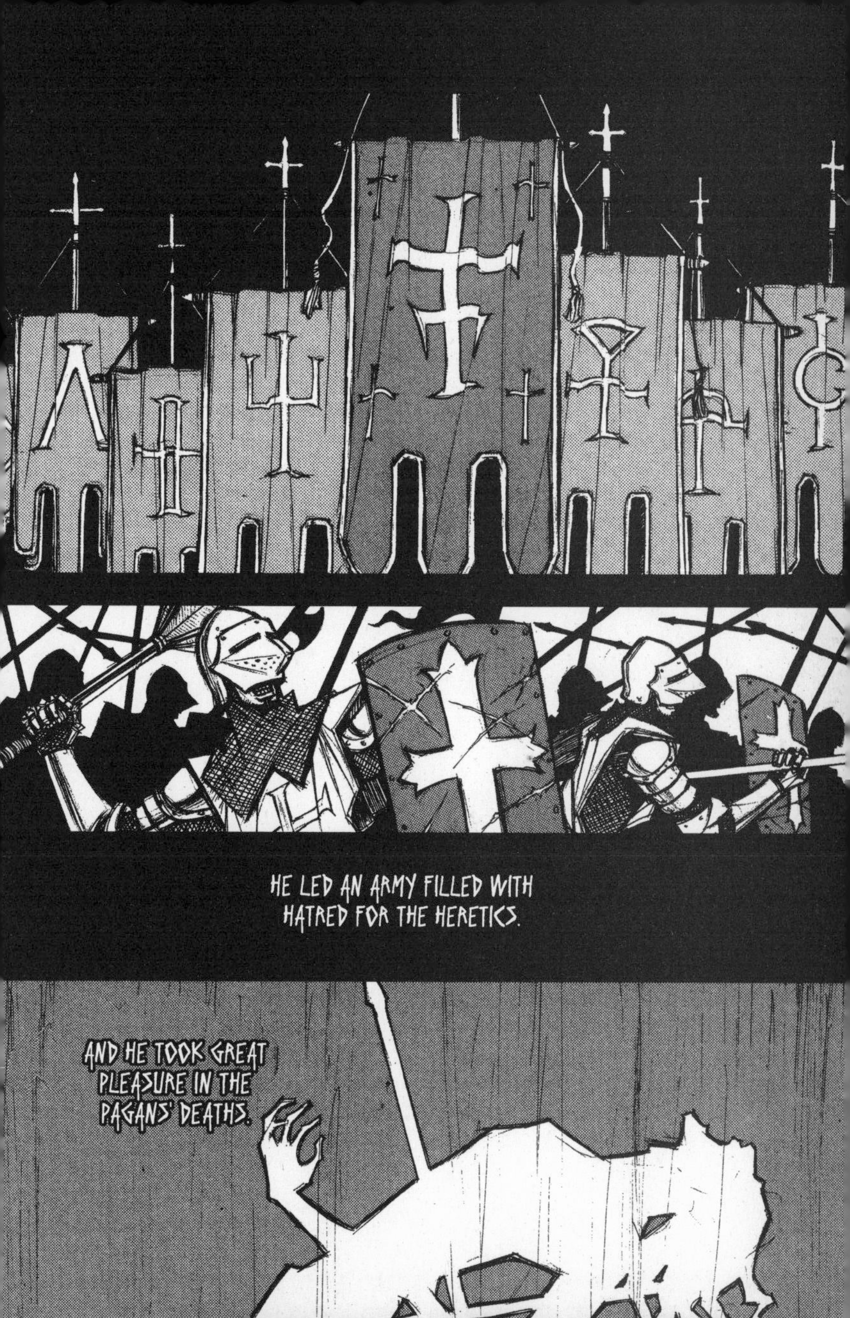
HE LED AN ARMY FILLED WITH HATRED FOR THE HERETICS.
AND HE TOOK GREAT PLEASURE IN THE PAGANS' DEATHS.

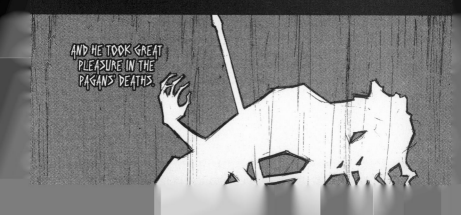

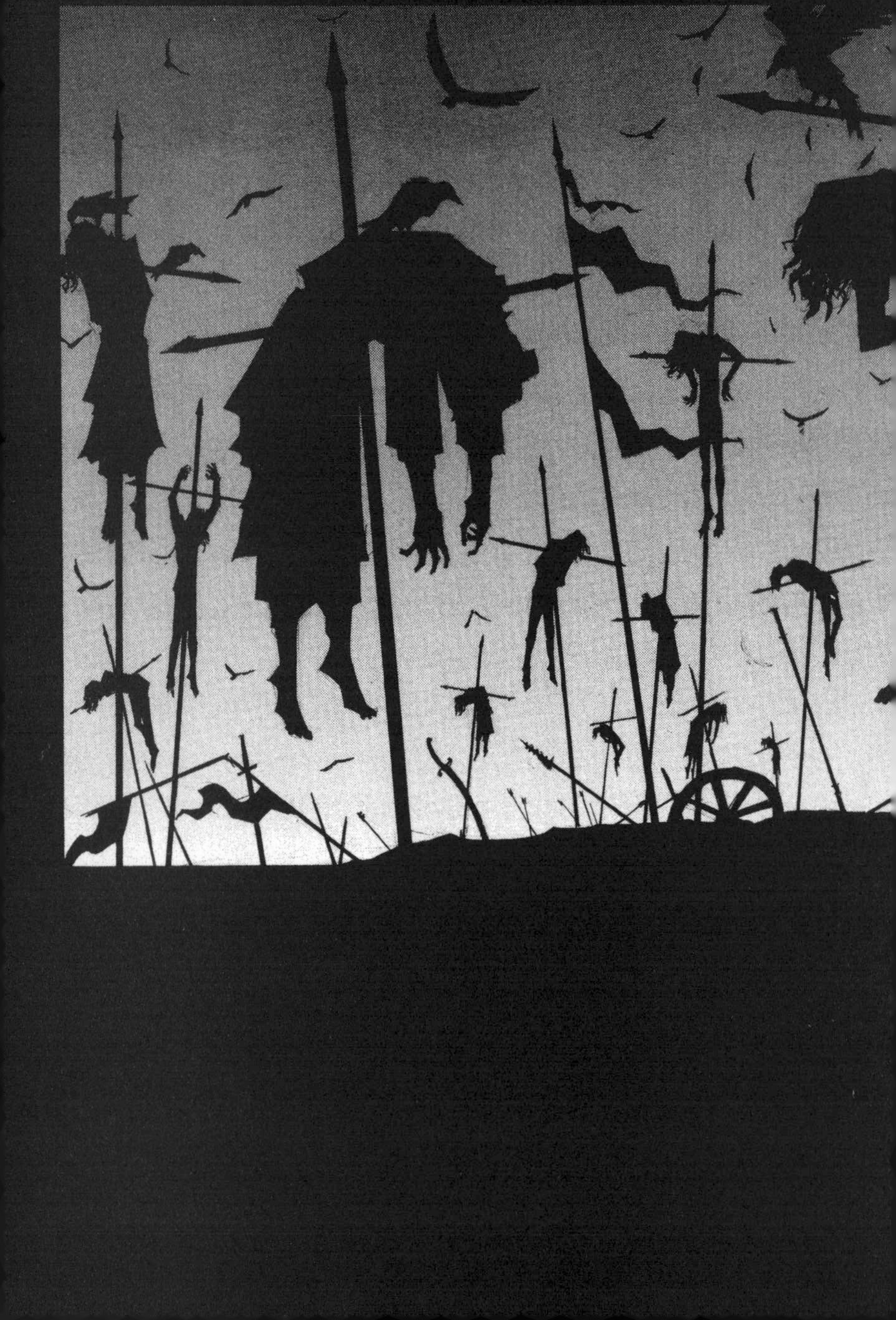

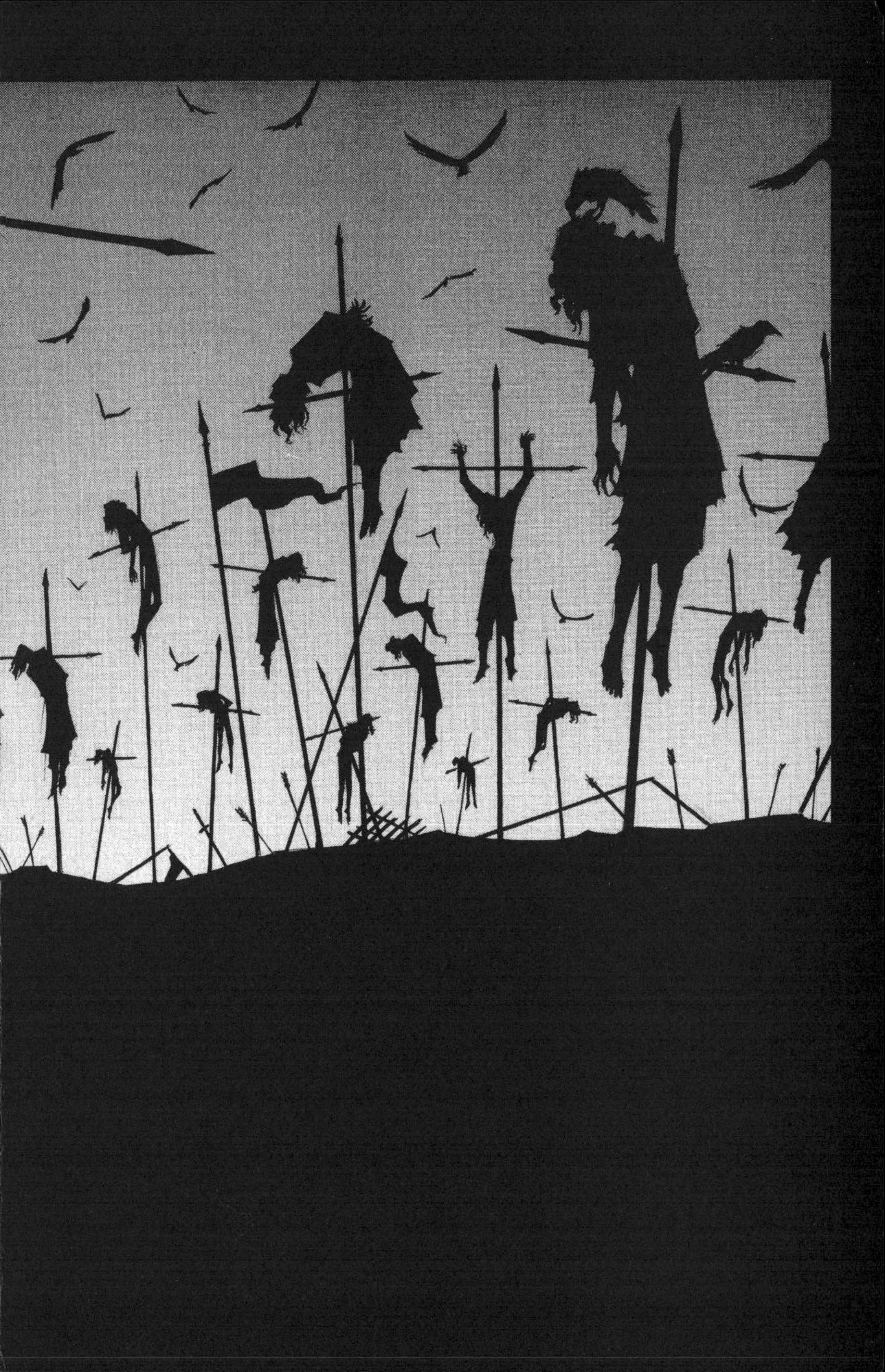

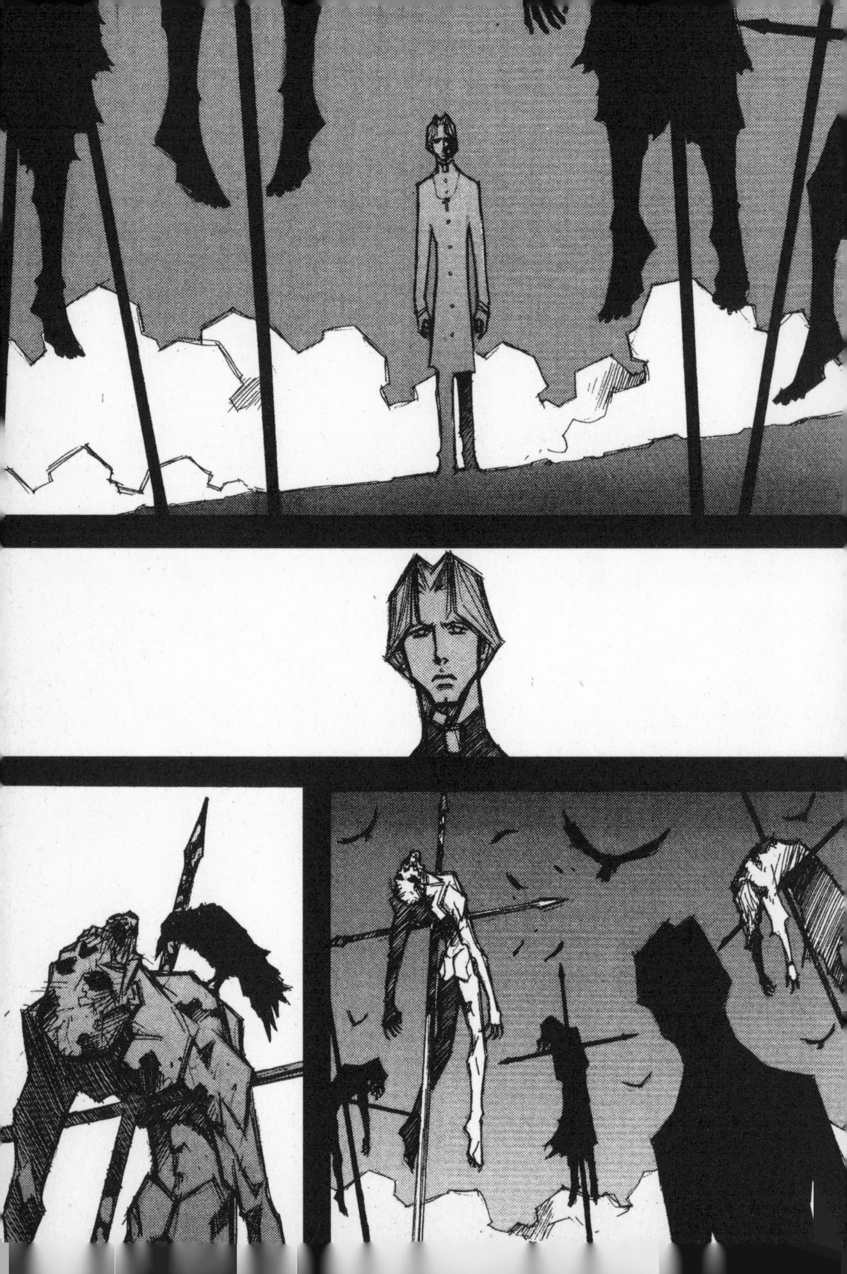

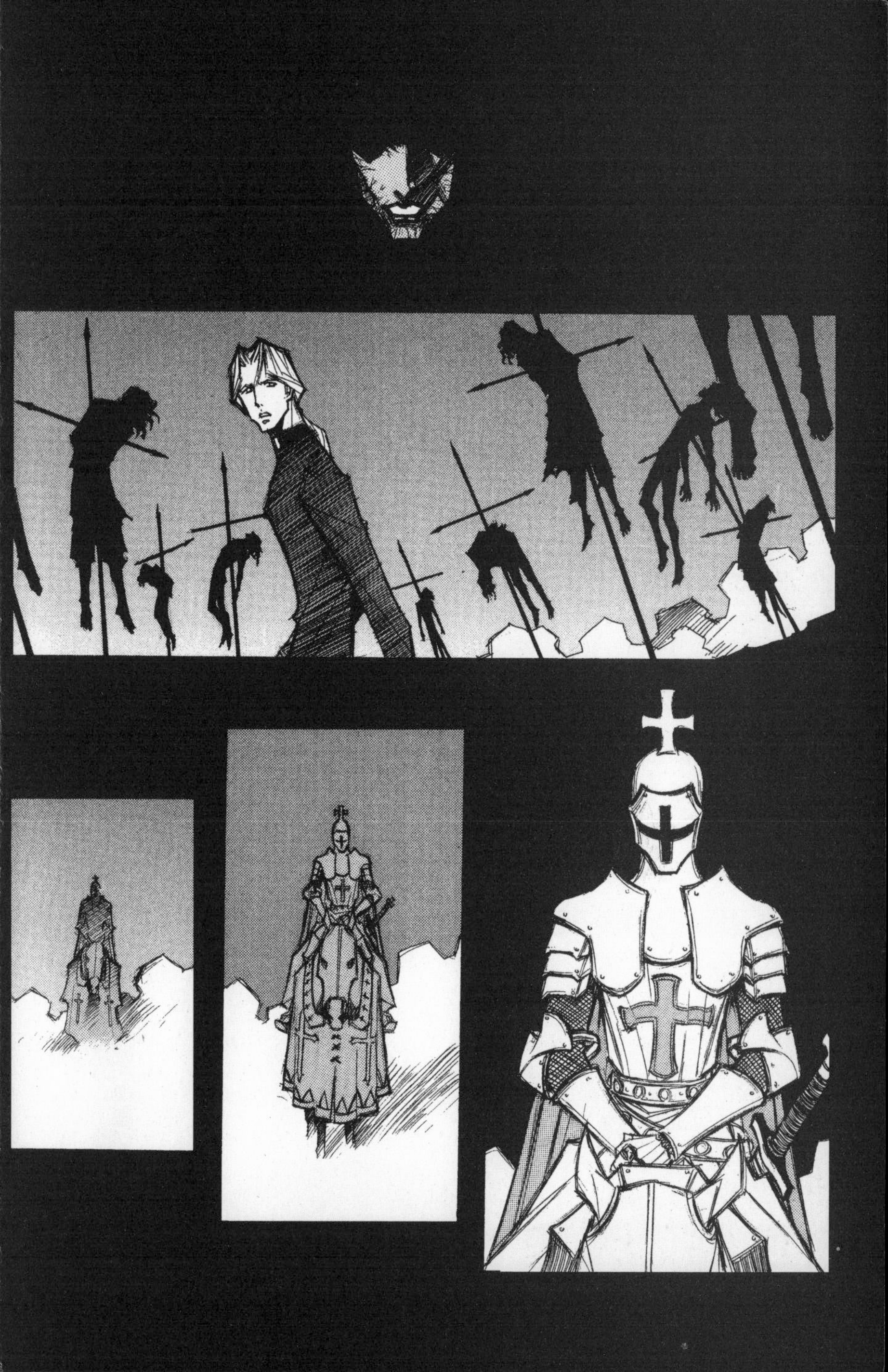

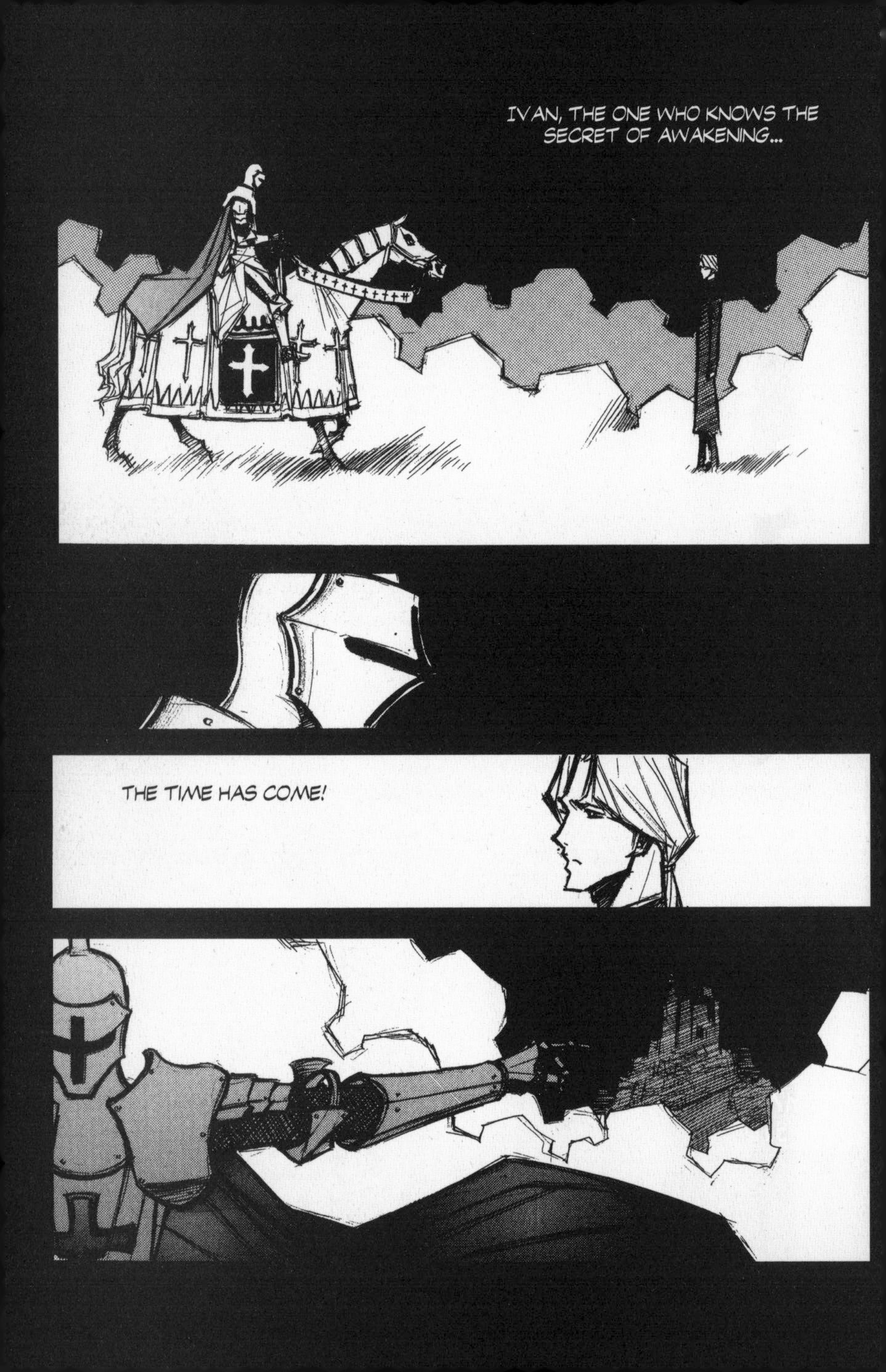
IVAN, THE ONE WHO KNOWS THE SECRET OF AWAKENING...
THE TIME HAS COME!

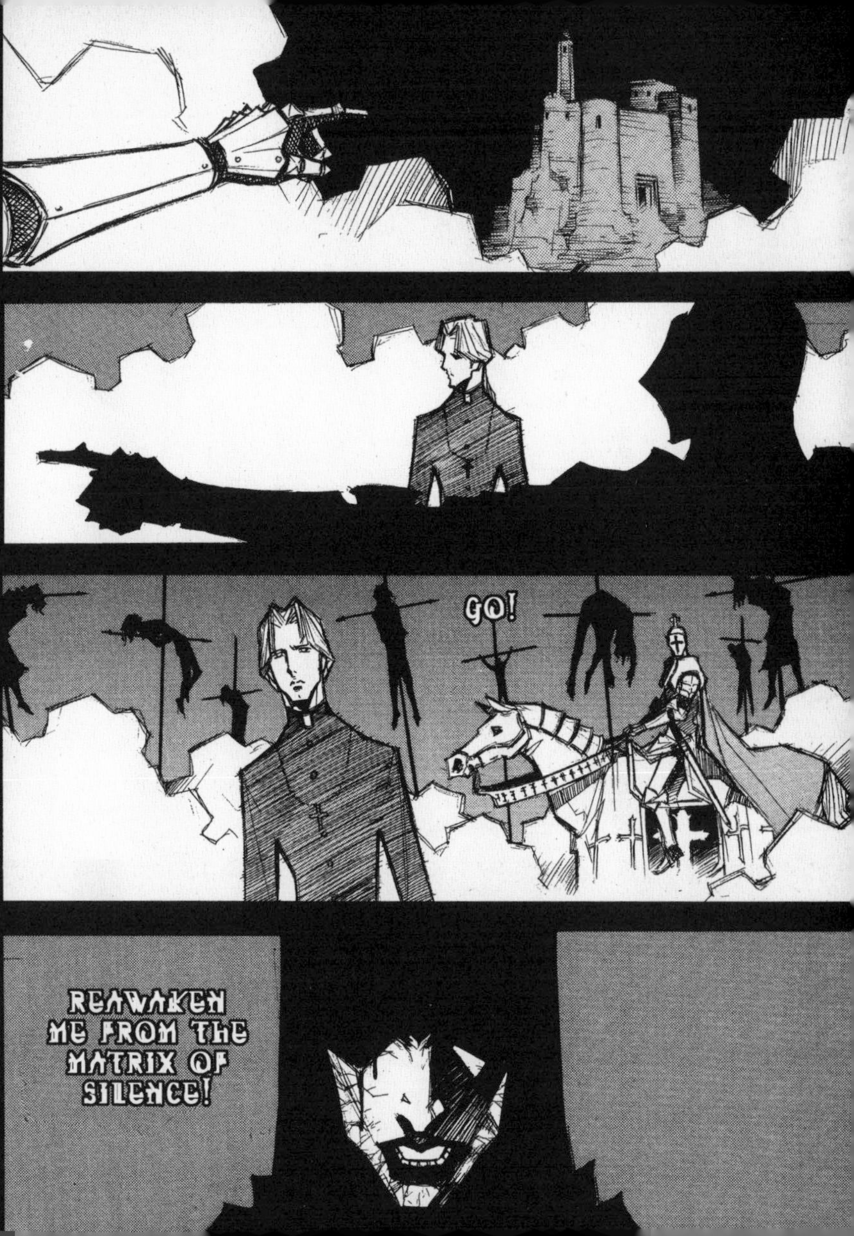
GO!
REAWAKEN ME FROM THE MATRIX OF SILENCE!

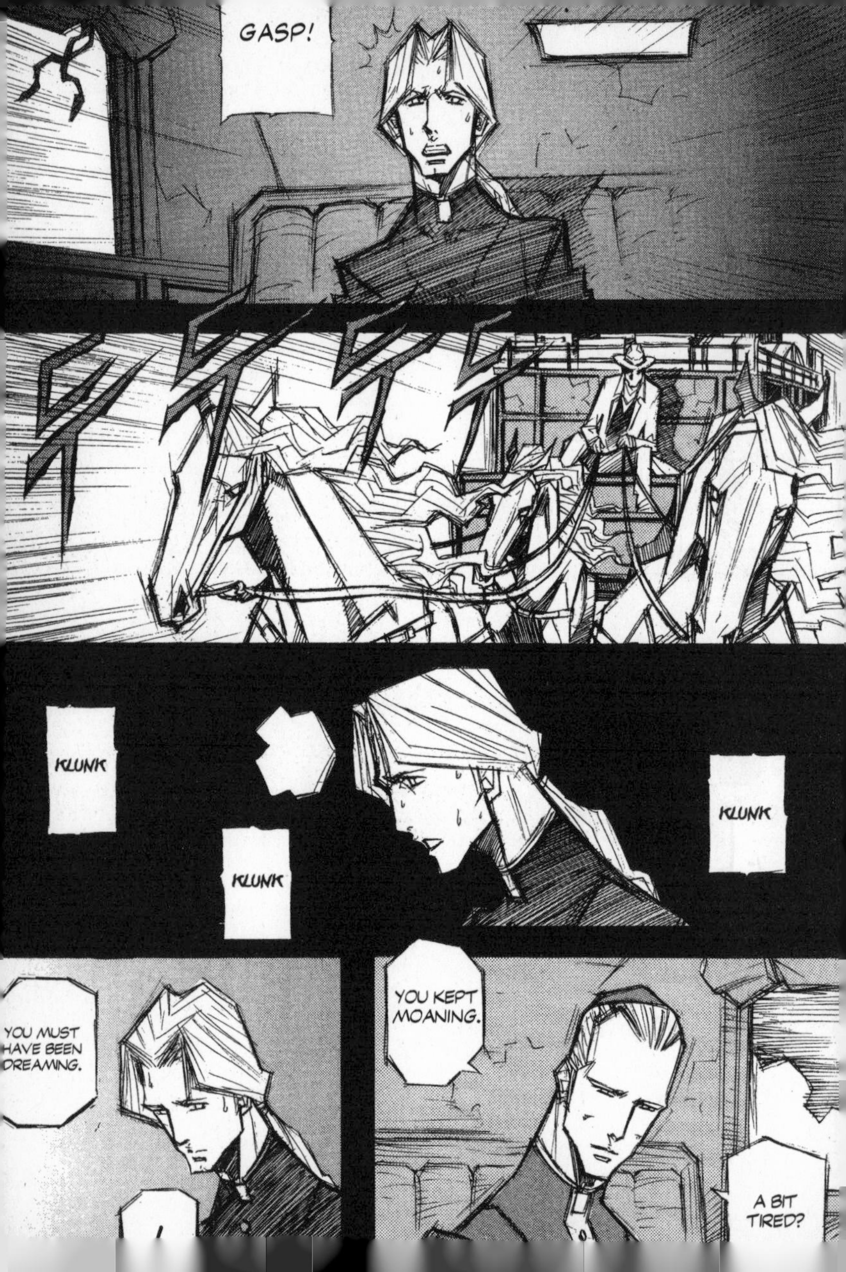
GASP!
KLUNK
KLUNK
KLUNK
YOU MUST HAVE BEEN DREAMING.
YOU KEPT MOANING.
A BIT TIRED?

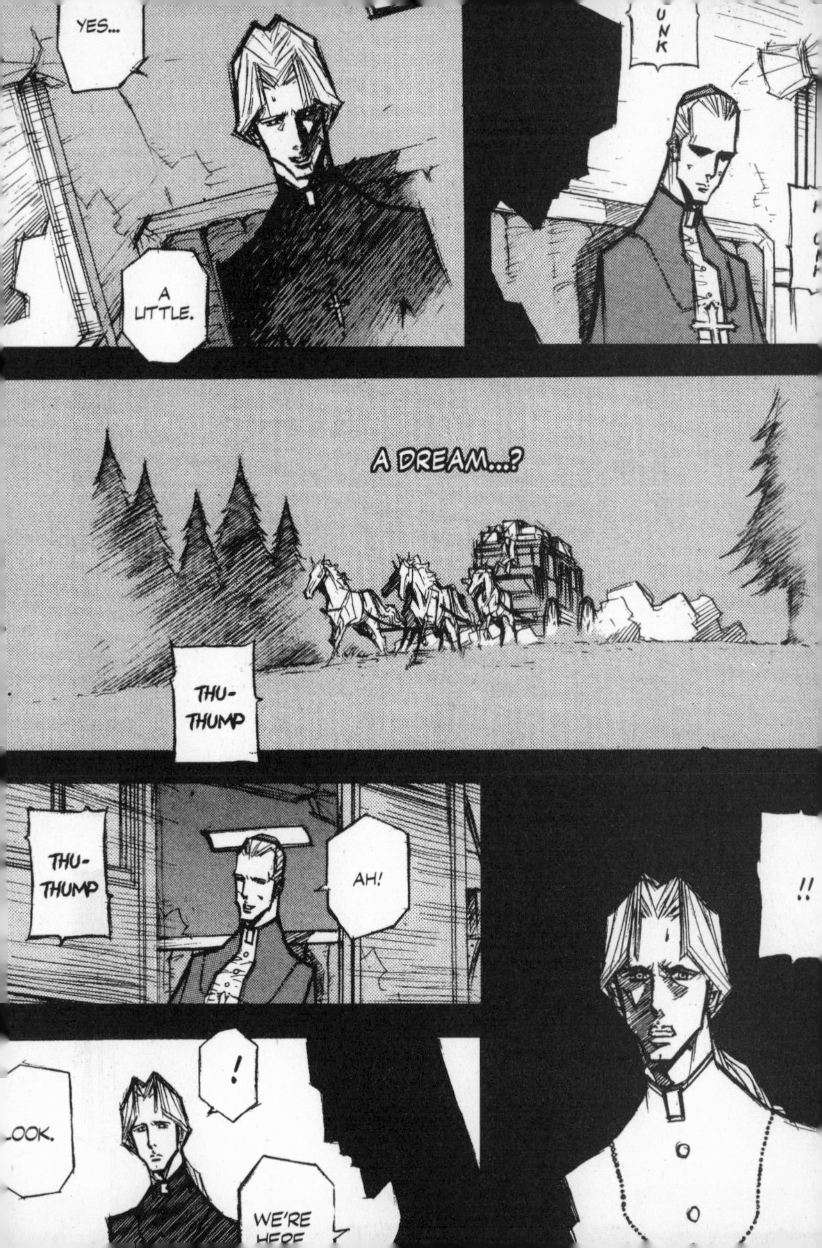
YES...
A LITTLE.
UNK
A DREAM...?
THU-THUMP
THU-THUMP
AH!
OOK.
!
WE'RE
!!

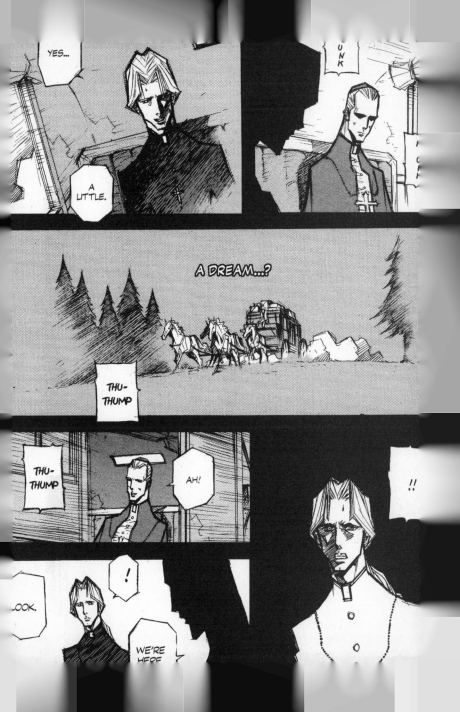

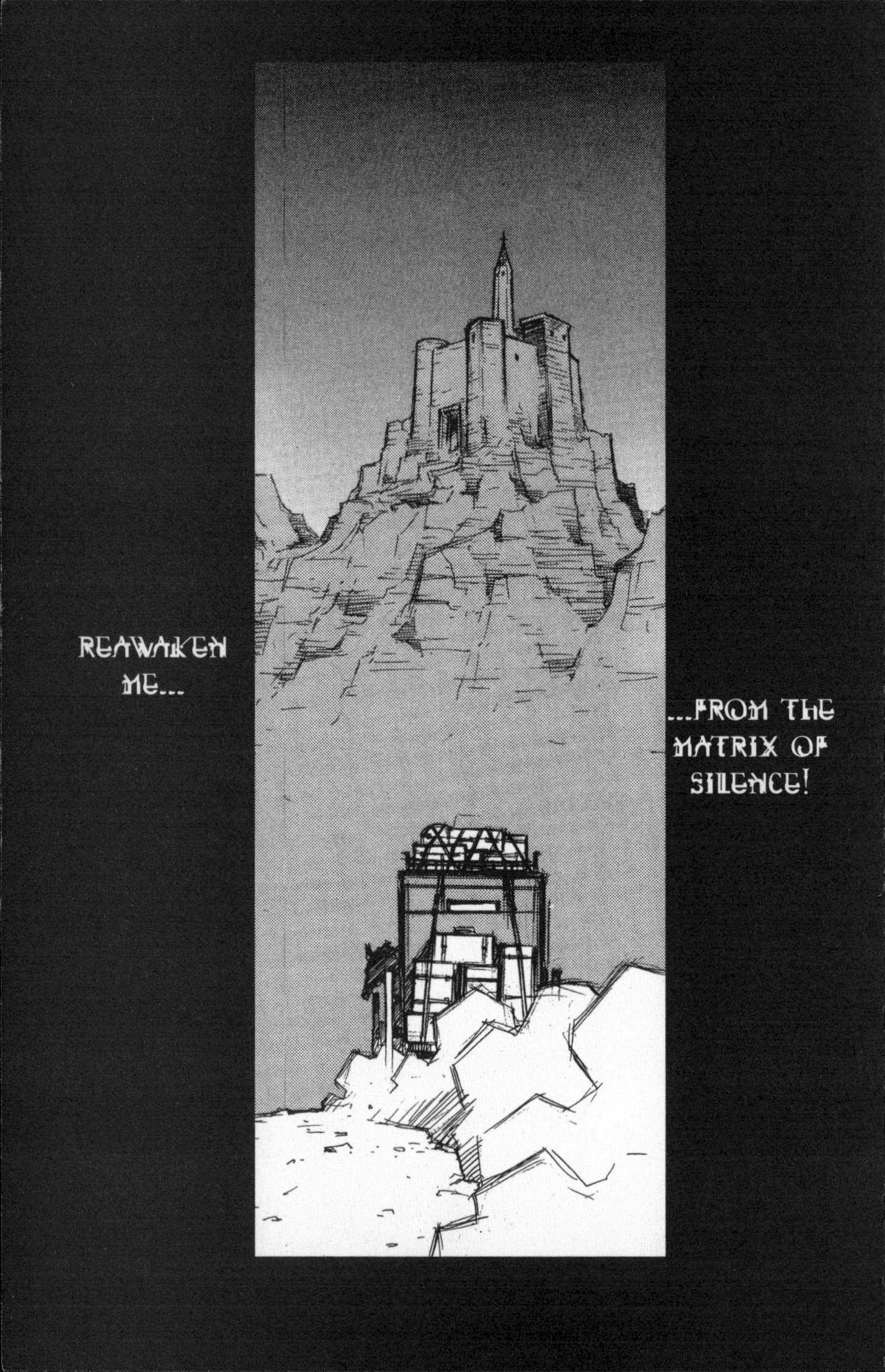
REAWAKEN ME...
...FROM THE MATRIX OF SILENCE!

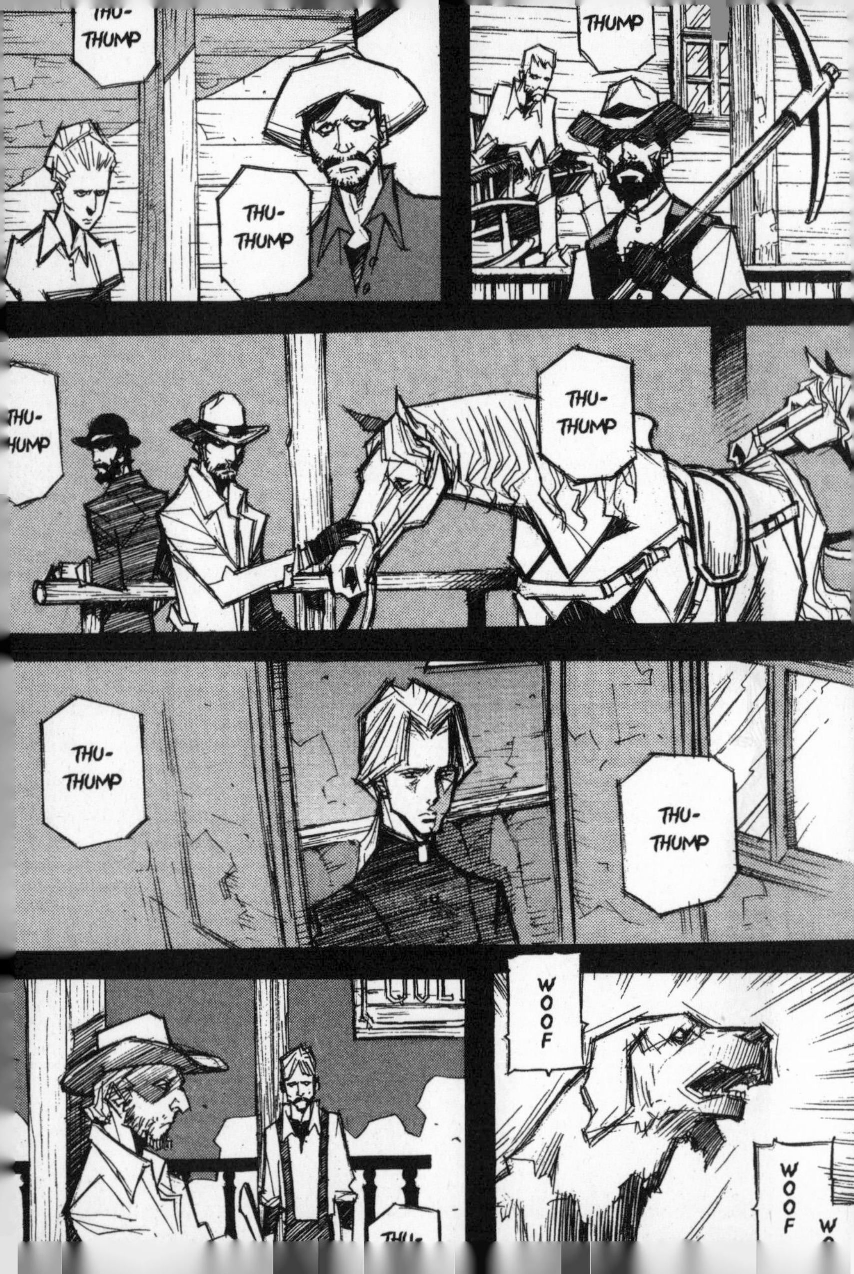
THU-THUMP
THU-THUMP
THUMP
THU-THUMP
THU-THUMP
THU-THUMP
THU-THUMP
WOOF
WOOF

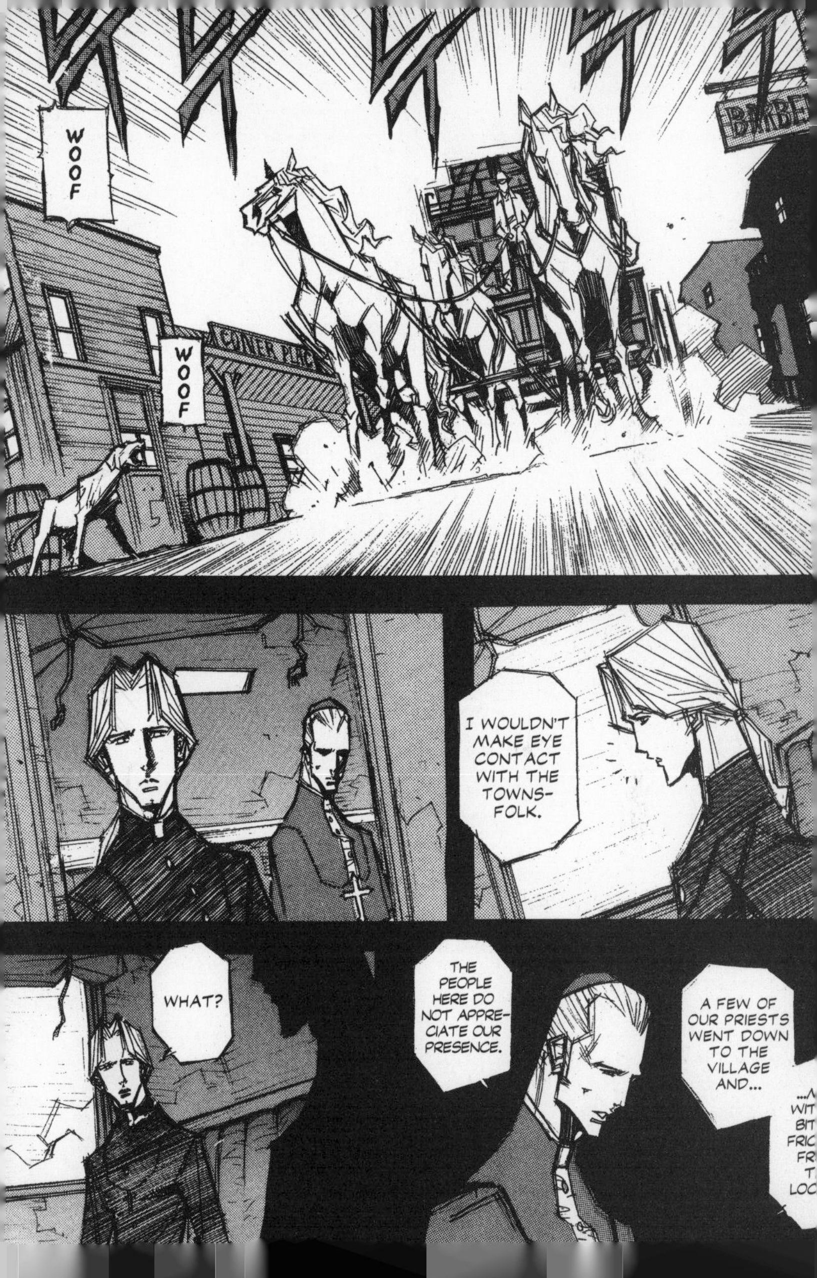
WOOF
WOOF
I WOULDN'T MAKE EYE CONTACT WITH THE TOWNS-FOLK.
WHAT?
THE PEOPLE HERE DO NOT APPRE-CIATE OUR PRESENCE.
A FEW OF OUR PRIESTS WENT DOWN TO THE VILLAGE AND...

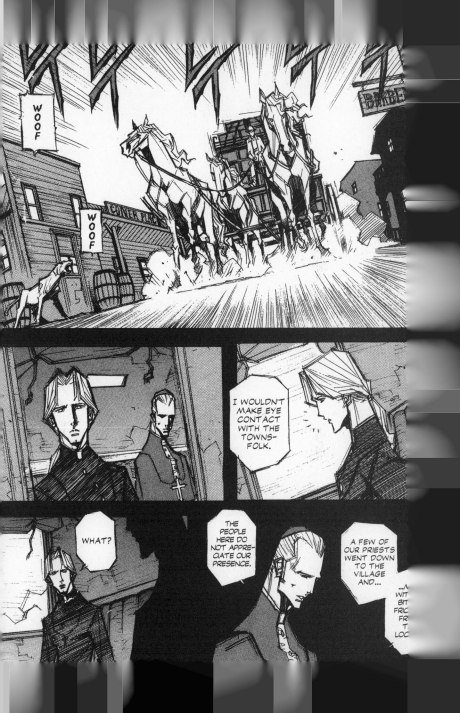

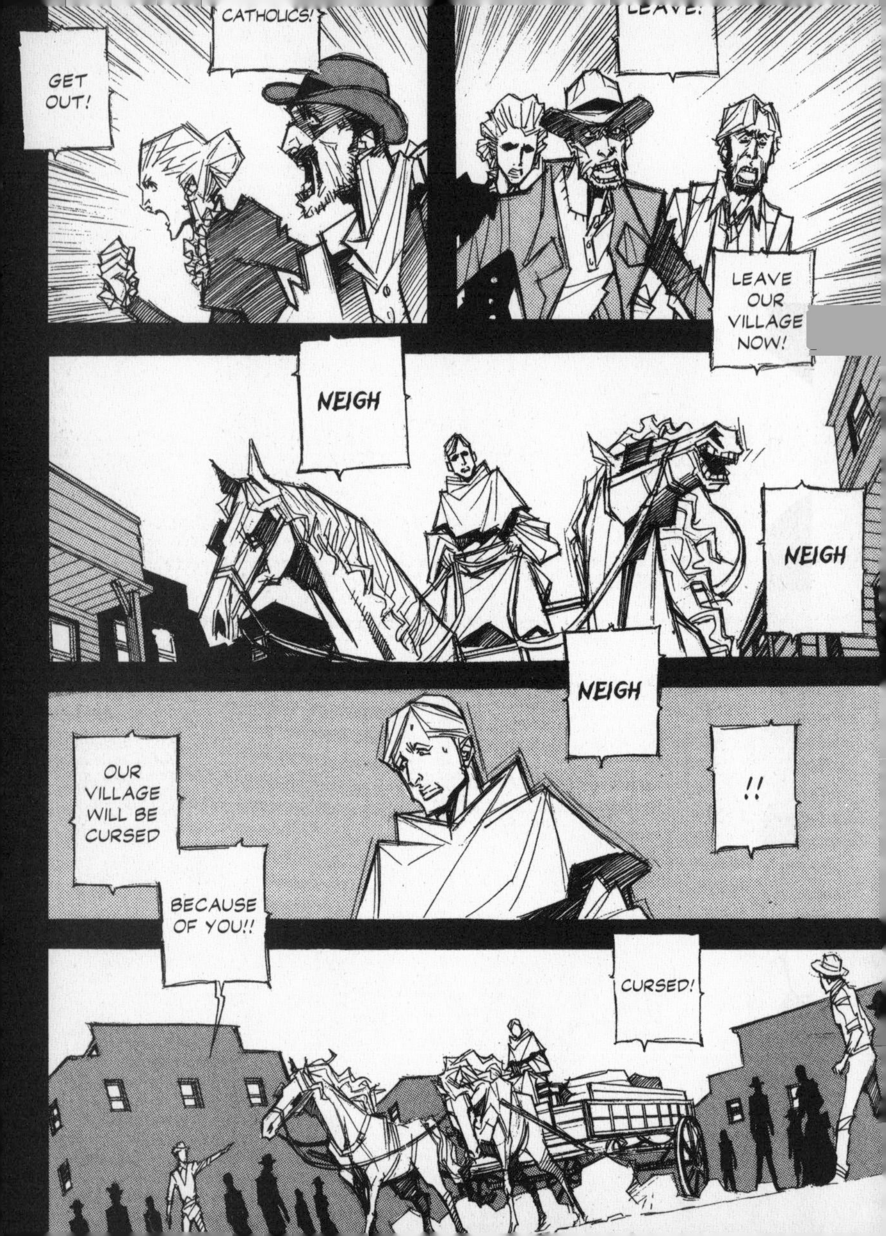
CATHOLICS!
GET OUT!
LEAVE!
LEAVE OUR VILLAGE NOW!
NEIGH
NEIGH
NEIGH
OUR VILLAGE WILL BE CURSED
BECAUSE OF YOU!!
!!
CURSED!

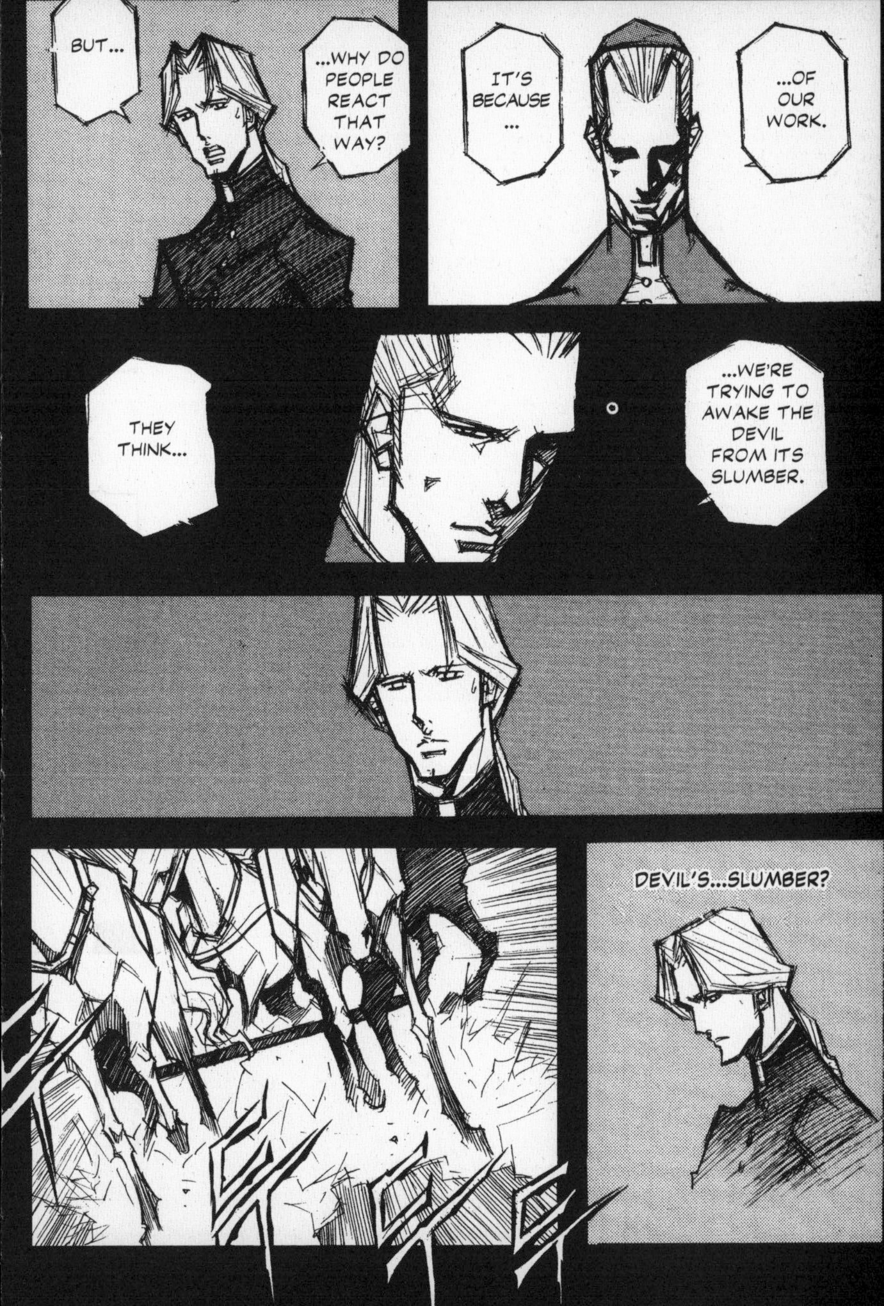
BUT...
...WHY DO PEOPLE REACT THAT WAY?
IT'S BECAUSE ...
...OF OUR WORK.
THEY THINK...
...WE'RE TRYING TO AWAKE THE DEVIL FROM ITS SLUMBER.
DEVIL'S...SLUMBER?

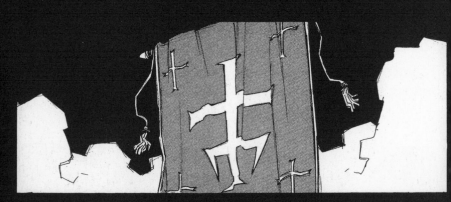

THAT DREAM...
WAS IT A
VISION?

BUT, WHY?
WHY WOULD THOSE IMAGES
APPEAR IN MY DREAM?

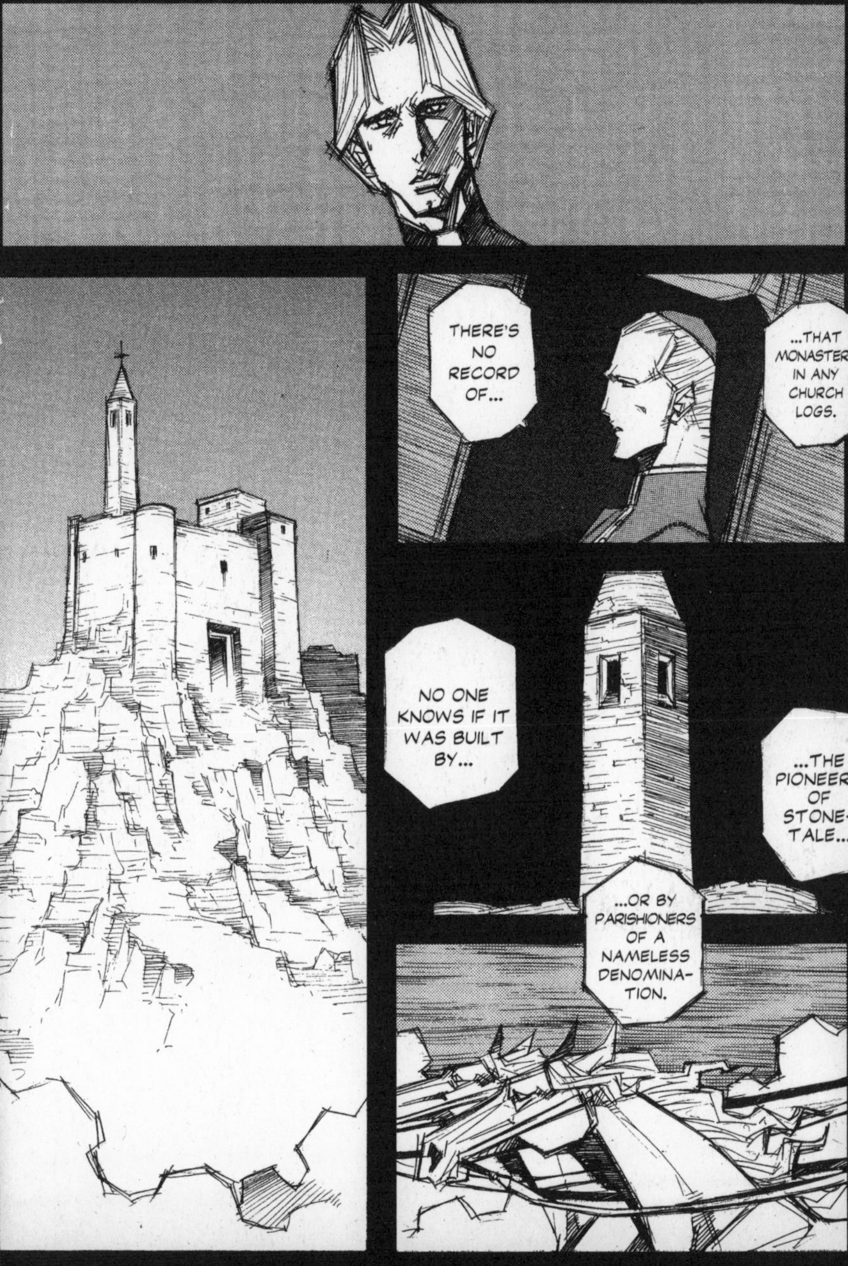
THERE'S NO RECORD OF...
...THAT MONASTERY IN ANY CHURCH LOGS.
NO ONE KNOWS IF IT WAS BUILT BY...
...THE PIONEERS OF STONE-TALE...
...OR BY PARISHIONERS OF A NAMELESS DENOMINA-TION.

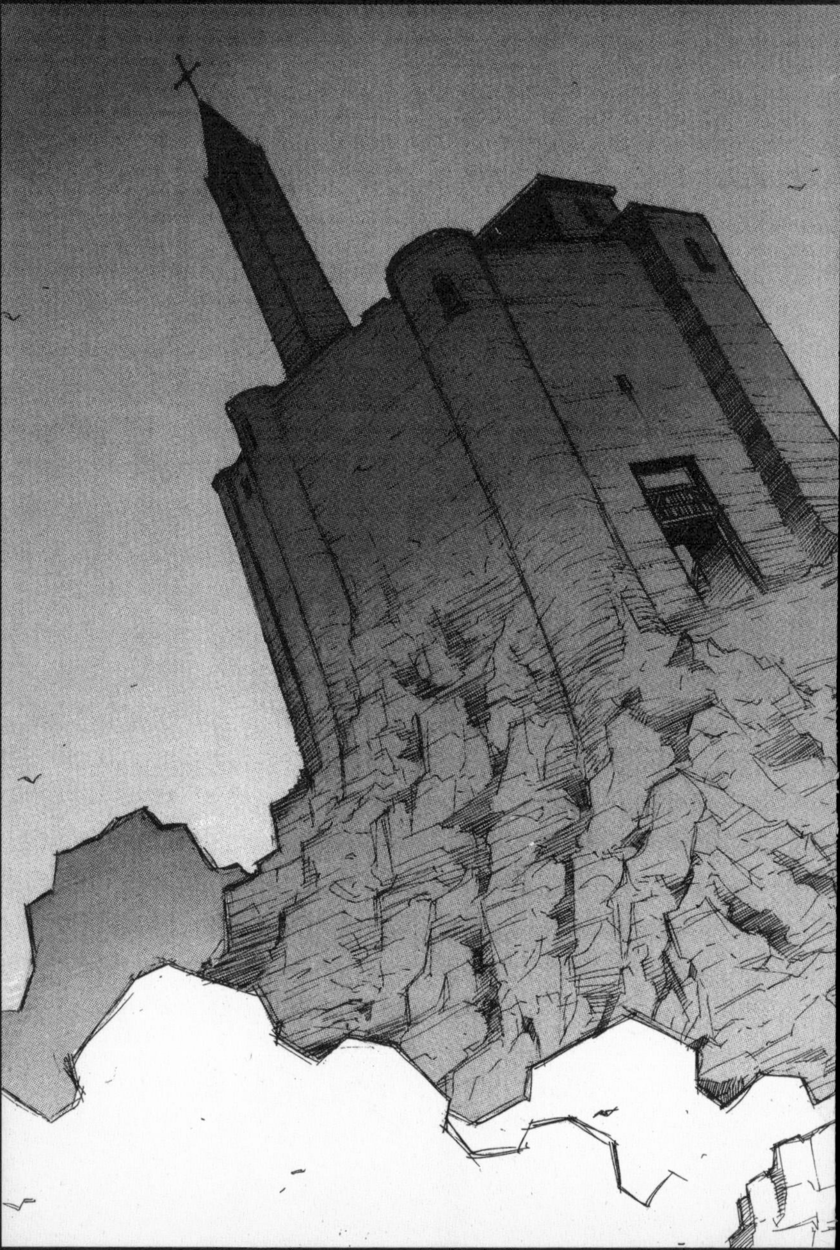

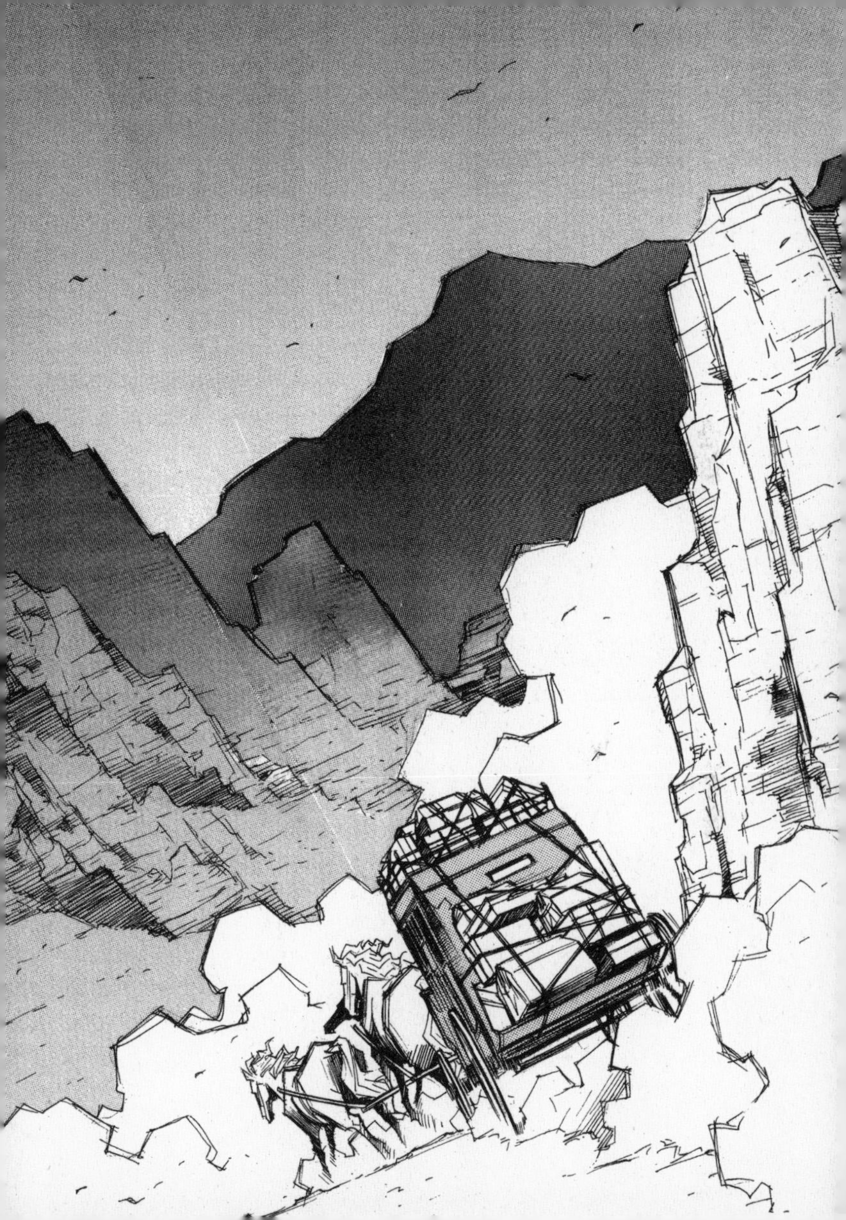

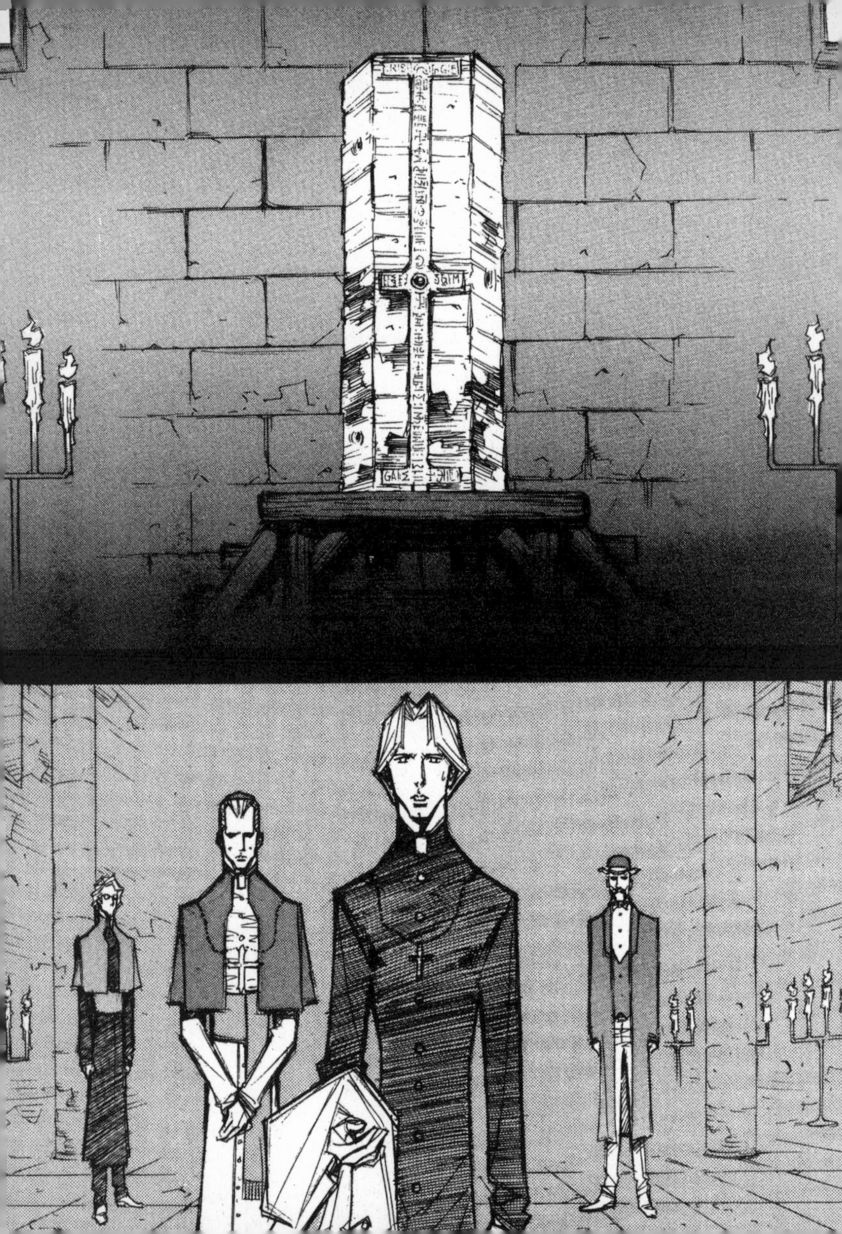

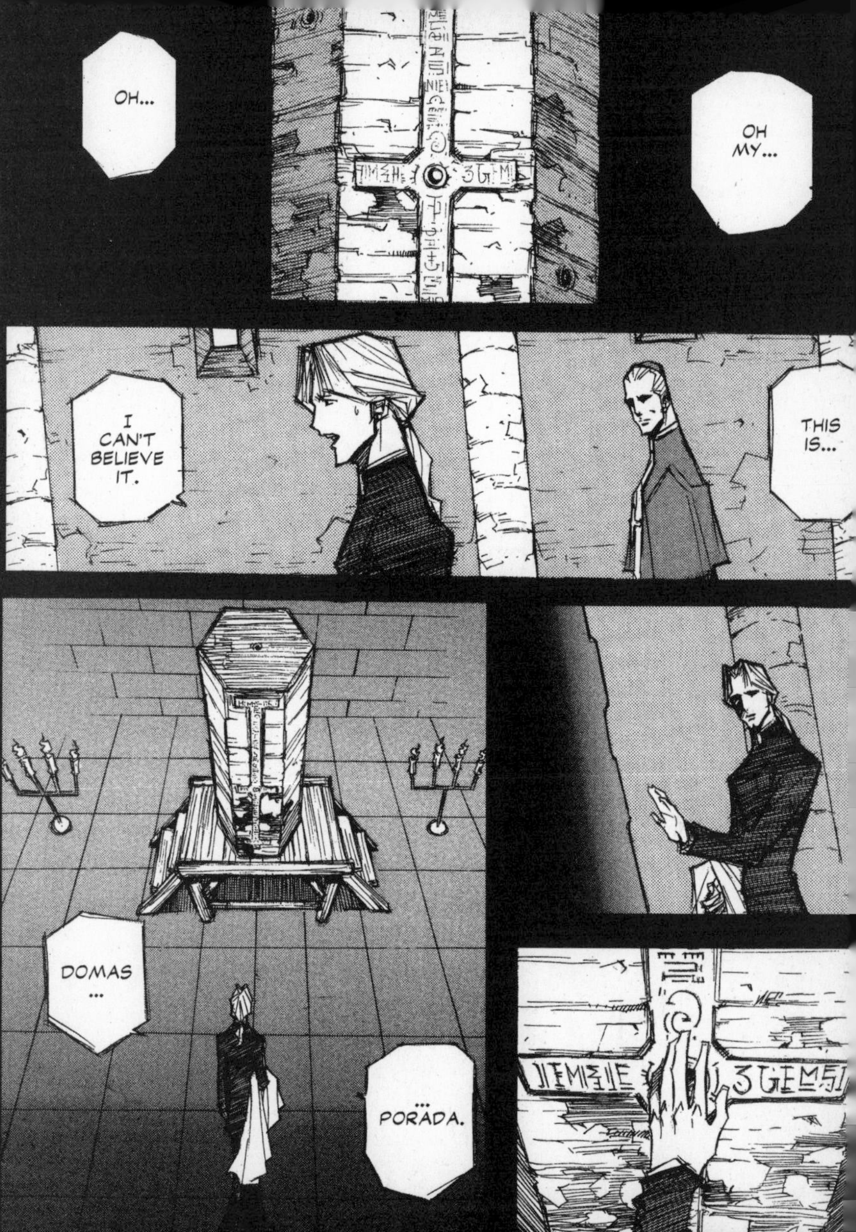
OH...
OH MY...
I CAN'T BELIEVE IT.
THIS IS...
DOMAS ...
... PORADA.

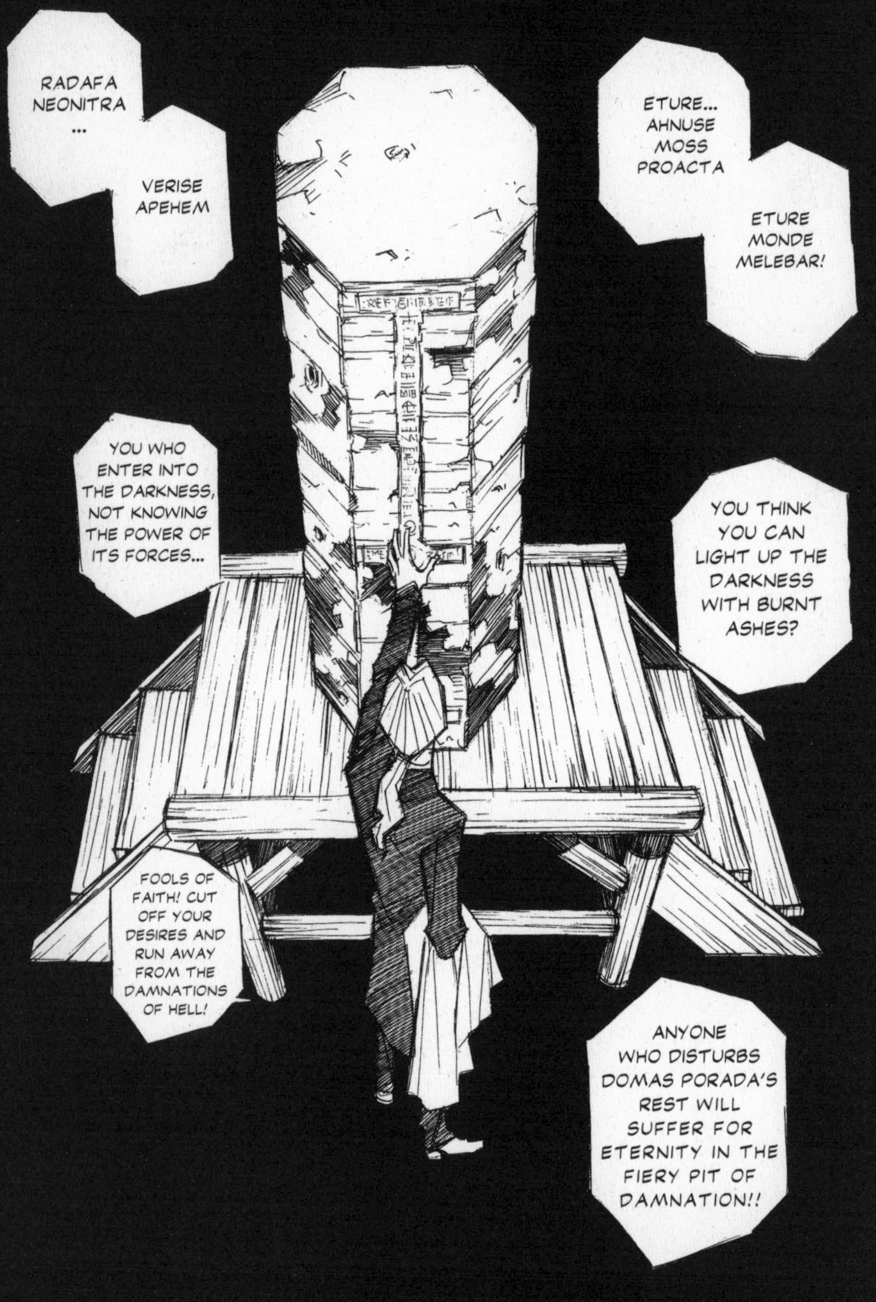
RADAFA NEONITRA ...
VERISE APEHEM
ETURE... AHNUSE MOSS PROACTA
ETURE MONDE MELEBAR!
YOU WHO ENTER INTO THE DARKNESS, NOT KNOWING THE POWER OF ITS FORCES...
YOU THINK YOU CAN LIGHT UP THE DARKNESS WITH BURNT ASHES?
FOOLS OF FAITH! CUT OFF YOUR DESIRES AND RUN AWAY FROM THE DAMNATIONS OF HELL!
ANYONE WHO DISTURBS DOMAS PORADA'S REST WILL SUFFER FOR ETERNITY IN THE FIERY PIT OF DAMNATION!!

# Dante's Inferno

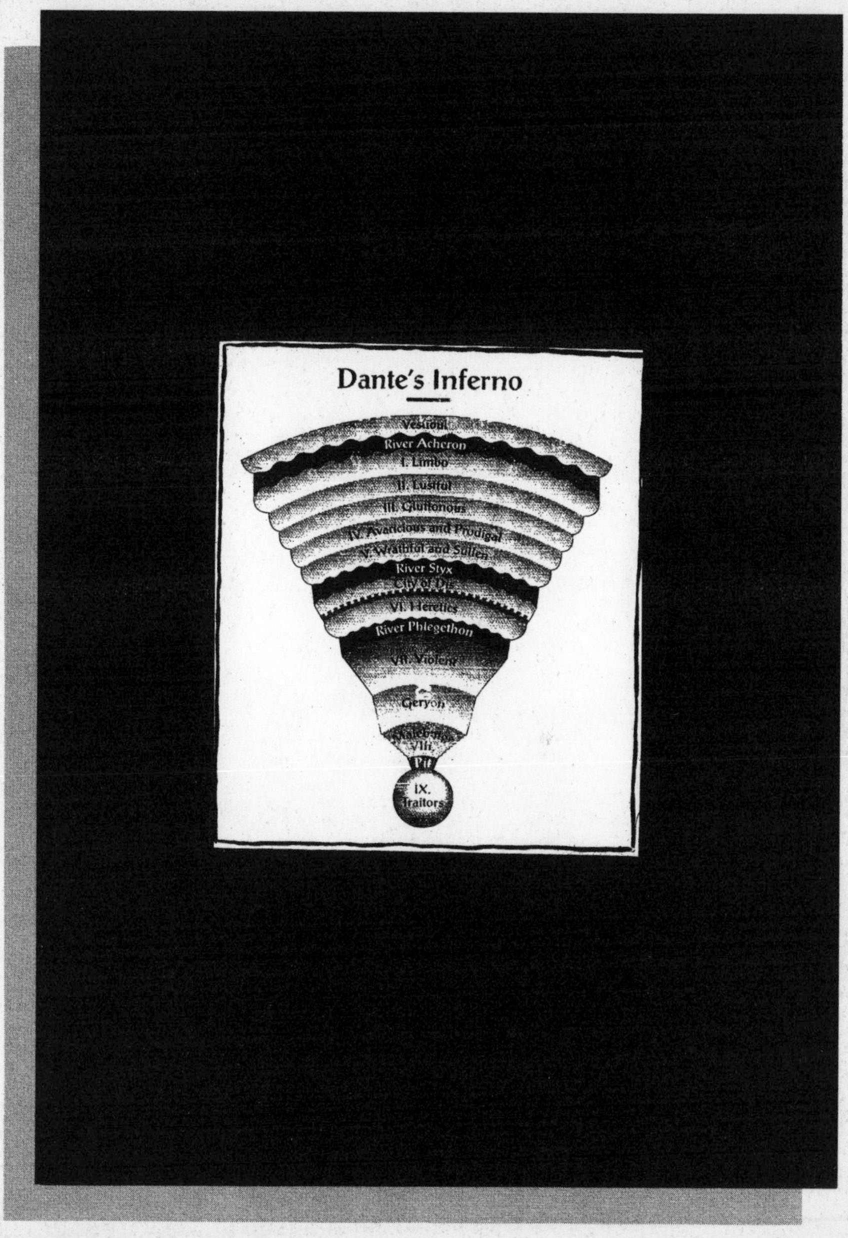
Vestibul
River Acheron
I. Limbo
II. Lustful
III. Gluttonous
IV. Avaricious and Prodigal
V. Wrathful and Sullen
River Styx
City of Dis
VI. Heretics
River Phlegethon
VII. Violent
Geryon
VIII.
Pit
IX.
Traitors

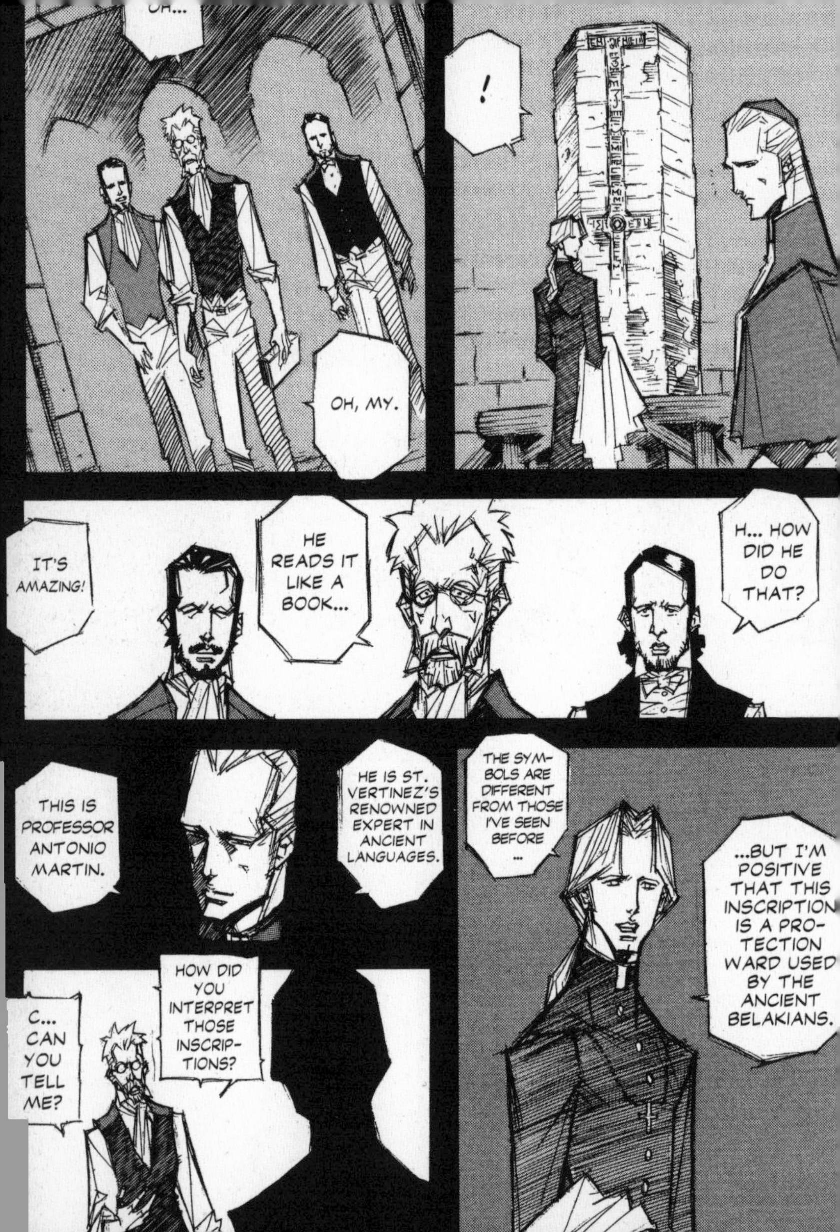
OH...
!
OH, MY.
IT'S AMAZING!
HE READS IT LIKE A BOOK...
H... HOW DID HE DO THAT?
THIS IS PROFESSOR ANTONIO MARTIN.
HE IS ST. VERTINEZ'S RENOWNED EXPERT IN ANCIENT LANGUAGES.
THE SYMBOLS ARE DIFFERENT FROM THOSE I'VE SEEN BEFORE ...
...BUT I'M POSITIVE THAT THIS INSCRIPTION IS A PROTECTION WARD USED BY THE ANCIENT BELAKIANS.
C... CAN YOU TELL ME?
HOW DID YOU INTERPRET THOSE INSCRIPTIONS?

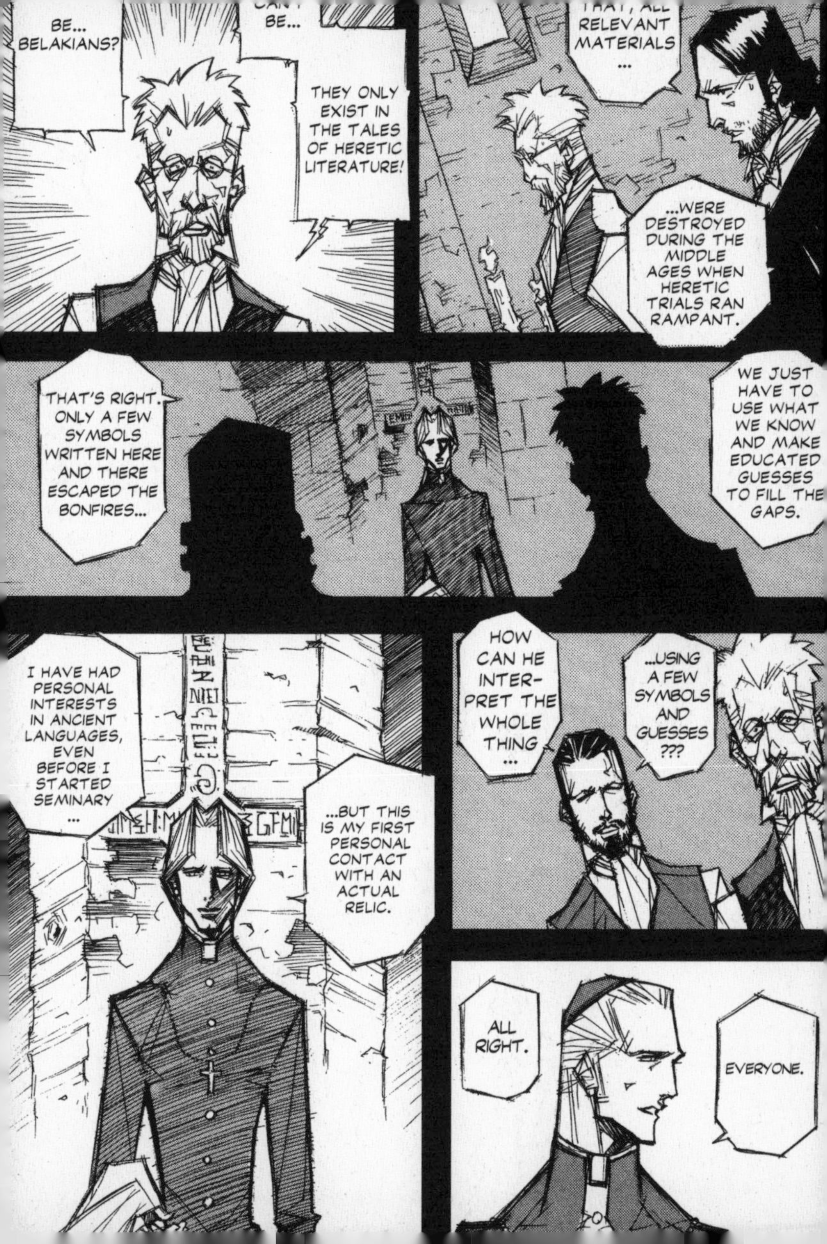
BE... BELAKIANS?
BE...
THEY ONLY EXIST IN THE TALES OF HERETIC LITERATURE!
THAT, ALL RELEVANT MATERIALS ...
...WERE DESTROYED DURING THE MIDDLE AGES WHEN HERETIC TRIALS RAN RAMPANT.
THAT'S RIGHT. ONLY A FEW SYMBOLS WRITTEN HERE AND THERE ESCAPED THE BONFIRES...
WE JUST HAVE TO USE WHAT WE KNOW AND MAKE EDUCATED GUESSES TO FILL THE GAPS.
I HAVE HAD PERSONAL INTERESTS IN ANCIENT LANGUAGES, EVEN BEFORE I STARTED SEMINARY ...
...BUT THIS IS MY FIRST PERSONAL CONTACT WITH AN ACTUAL RELIC.
HOW CAN HE INTER-PRET THE WHOLE THING ...
...USING A FEW SYMBOLS AND GUESSES ???
ALL RIGHT.
EVERYONE.

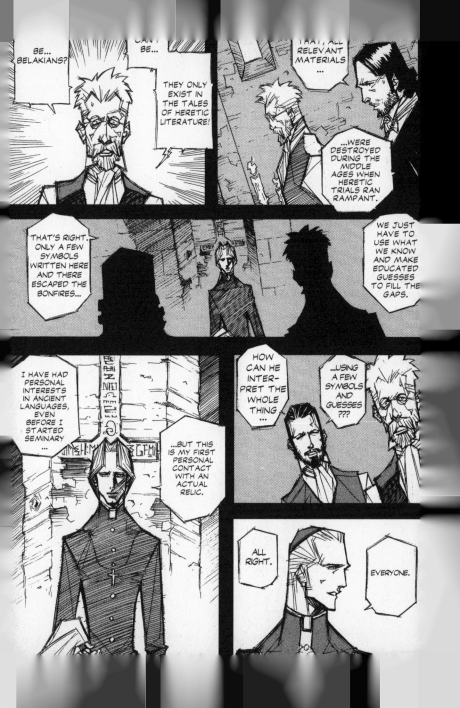

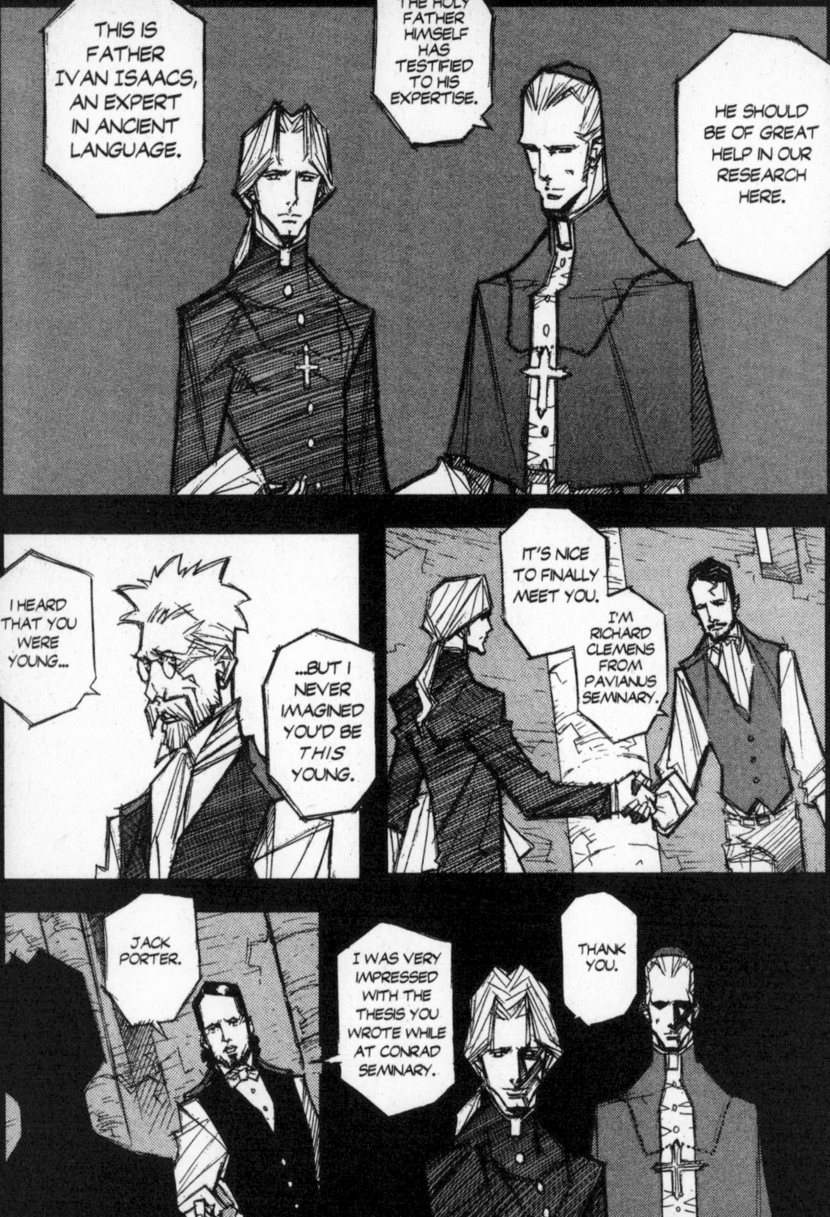
THIS IS FATHER IVAN ISAACS, AN EXPERT IN ANCIENT LANGUAGE.
THE HOLY FATHER HIMSELF HAS TESTIFIED TO HIS EXPERTISE.
HE SHOULD BE OF GREAT HELP IN OUR RESEARCH HERE.
I HEARD THAT YOU WERE YOUNG...
...BUT I NEVER IMAGINED YOU'D BE *THIS* YOUNG.
IT'S NICE TO FINALLY MEET YOU.
I'M RICHARD CLEMENS FROM PAVIANUS SEMINARY.
JACK PORTER.
I WAS VERY IMPRESSED WITH THE THESIS YOU WROTE WHILE AT CONRAD SEMINARY.
THANK YOU.

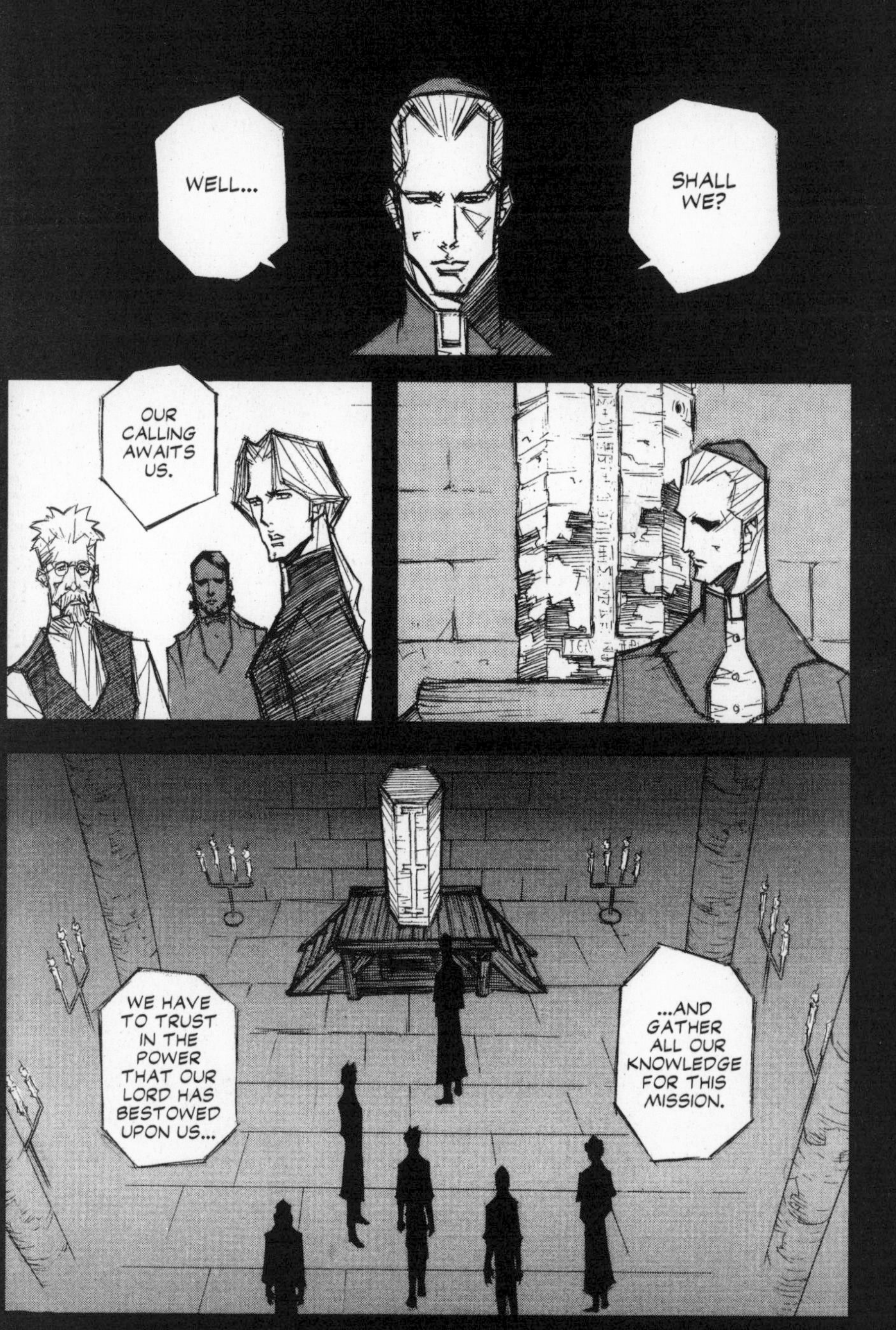
WELL...
SHALL WE?
OUR CALLING AWAITS US.
WE HAVE TO TRUST IN THE POWER THAT OUR LORD HAS BESTOWED UPON US...
...AND GATHER ALL OUR KNOWLEDGE FOR THIS MISSION.

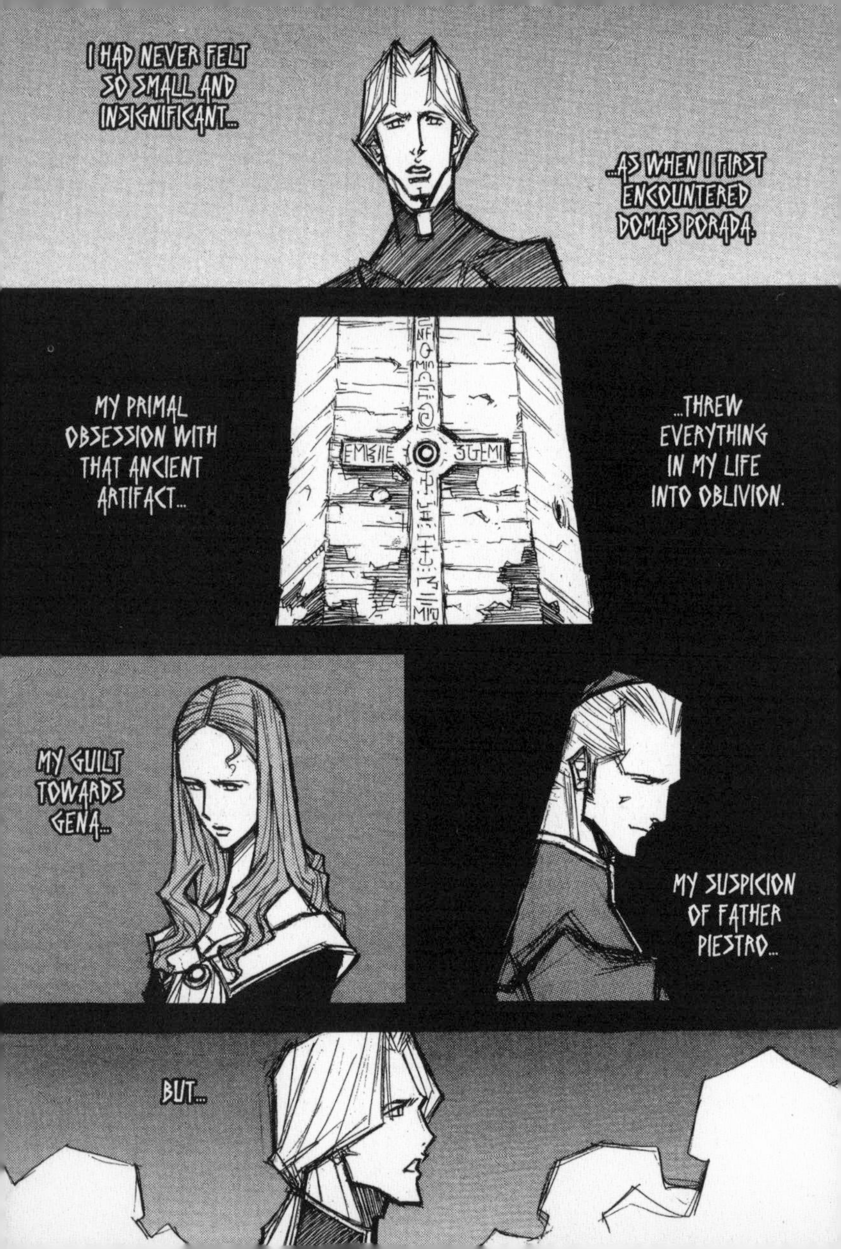
I HAD NEVER FELT SO SMALL AND INSIGNIFICANT...
...AS WHEN I FIRST ENCOUNTERED DOMAS PORADA.
MY PRIMAL OBSESSION WITH THAT ANCIENT ARTIFACT...
...THREW EVERYTHING IN MY LIFE INTO OBLIVION.
MY GUILT TOWARDS GENA...
MY SUSPICION OF FATHER PIESTRO...
BUT...

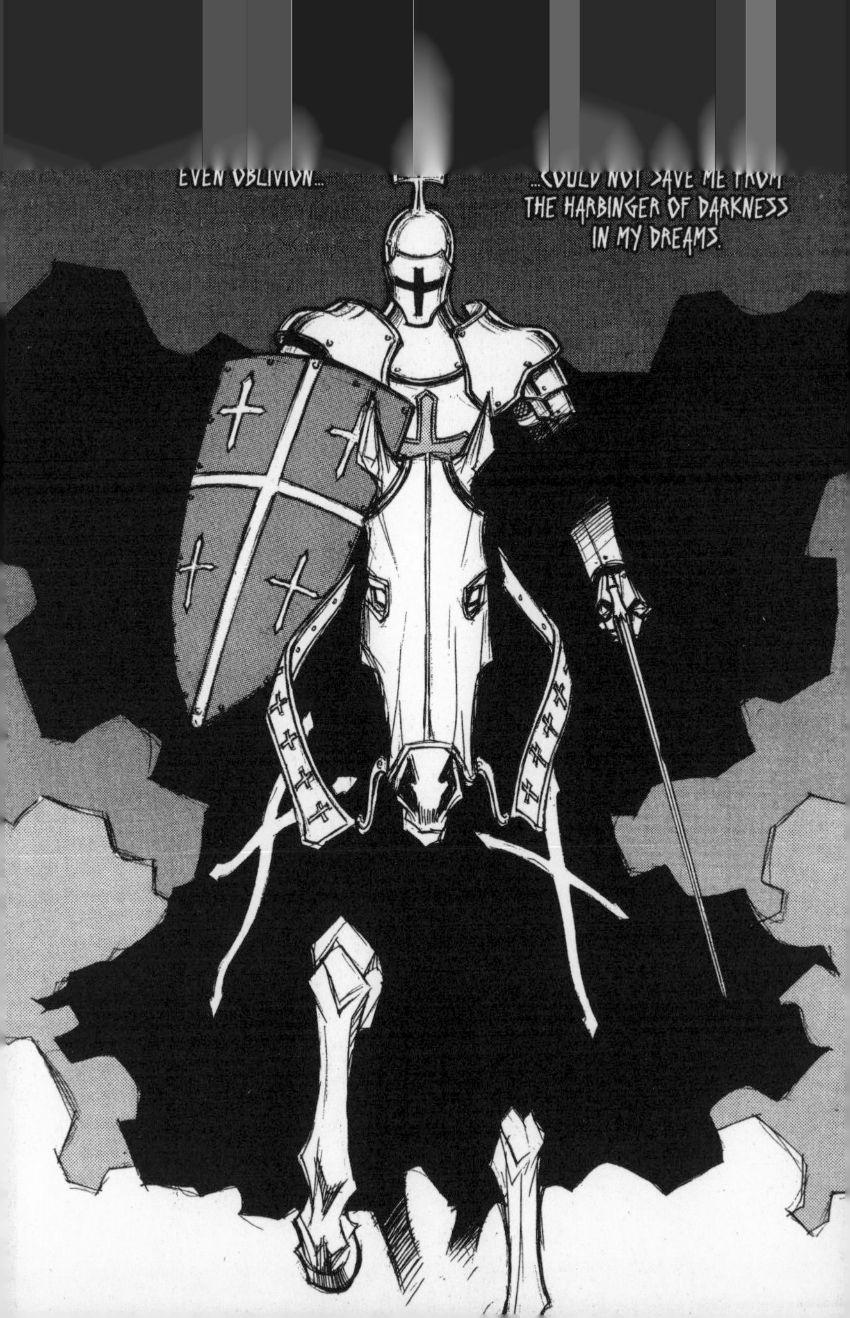
EVEN OBLIVION...
...COULD NOT SAVE ME FROM THE HARBINGER OF DARKNESS IN MY DREAMS.

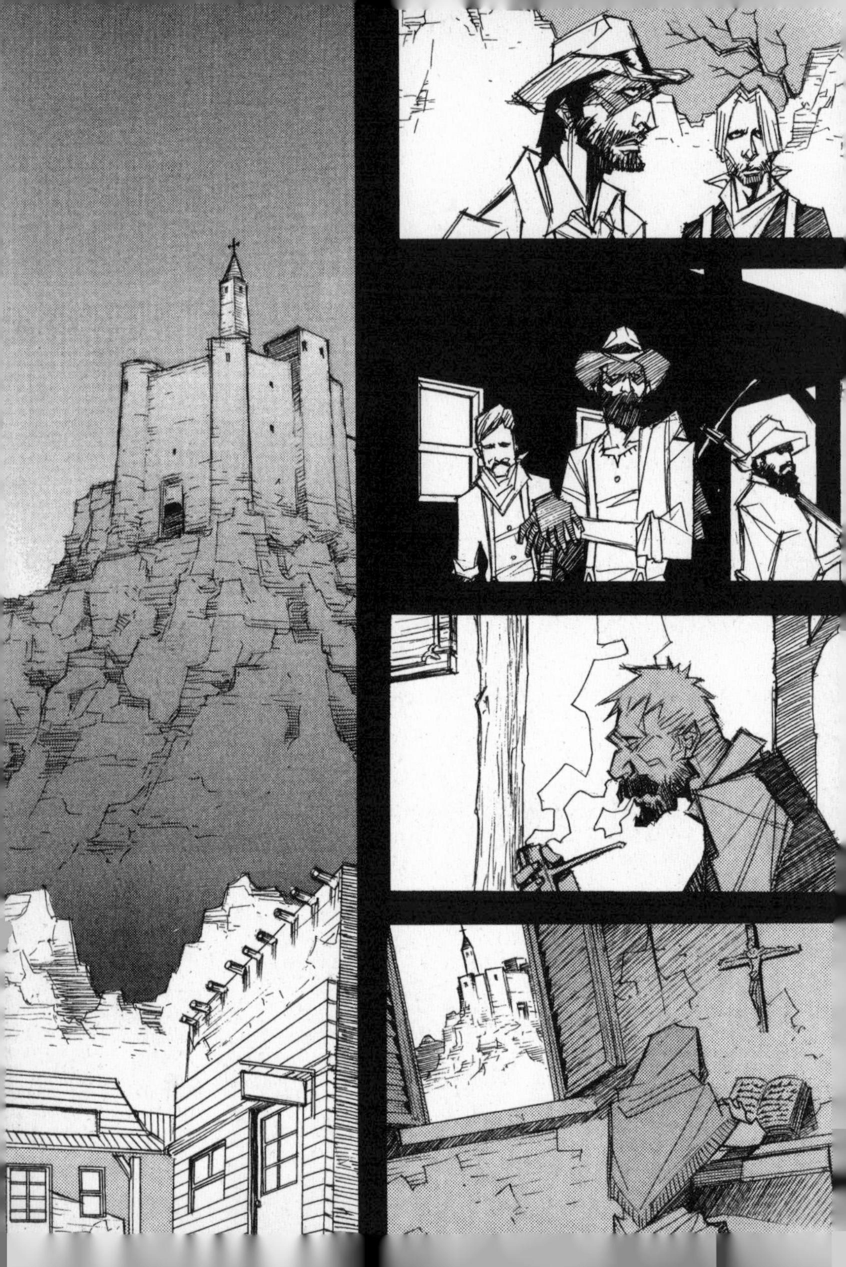

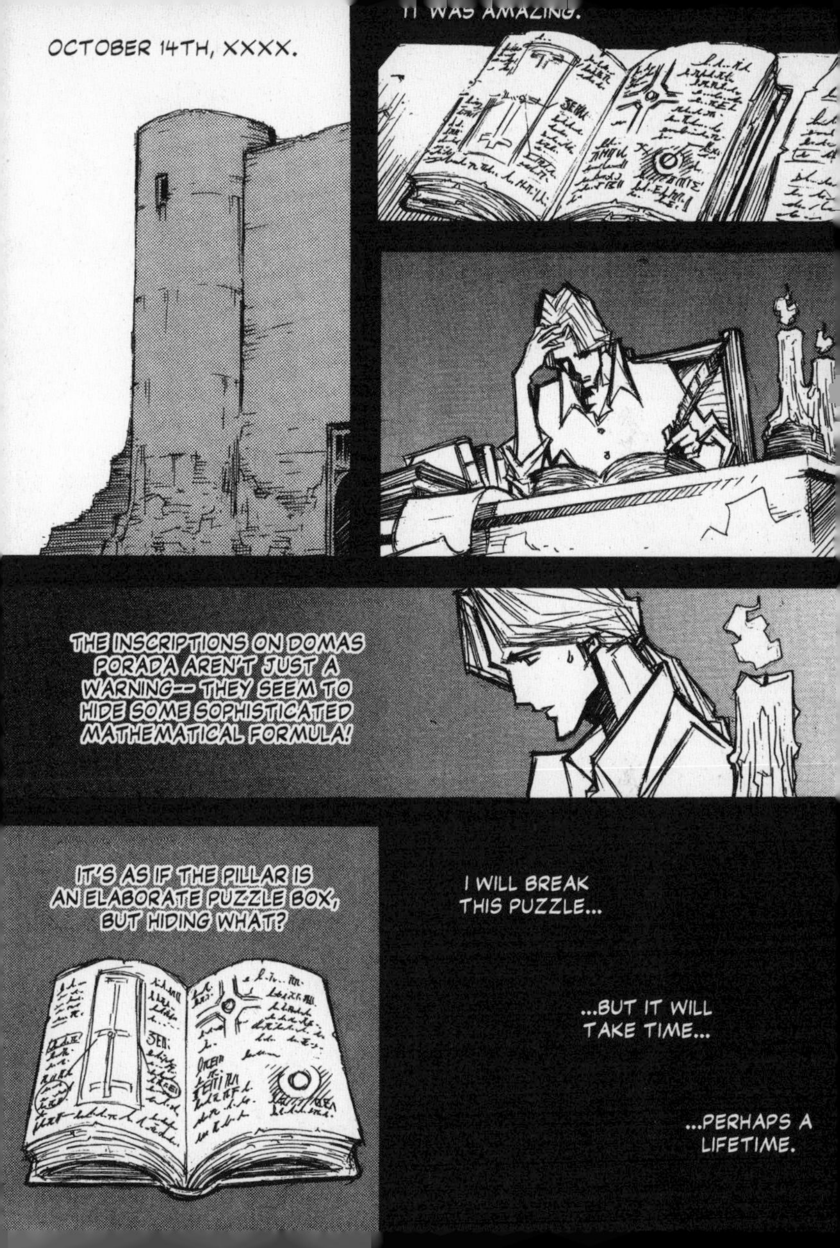
OCTOBER 14TH, XXXX.
IT WAS AMAZING.
THE INSCRIPTIONS ON DOMAS PORADA AREN'T JUST A WARNING-- THEY SEEM TO HIDE SOME SOPHISTICATED MATHEMATICAL FORMULA!
IT'S AS IF THE PILLAR IS AN ELABORATE PUZZLE BOX, BUT HIDING WHAT?
I WILL BREAK THIS PUZZLE...
...BUT IT WILL TAKE TIME...
...PERHAPS A LIFETIME.

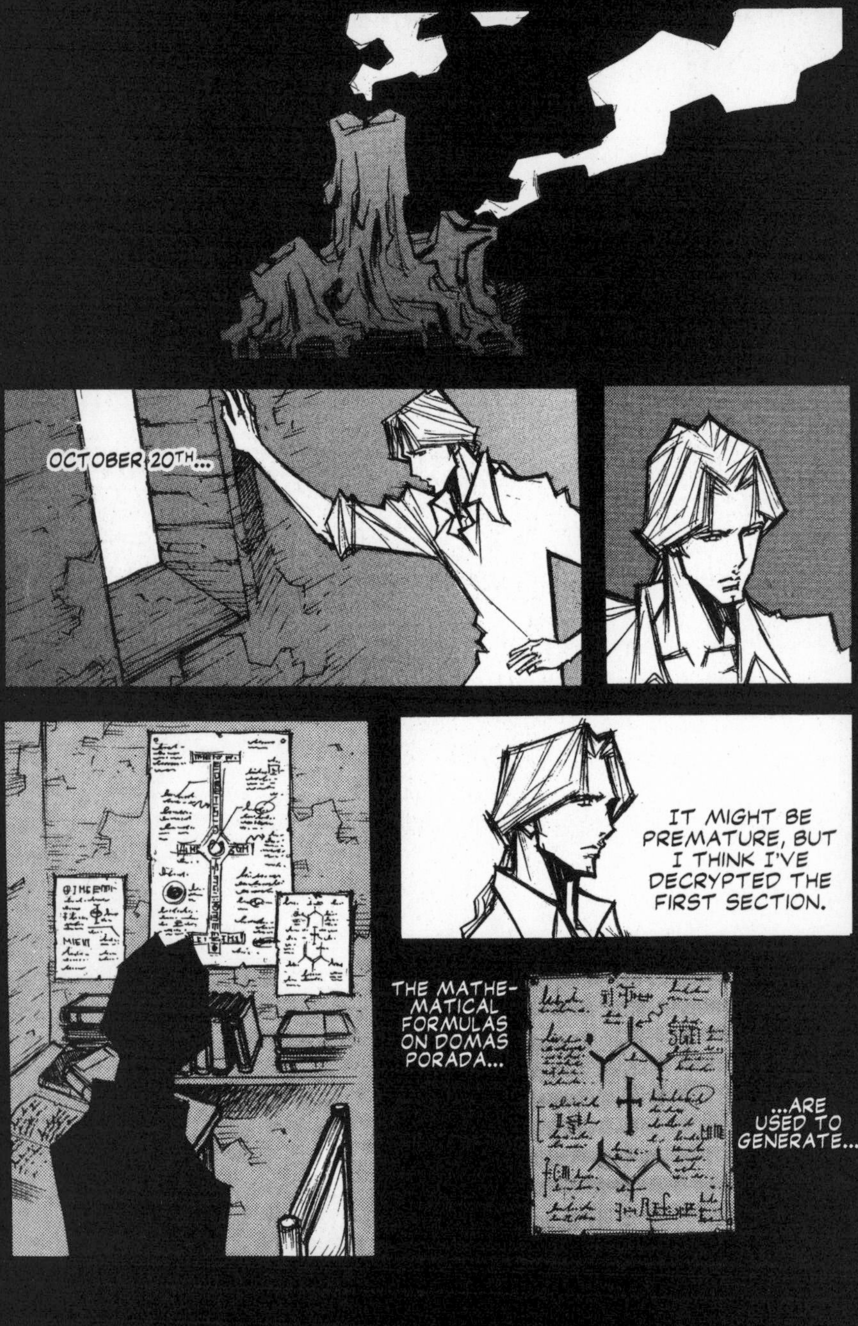
OCTOBER 20TH...
IT MIGHT BE PREMATURE, BUT I THINK I'VE DECRYPTED THE FIRST SECTION.
THE MATHE-MATICAL FORMULAS ON DOMAS PORADA...
...ARE USED TO GENERATE...

...SOME SORT OF HIEROGLYPHS.

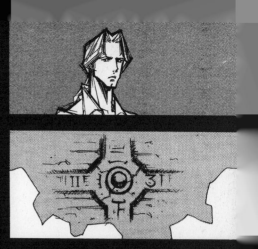

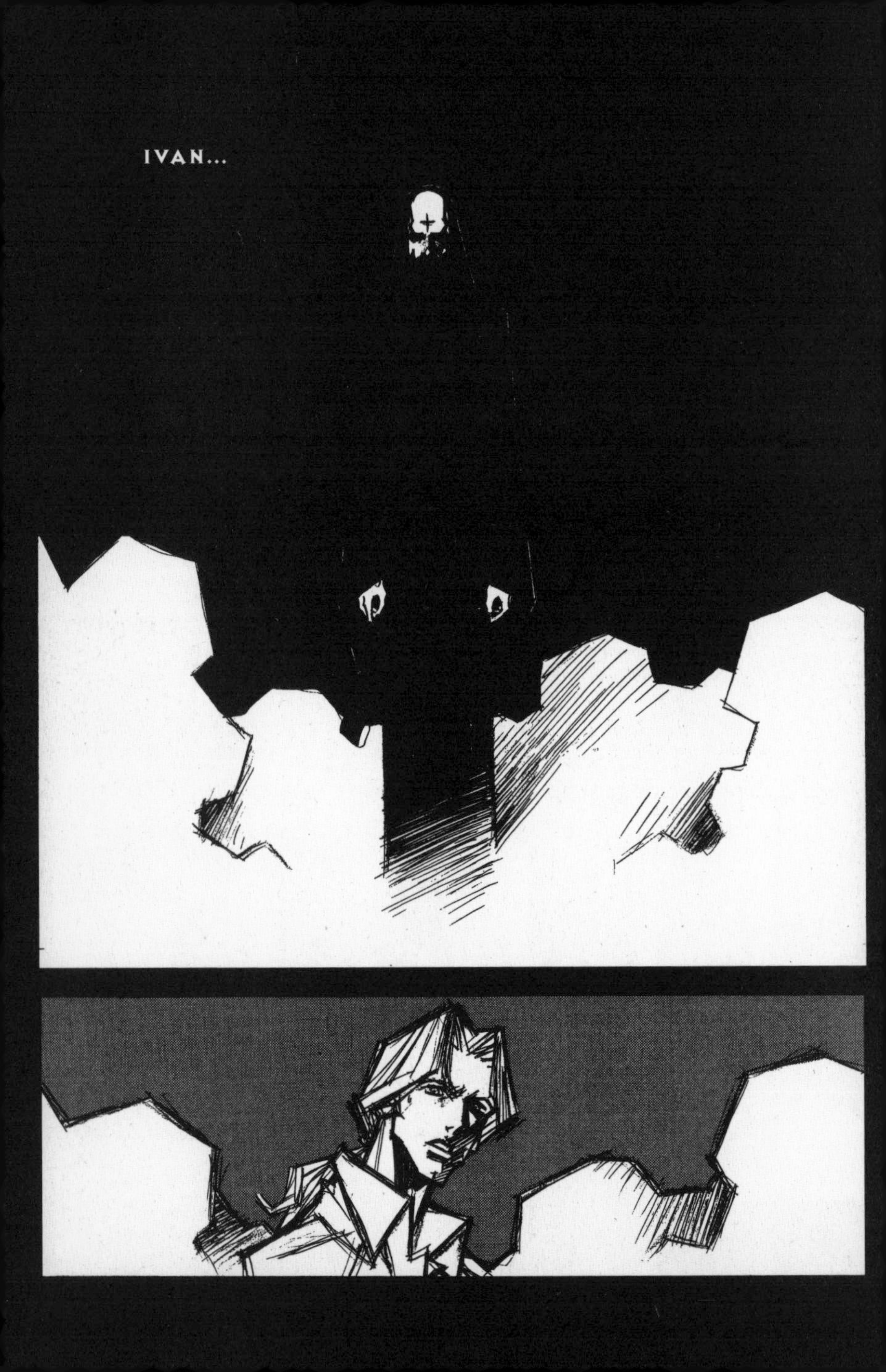
IVAN...

WHA+ DO
YOU HOPE
+O FIND
HERE?

WHO...
WHO
ARE
YOU?!

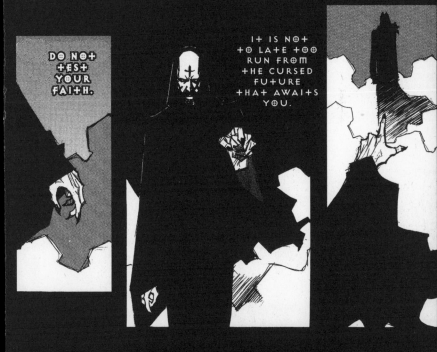

DO NO+
+ES+
YOUR
FAI+H.

I+ IS NO+
+O LA+E +OO
RUN FROM
+HE CURSED
FU+URE
+HA+ AWAI+S
YOU.

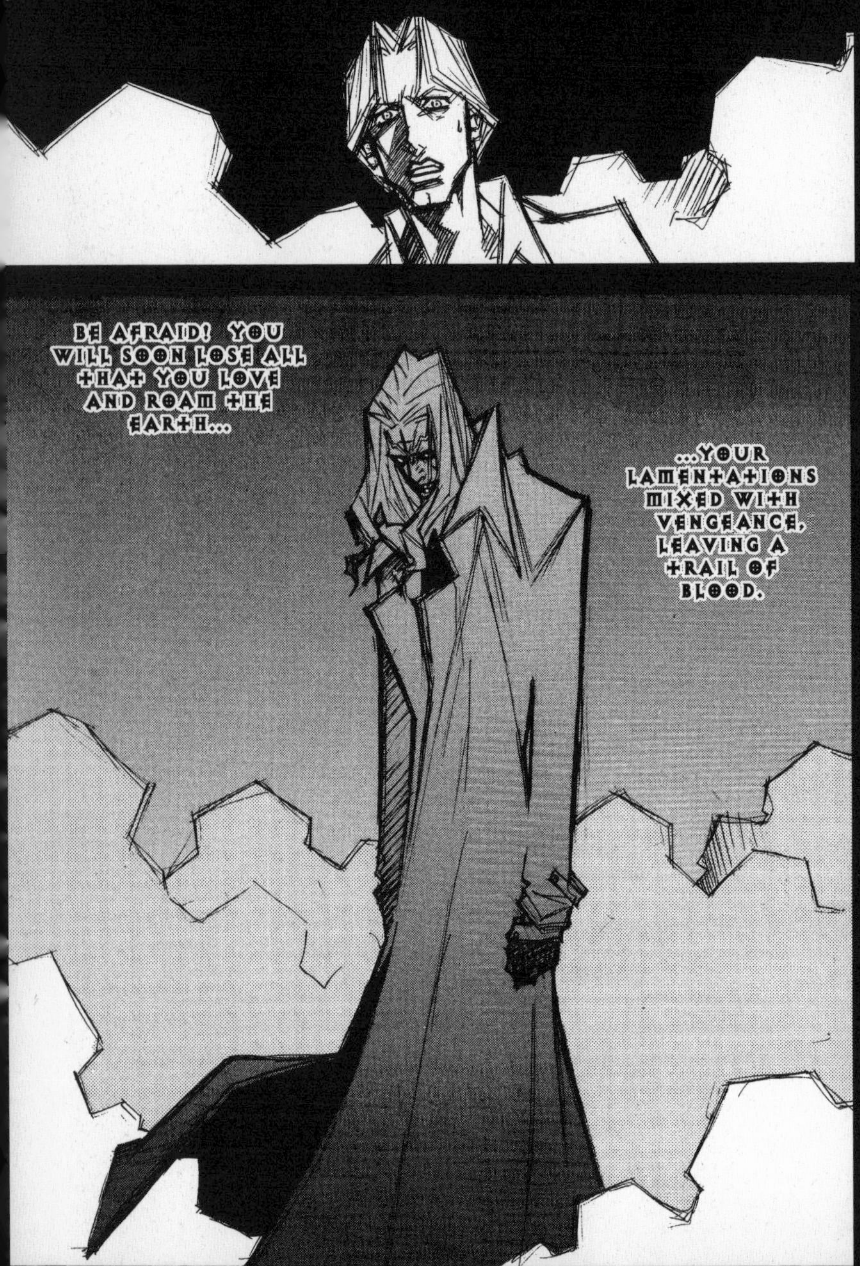
BE AFRAID! YOU WILL SOON LOSE ALL THAT YOU LOVE AND ROAM THE EARTH...
...YOUR LAMENTATIONS MIXED WITH VENGEANCE, LEAVING A TRAIL OF BLOOD.

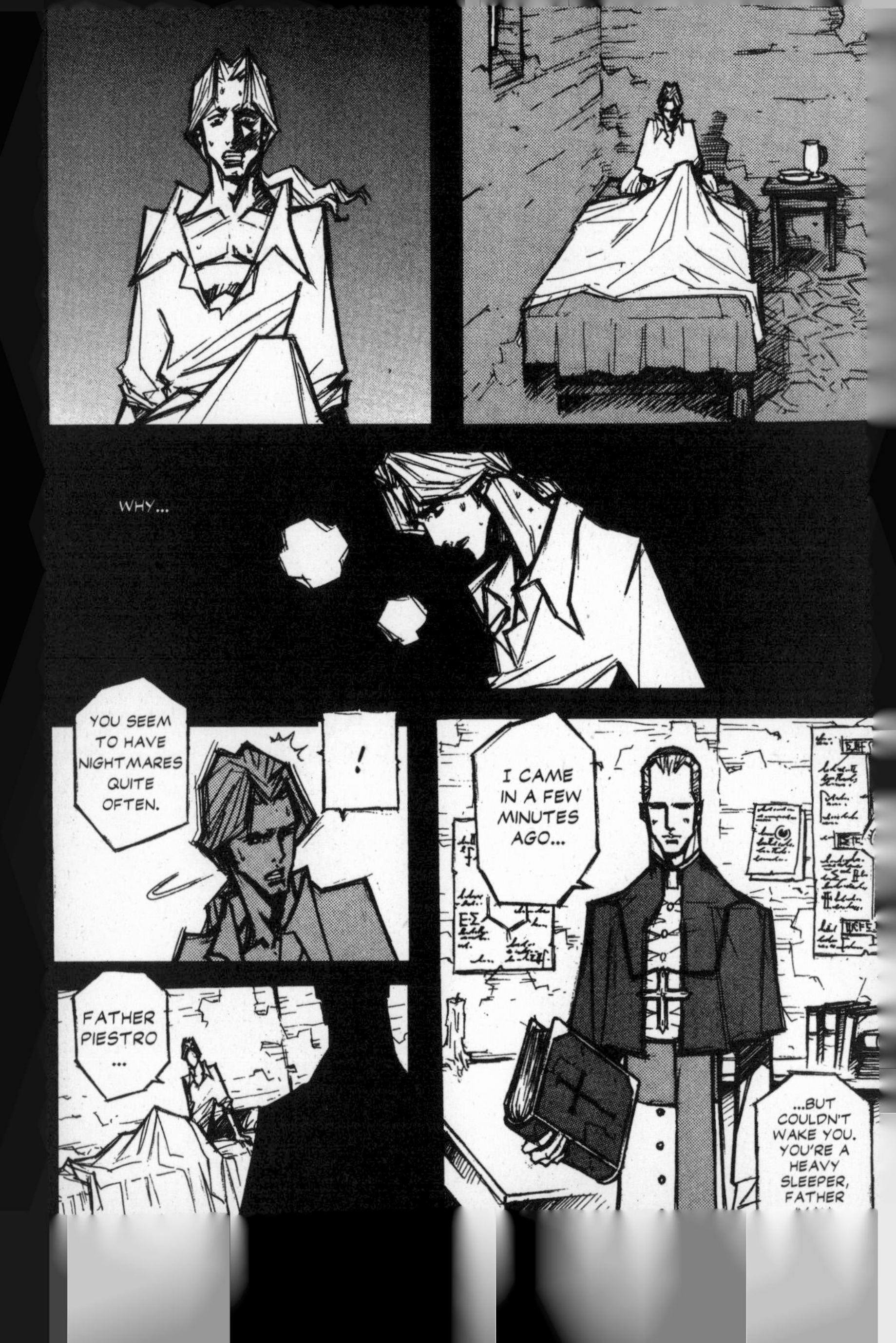
WHY...
YOU SEEM TO HAVE NIGHTMARES QUITE OFTEN.
!
FATHER PIESTRO ...
I CAME IN A FEW MINUTES AGO...
...BUT COULDN'T WAKE YOU. YOU'RE A HEAVY SLEEPER, FATHER

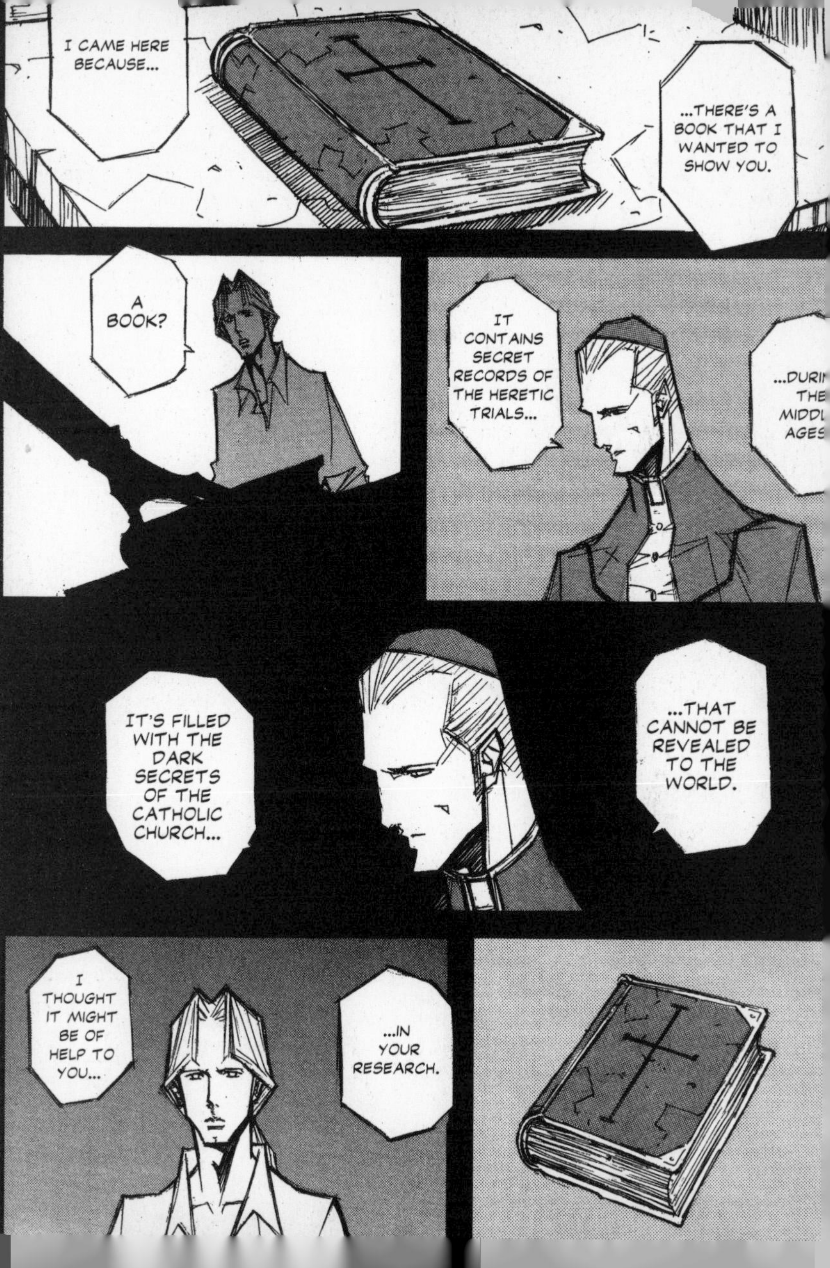
I CAME HERE BECAUSE...
...THERE'S A BOOK THAT I WANTED TO SHOW YOU.
A BOOK?
IT CONTAINS SECRET RECORDS OF THE HERETIC TRIALS...
...DURIN THE MIDDL AGES
IT'S FILLED WITH THE DARK SECRETS OF THE CATHOLIC CHURCH...
...THAT CANNOT BE REVEALED TO THE WORLD.
I THOUGHT IT MIGHT BE OF HELP TO YOU...
...IN YOUR RESEARCH.

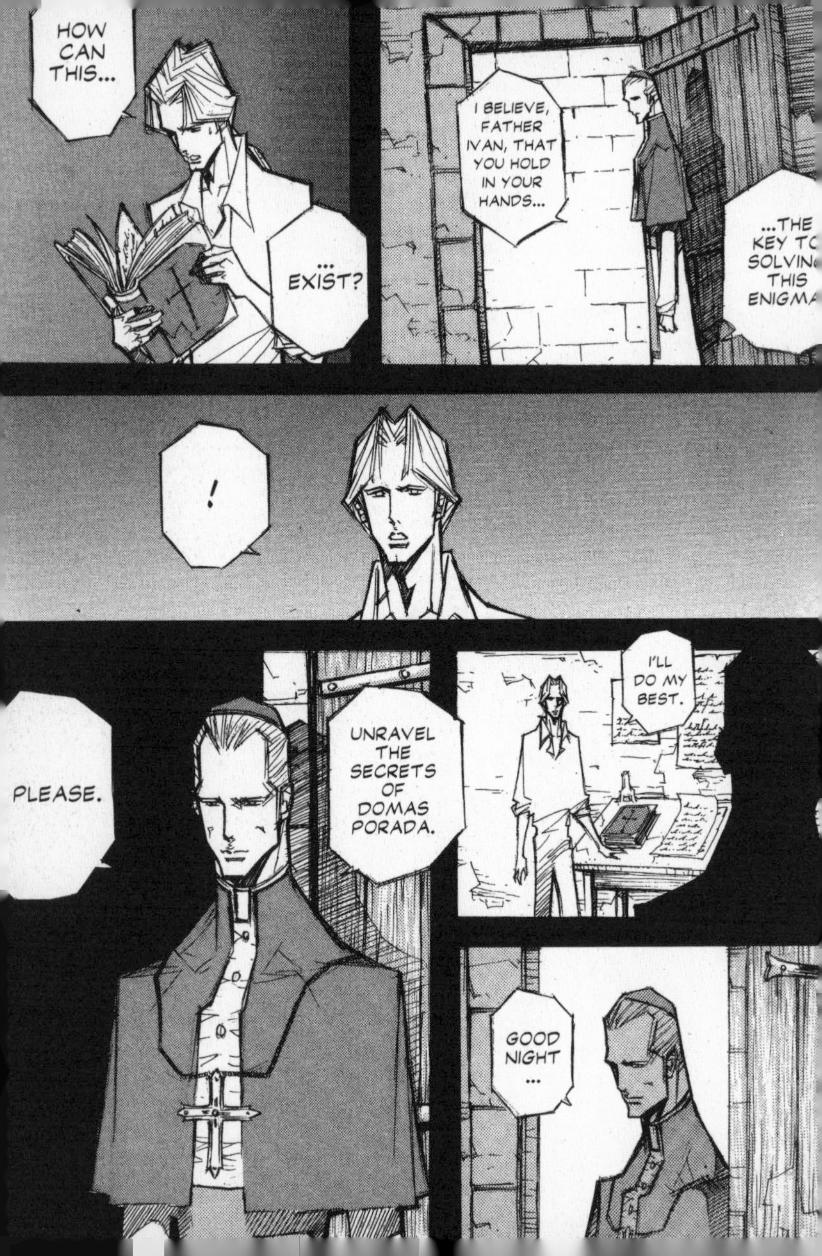
HOW CAN THIS...
... EXIST?
I BELIEVE, FATHER IVAN, THAT YOU HOLD IN YOUR HANDS...
...THE KEY TO SOLVING THIS ENIGMA
!
PLEASE.
UNRAVEL THE SECRETS OF DOMAS PORADA.
I'LL DO MY BEST.
GOOD NIGHT ...

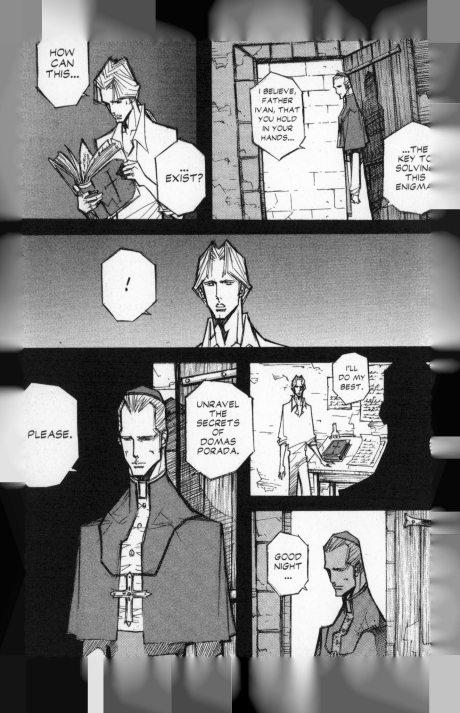

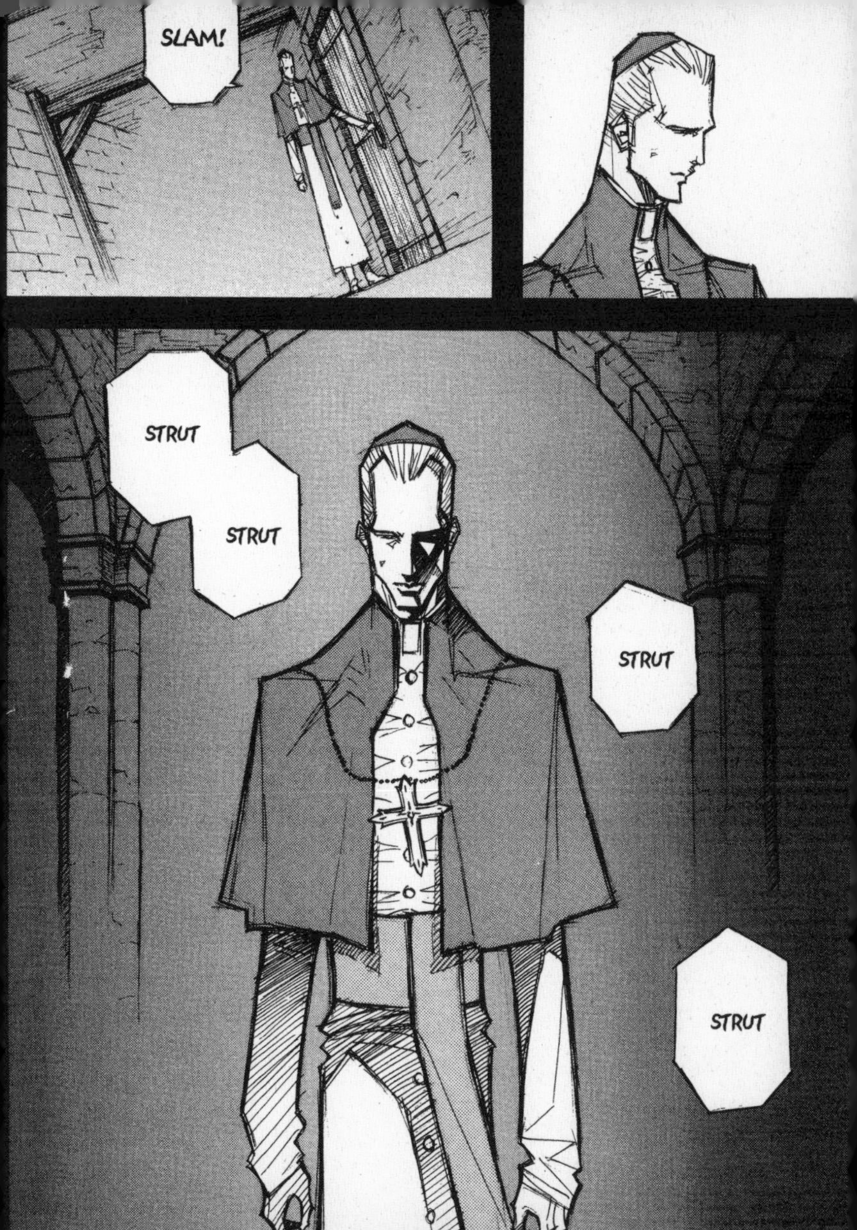
SLAM!
STRUT
STRUT
STRUT
STRUT

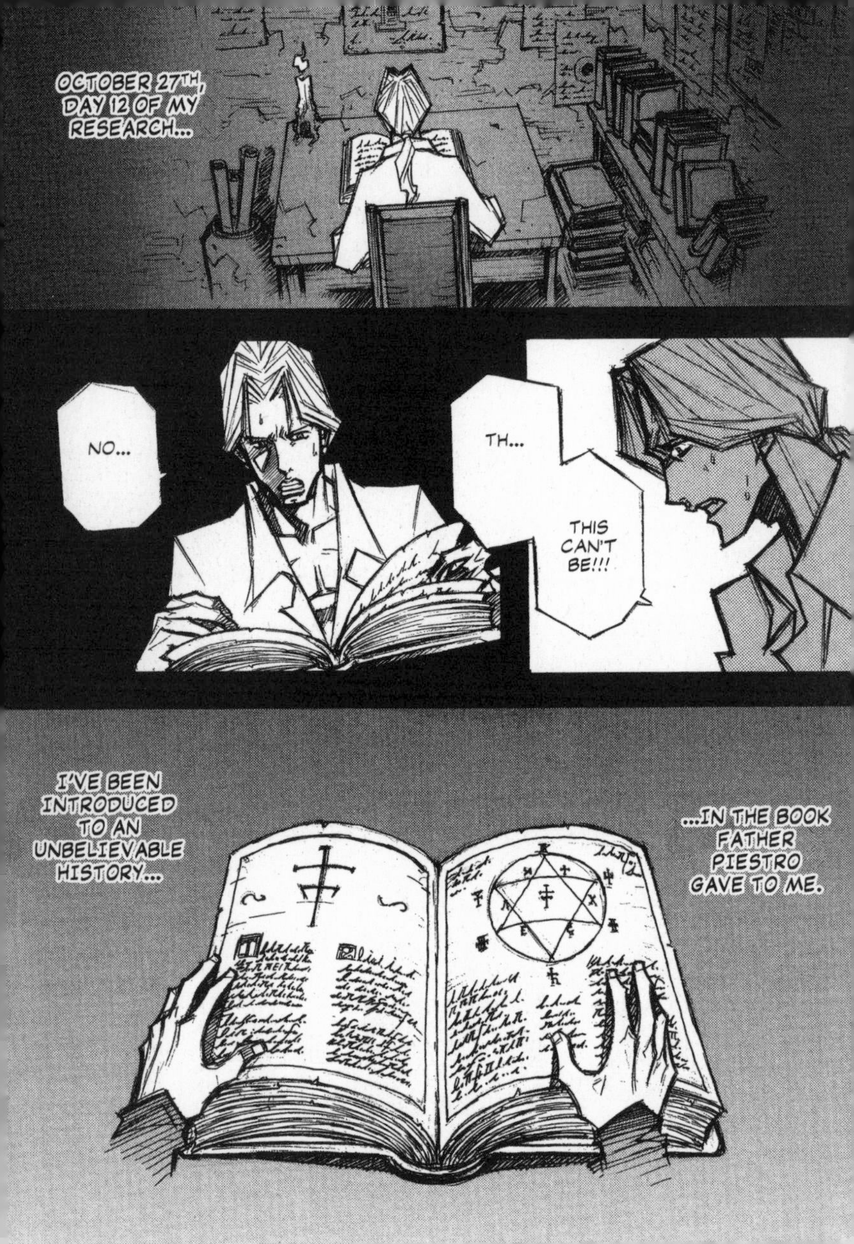
OCTOBER 27TH, DAY 12 OF MY RESEARCH...
NO...
TH...
THIS CAN'T BE!!!
I'VE BEEN INTRODUCED TO AN UNBELIEVABLE HISTORY...
...IN THE BOOK FATHER PIESTRO GAVE TO ME.

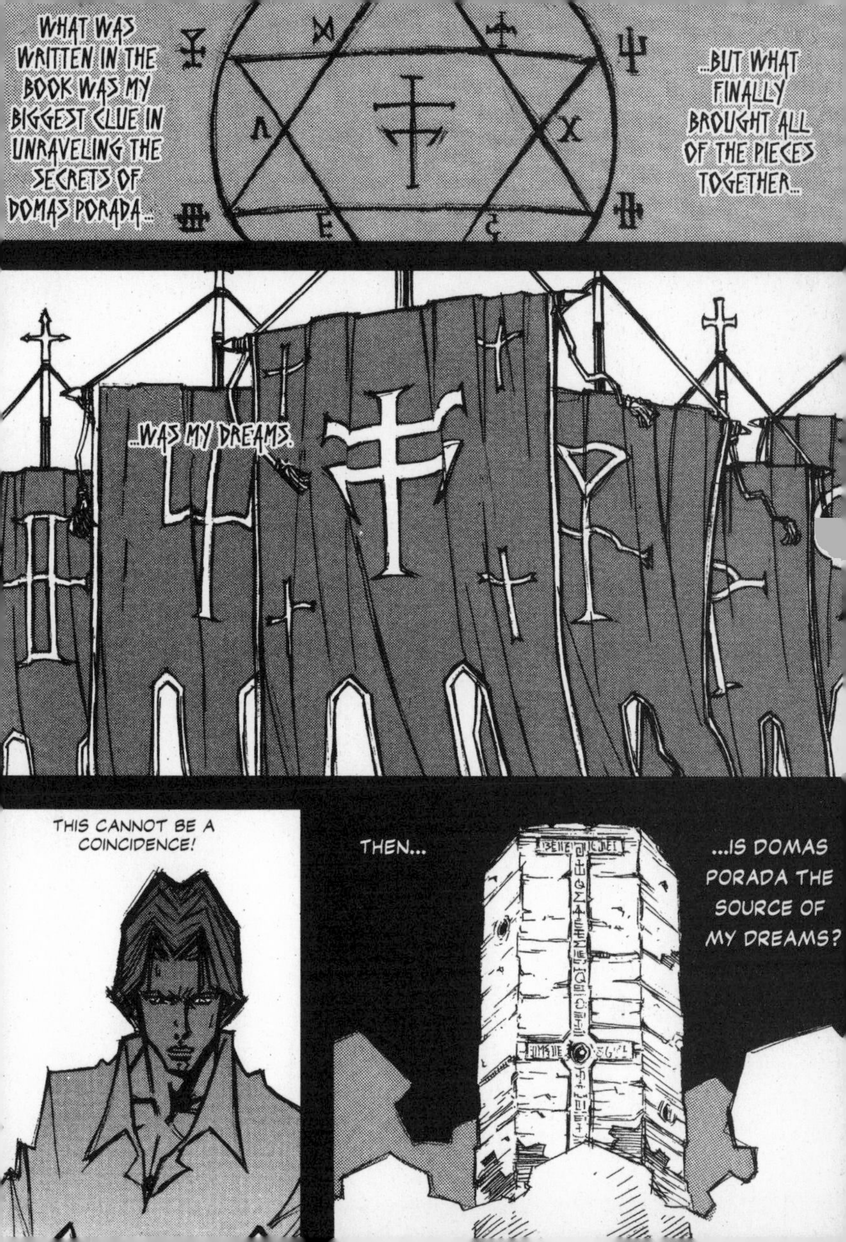
WHAT WAS WRITTEN IN THE BOOK WAS MY BIGGEST CLUE IN UNRAVELING THE SECRETS OF DOMAS PORADA...
...BUT WHAT FINALLY BROUGHT ALL OF THE PIECES TOGETHER...
...WAS MY DREAMS.
THIS CANNOT BE A COINCIDENCE!
THEN...
...IS DOMAS PORADA THE SOURCE OF MY DREAMS?

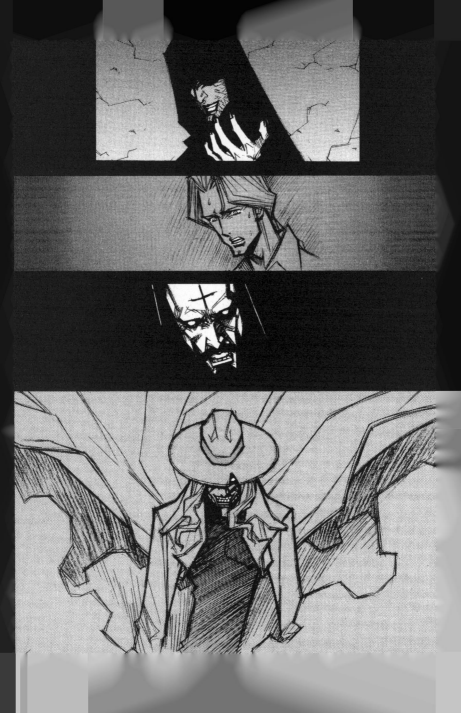

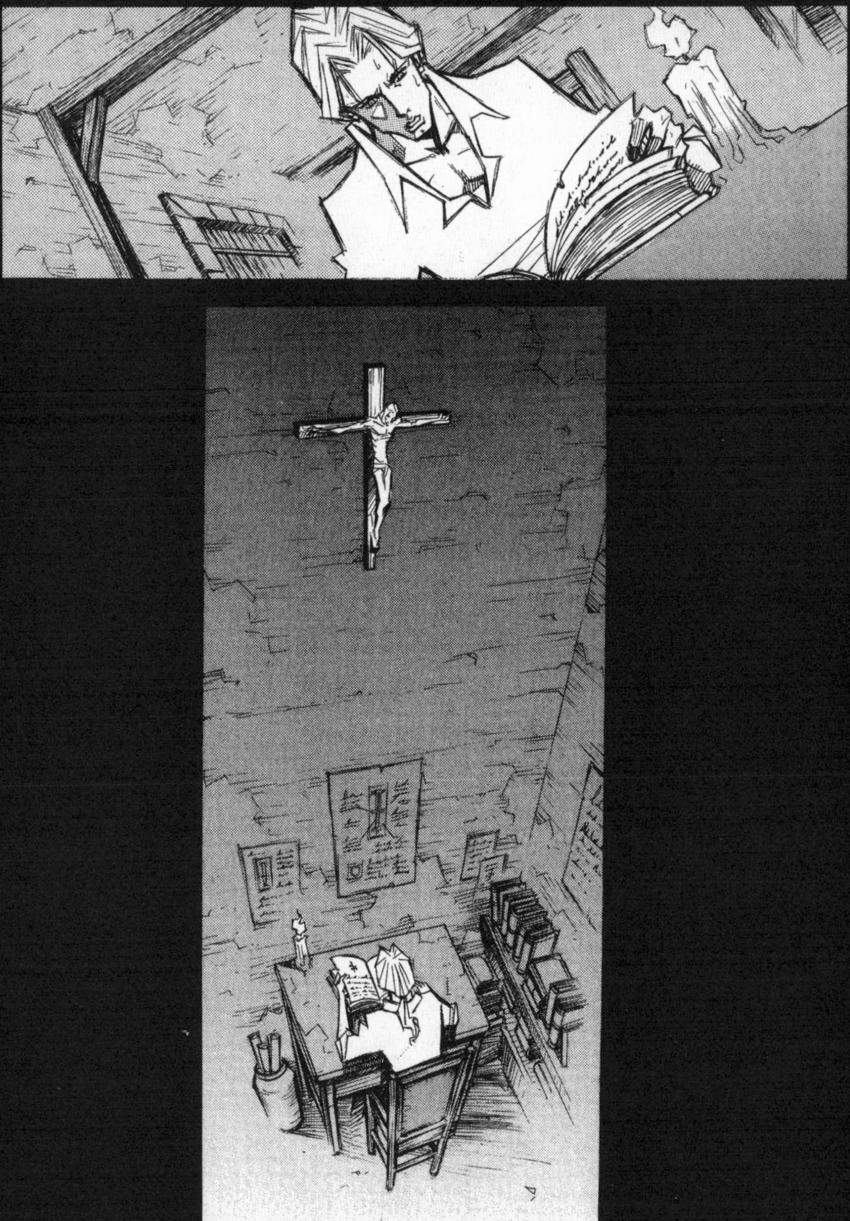

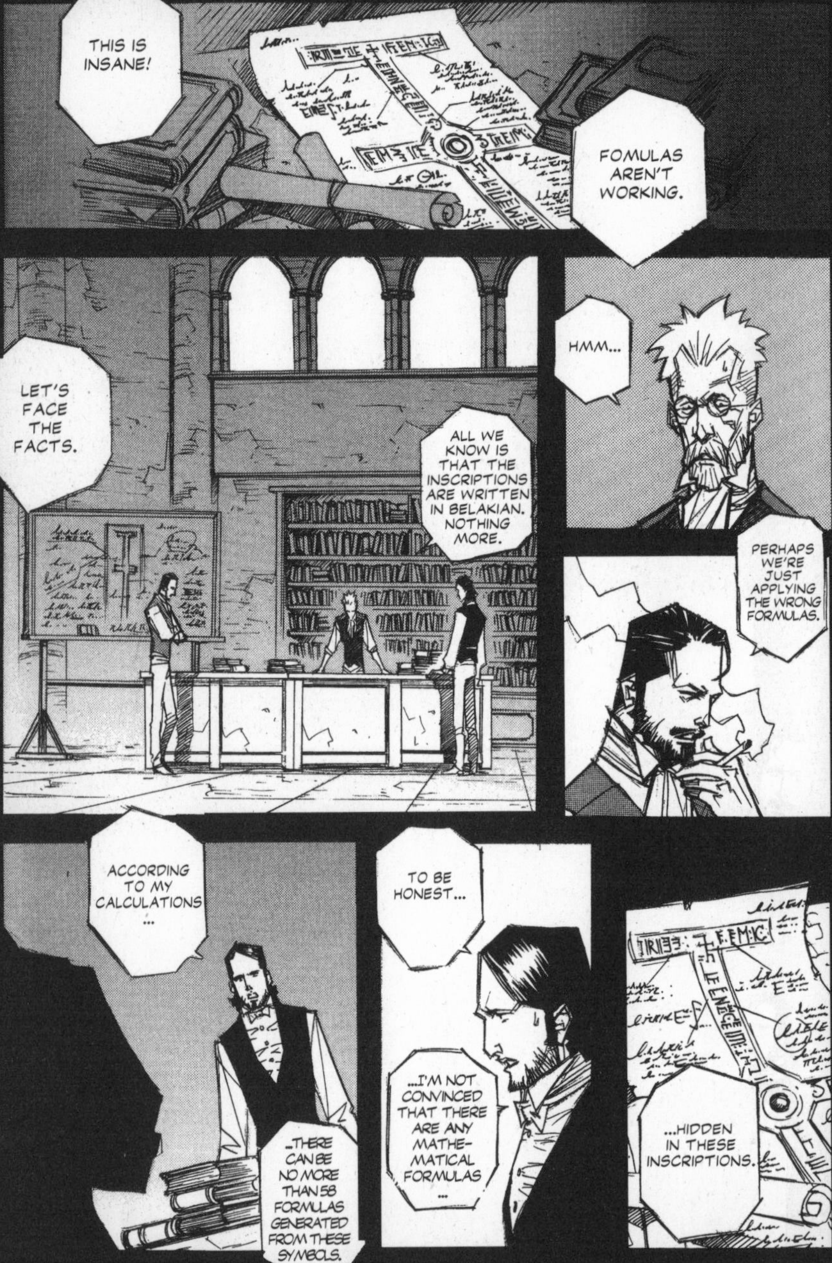
THIS IS INSANE!
FOMULAS AREN'T WORKING.
LET'S FACE THE FACTS.
ALL WE KNOW IS THAT THE INSCRIPTIONS ARE WRITTEN IN BELAKIAN. NOTHING MORE.
HMM...
PERHAPS WE'RE JUST APPLYING THE WRONG FORMULAS.
ACCORDING TO MY CALCULATIONS ...
...THERE CAN BE NO MORE THAN 58 FORMULAS GENERATED FROM THESE SYMBOLS.
TO BE HONEST...
...I'M NOT CONVINCED THAT THERE ARE ANY MATHE-MATICAL FORMULAS ...
...HIDDEN IN THESE INSCRIPTIONS.

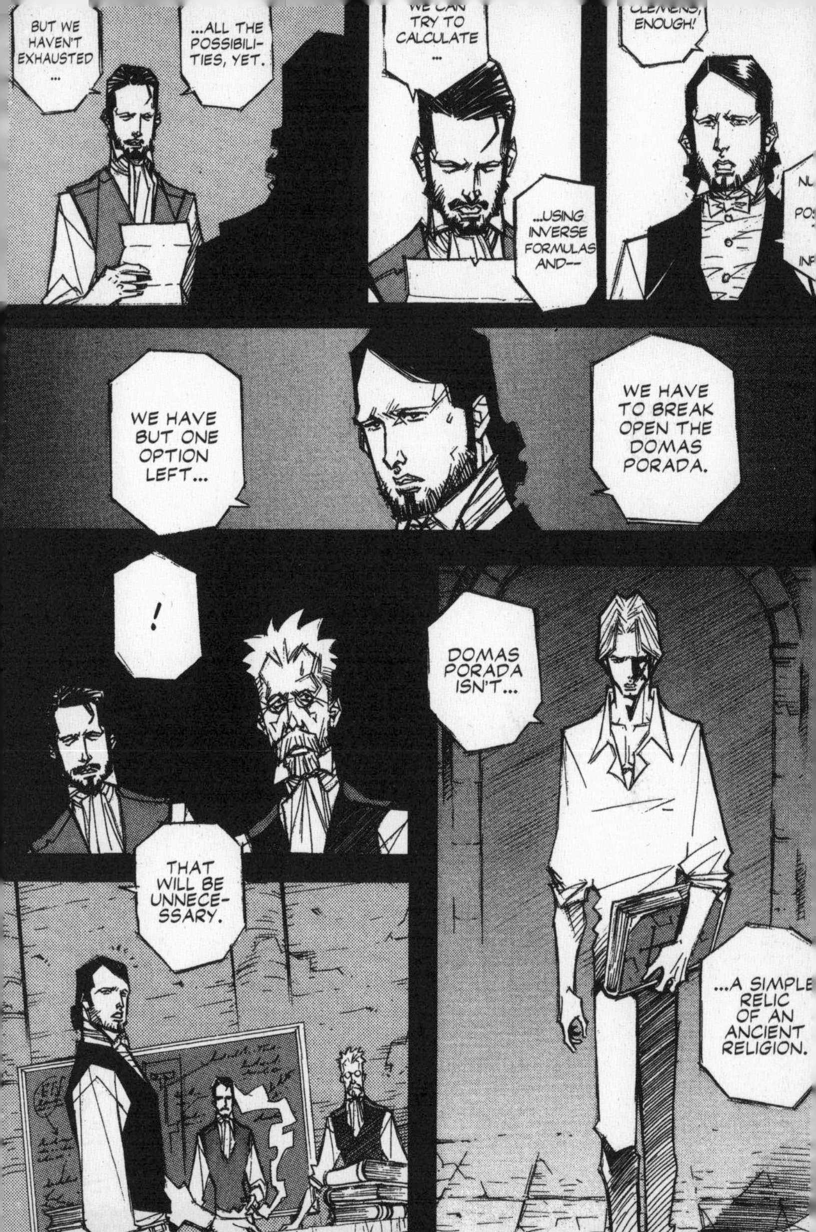

BUT WE HAVEN'T EXHAUSTED ...
...ALL THE POSSIBILITIES, YET.
TRY TO CALCULATE ...
...USING INVERSE FORMULAS AND--
ENOUGH!
WE HAVE BUT ONE OPTION LEFT...
WE HAVE TO BREAK OPEN THE DOMAS PORADA.
!
THAT WILL BE UNNECESSARY.
DOMAS PORADA ISN'T...
...A SIMPLE RELIC OF AN ANCIENT RELIGION.

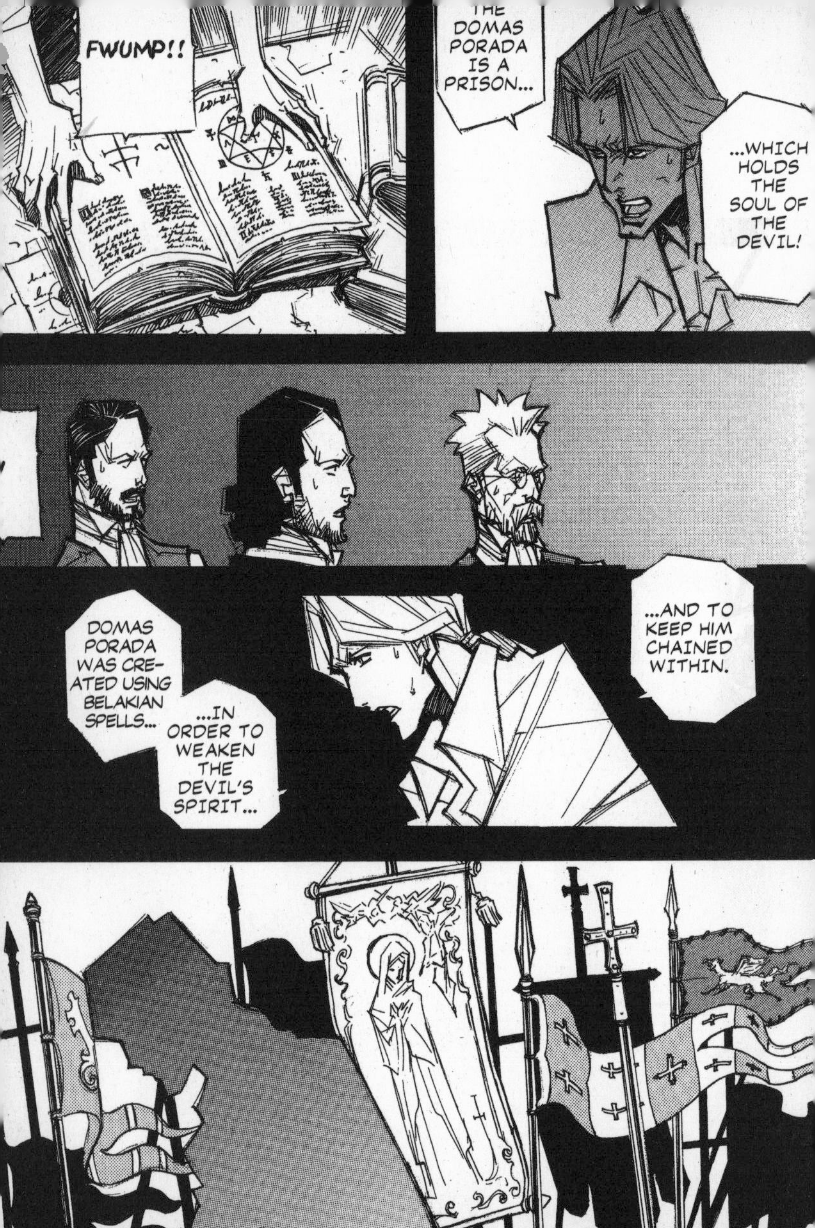
FWUMP!!
THE DOMAS PORADA IS A PRISON...
...WHICH HOLDS THE SOUL OF THE DEVIL!
DOMAS PORADA WAS CRE-ATED USING BELAKIAN SPELLS...
...IN ORDER TO WEAKEN THE DEVIL'S SPIRIT...
...AND TO KEEP HIM CHAINED WITHIN.

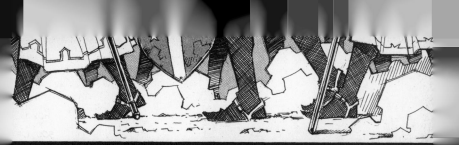

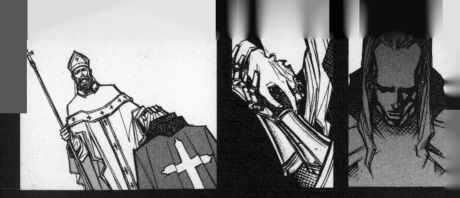

IT ALL STARTED 800 YEARS AGO, WITH A KNIGHT TEMPLAR OF THE CRUSADES NAMED VASCAR DE GUILLON...

...WHO WOULD LATER BE CALLED TEMOZARELA.

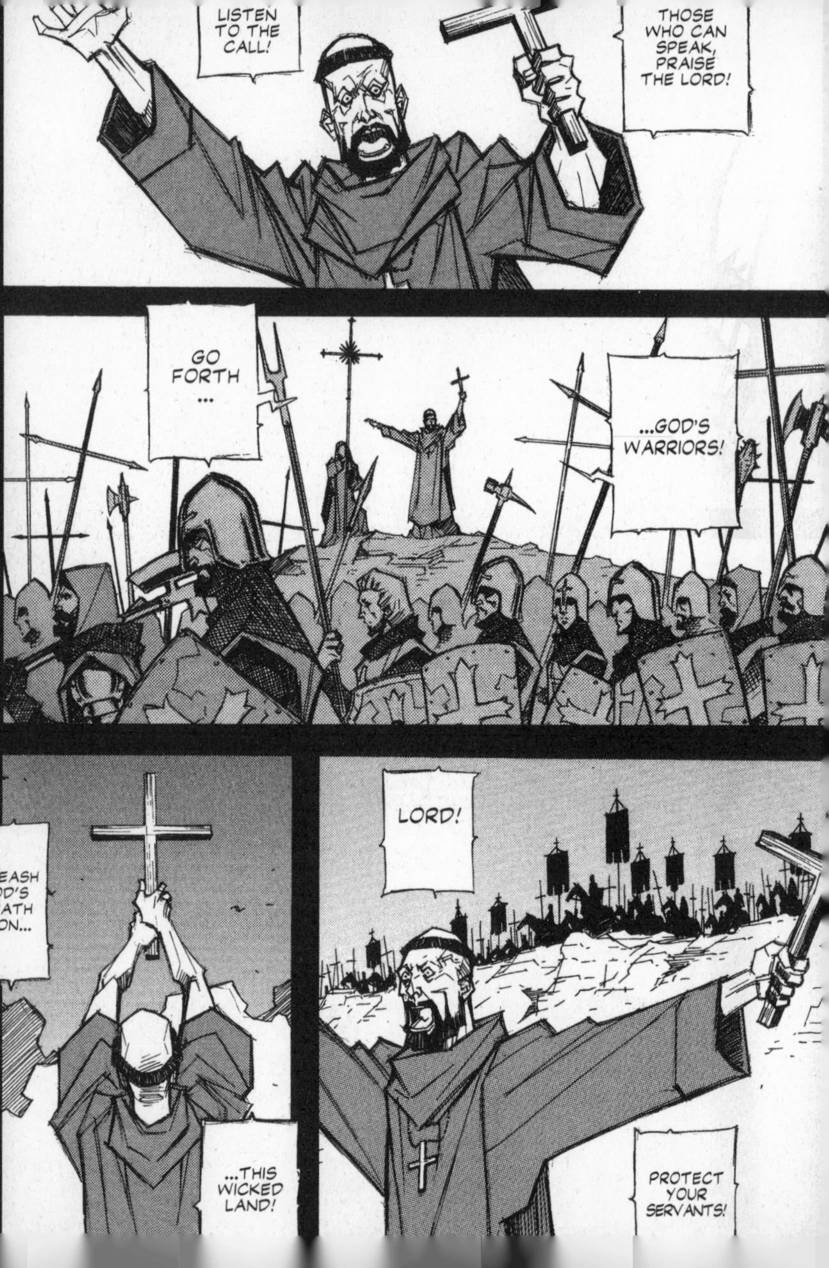
LISTEN TO THE CALL!
THOSE WHO CAN SPEAK, PRAISE THE LORD!
GO FORTH ...
...GOD'S WARRIORS!
UNLEASH GOD'S WRATH UPON...
...THIS WICKED LAND!
LORD!
PROTECT YOUR SERVANTS!

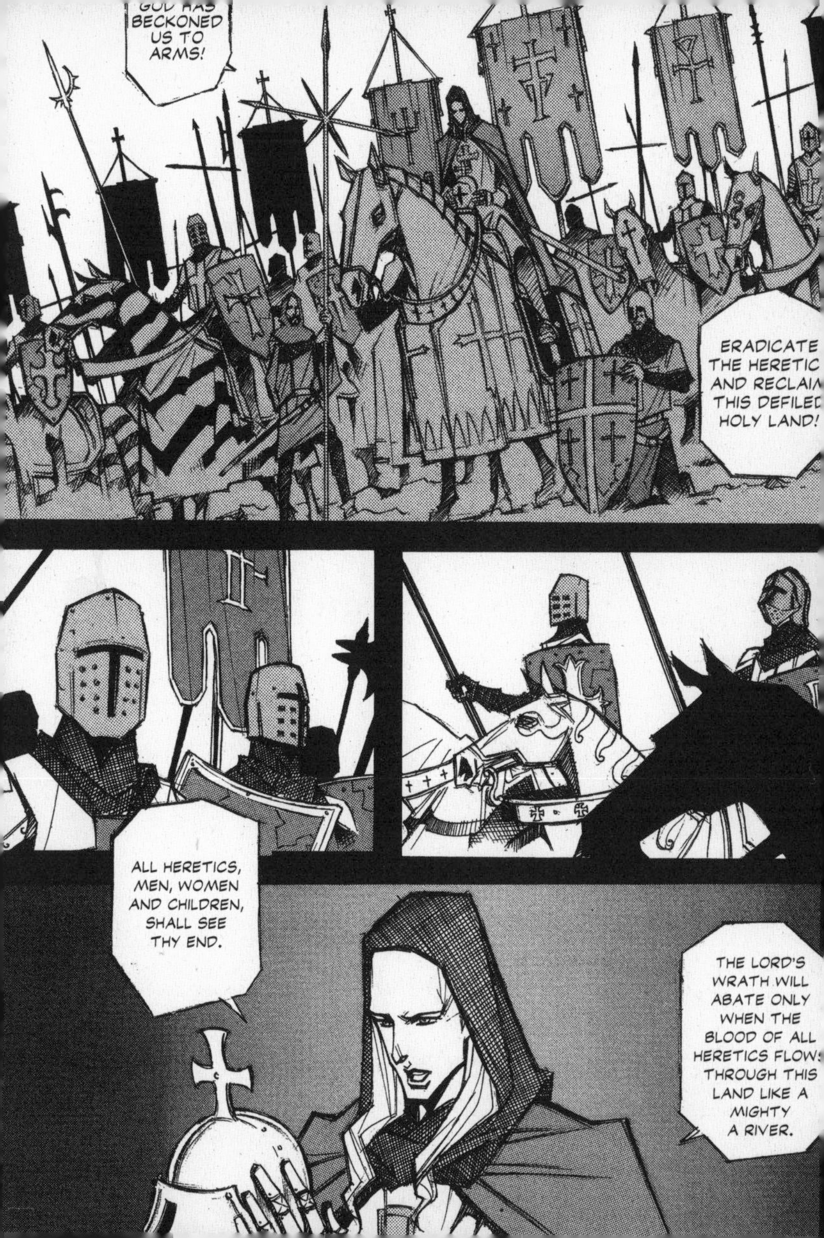
GOD HAS BECKONED US TO ARMS!
ERADICATE THE HERETIC AND RECLAIM THIS DEFILED HOLY LAND!
ALL HERETICS, MEN, WOMEN AND CHILDREN, SHALL SEE THY END.
THE LORD'S WRATH WILL ABATE ONLY WHEN THE BLOOD OF ALL HERETICS FLOWS THROUGH THIS LAND LIKE A MIGHTY A RIVER.

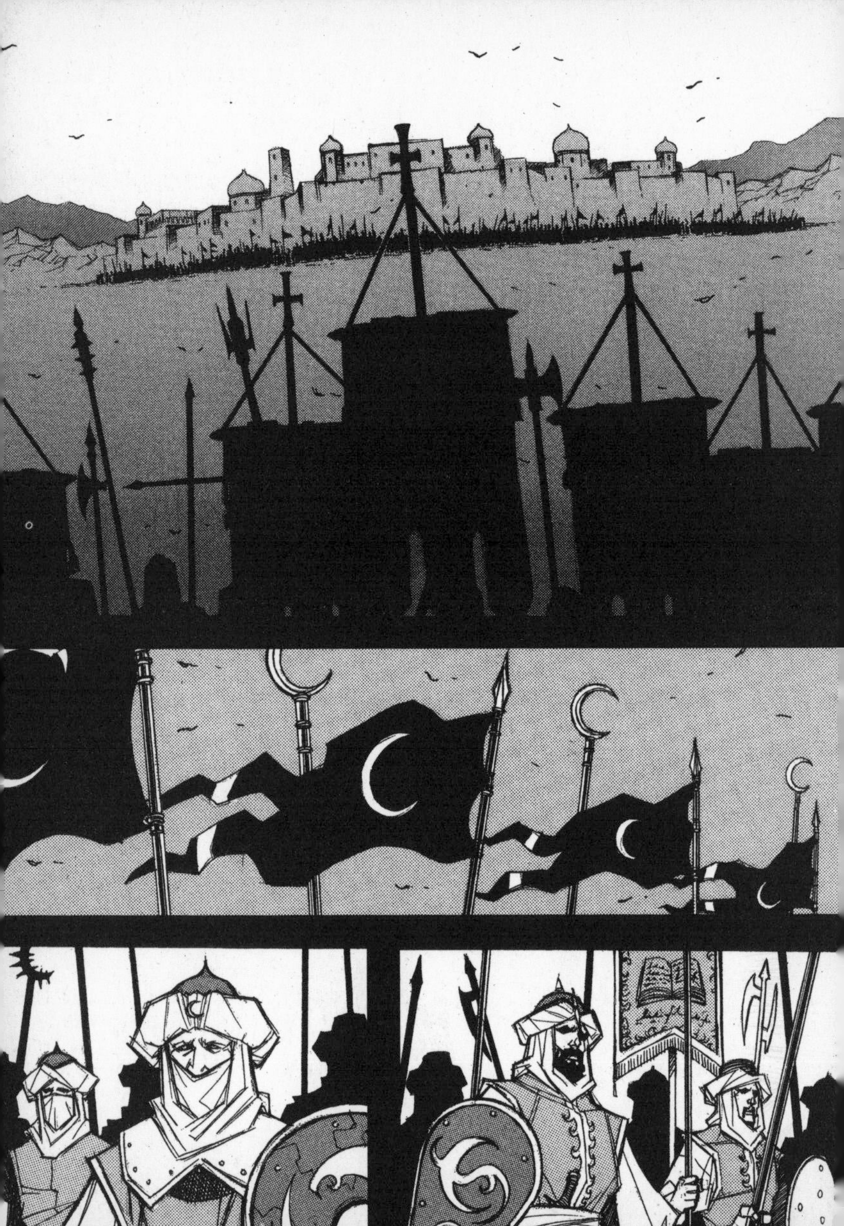

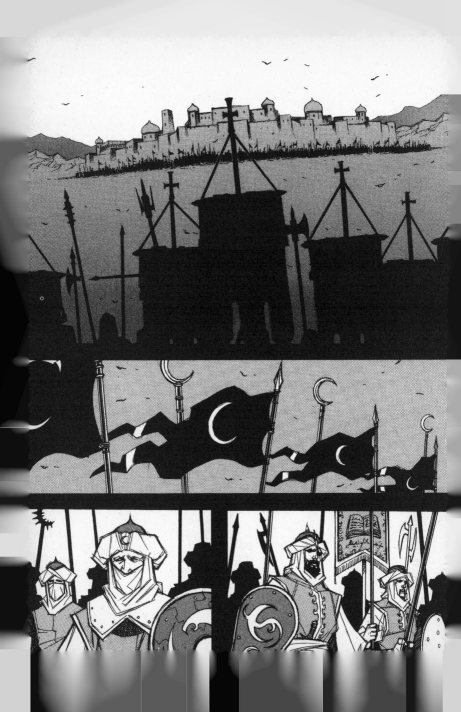

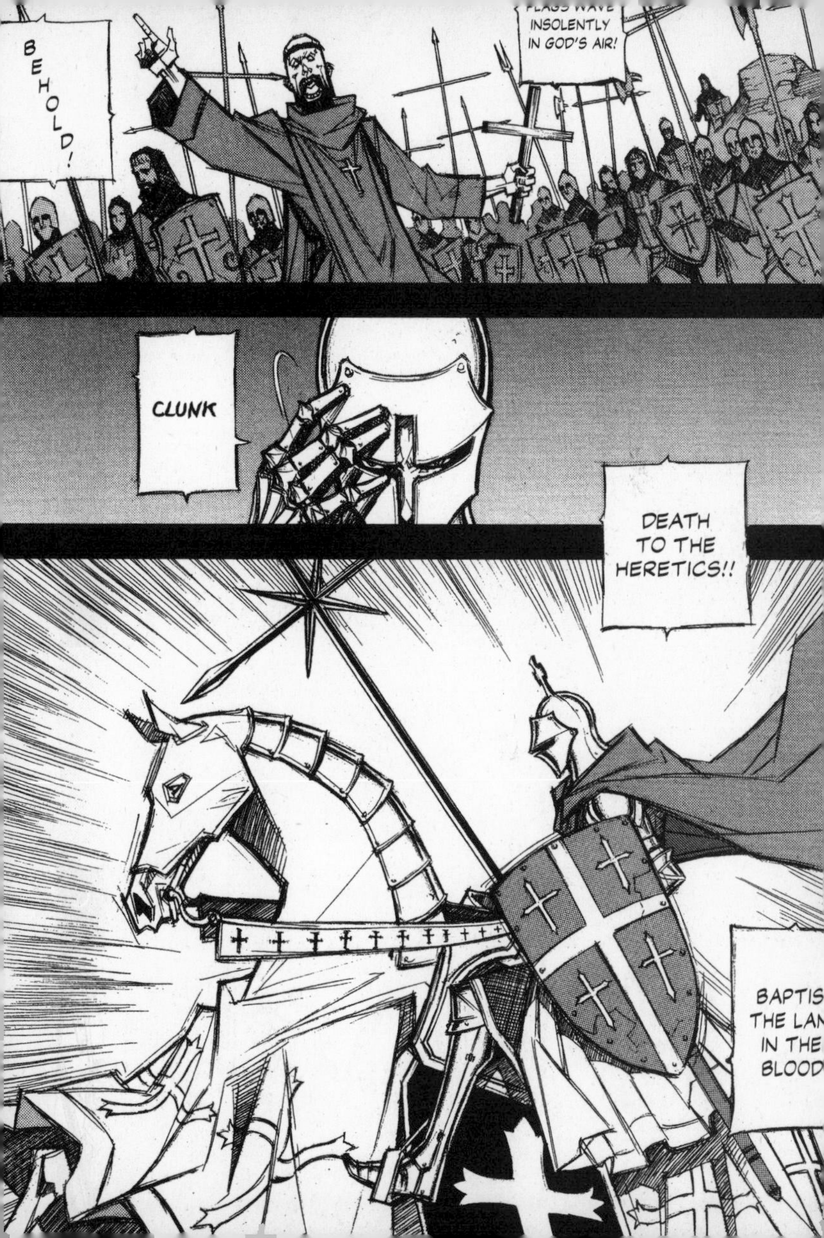
BEHOLD!
FLAGS WAVE INSOLENTLY IN GOD'S AIR!
CLUNK
DEATH TO THE HERETICS!!
BAPTIS THE LAN IN THE BLOOD

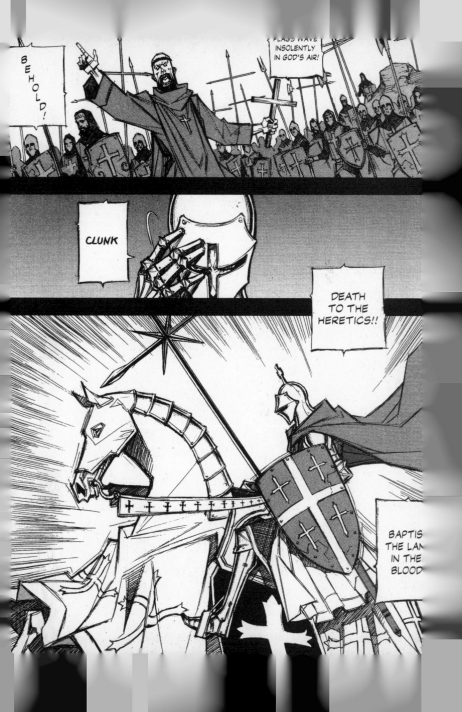

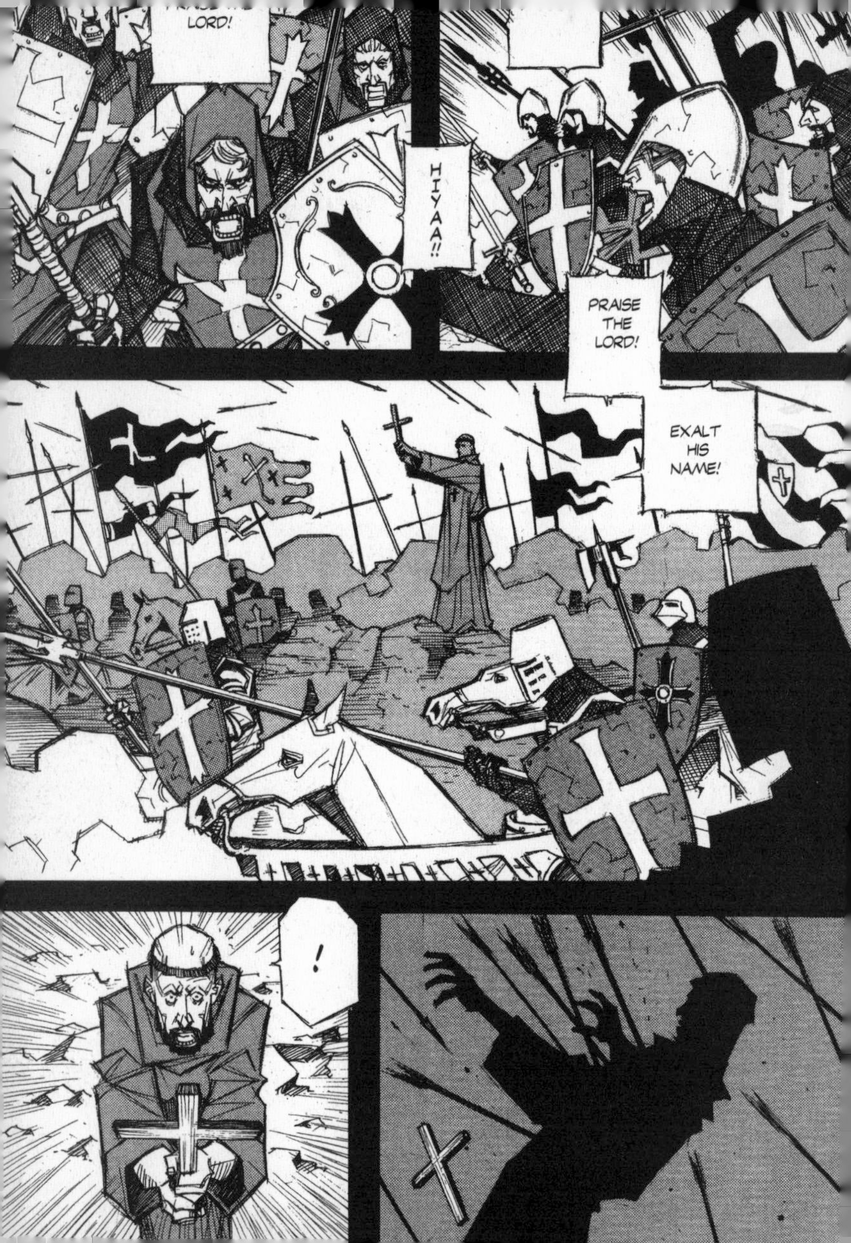
LORD!
HIYAA!!
PRAISE THE LORD!
EXALT HIS NAME!
!

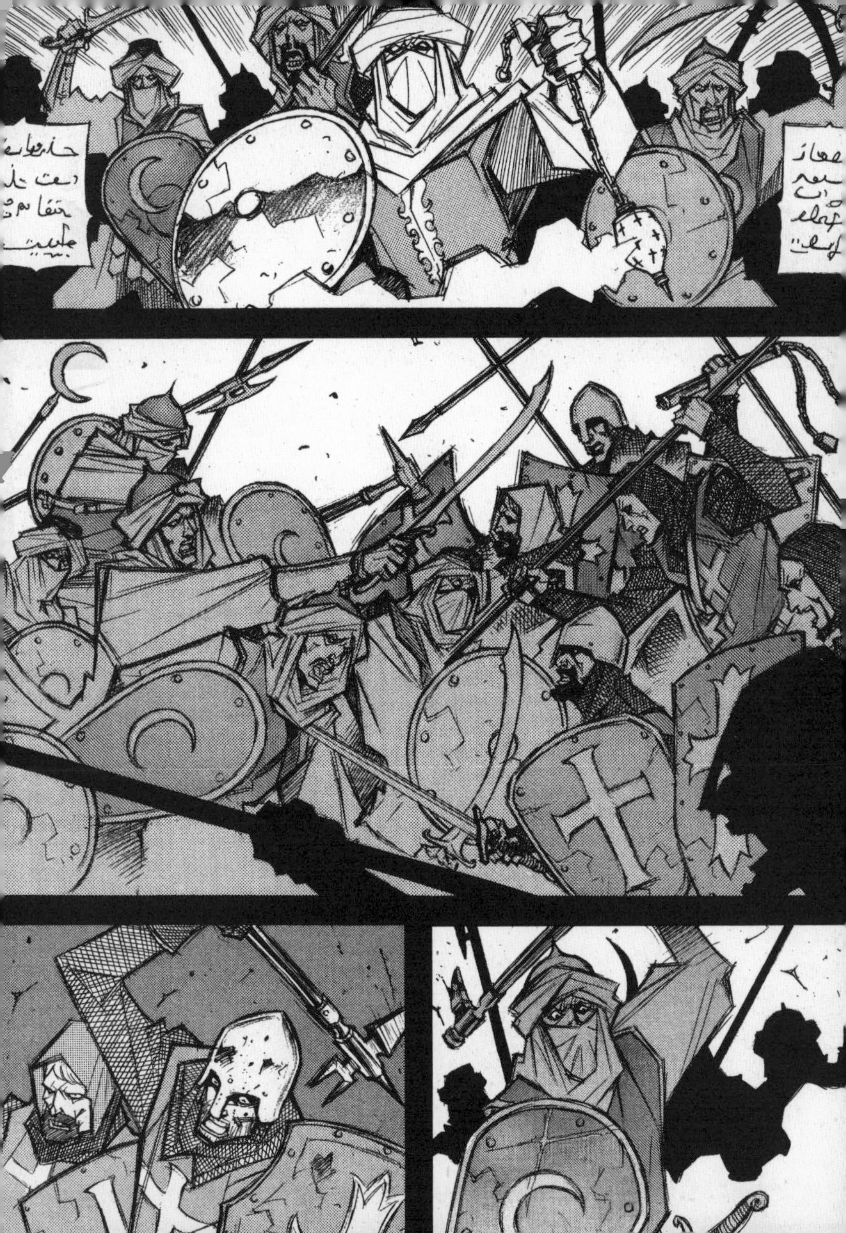

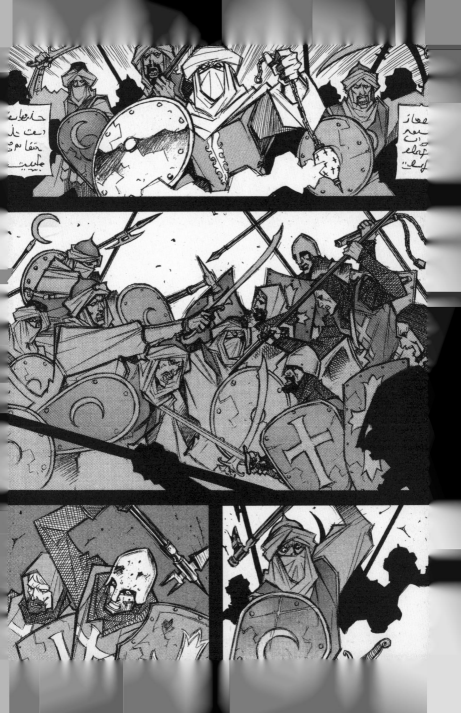

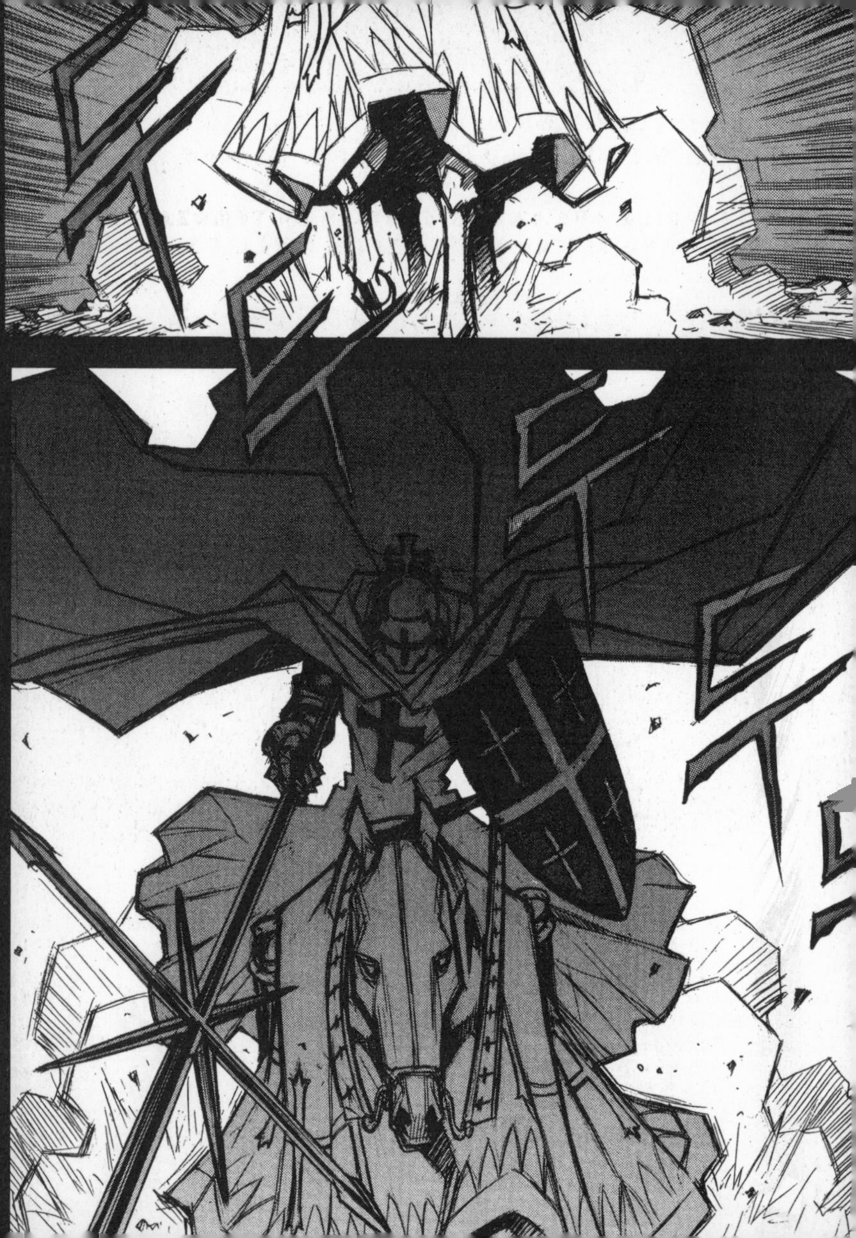

## IVAN ISAACS WILL RETURN IN
## PRIEST VOLUME 5: BALLAD OF A FALLEN ANGEL

IN WHICH THE DARK HISTORIES OF TEMOZARELA AND BELIAL ARE AT LAST REVEALED.

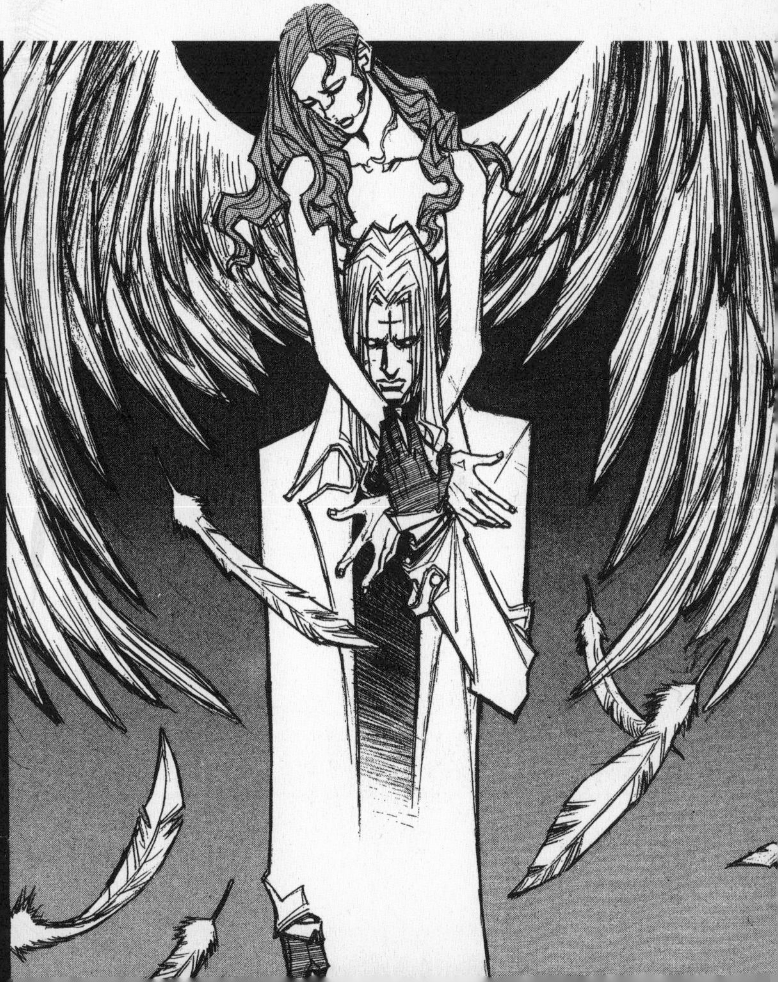

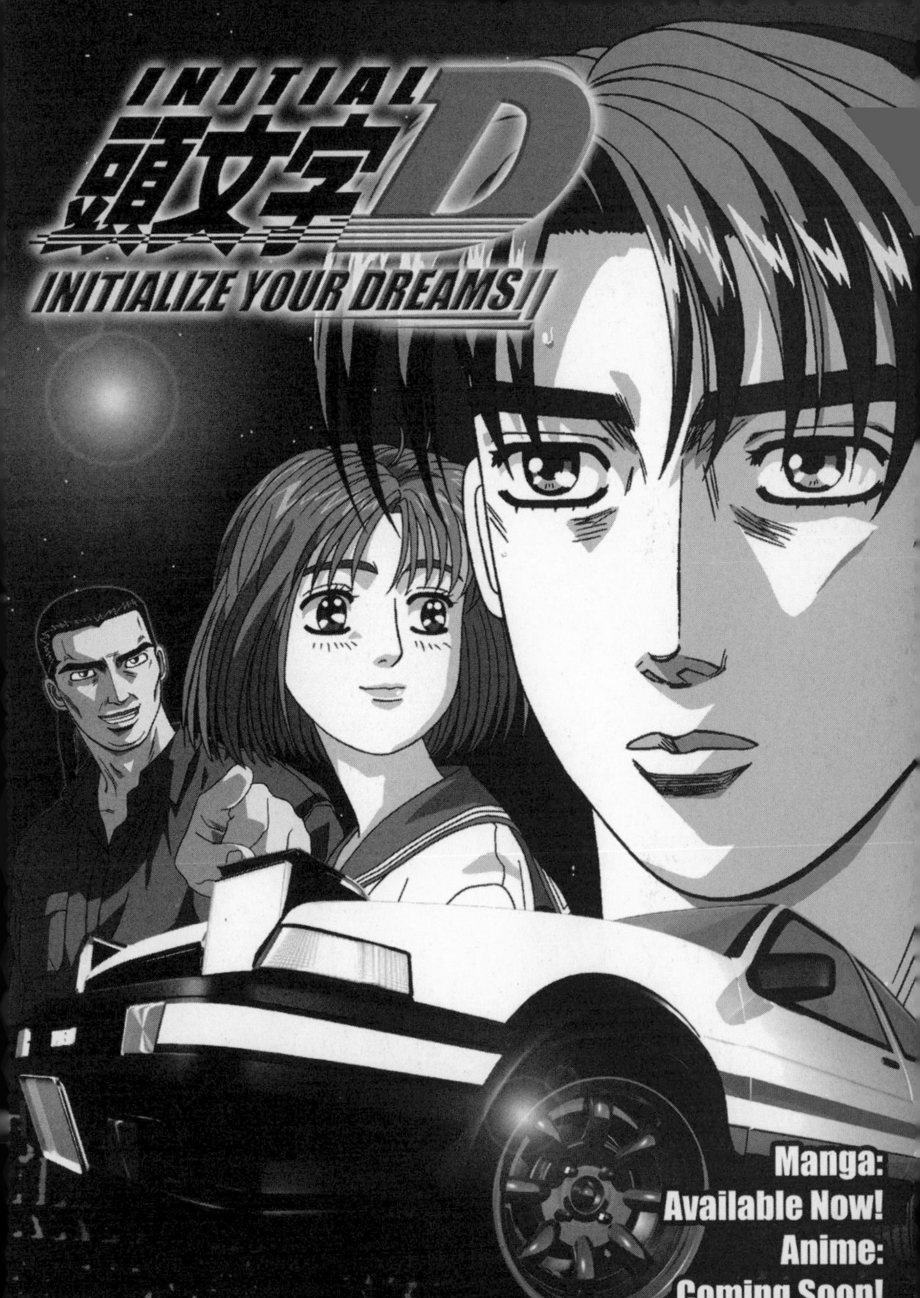
INITIAL
頭文字D
INITIALIZE YOUR DREAMS
Manga:
Available Now!
Anime:
Coming Soon!
TOKYOPOP

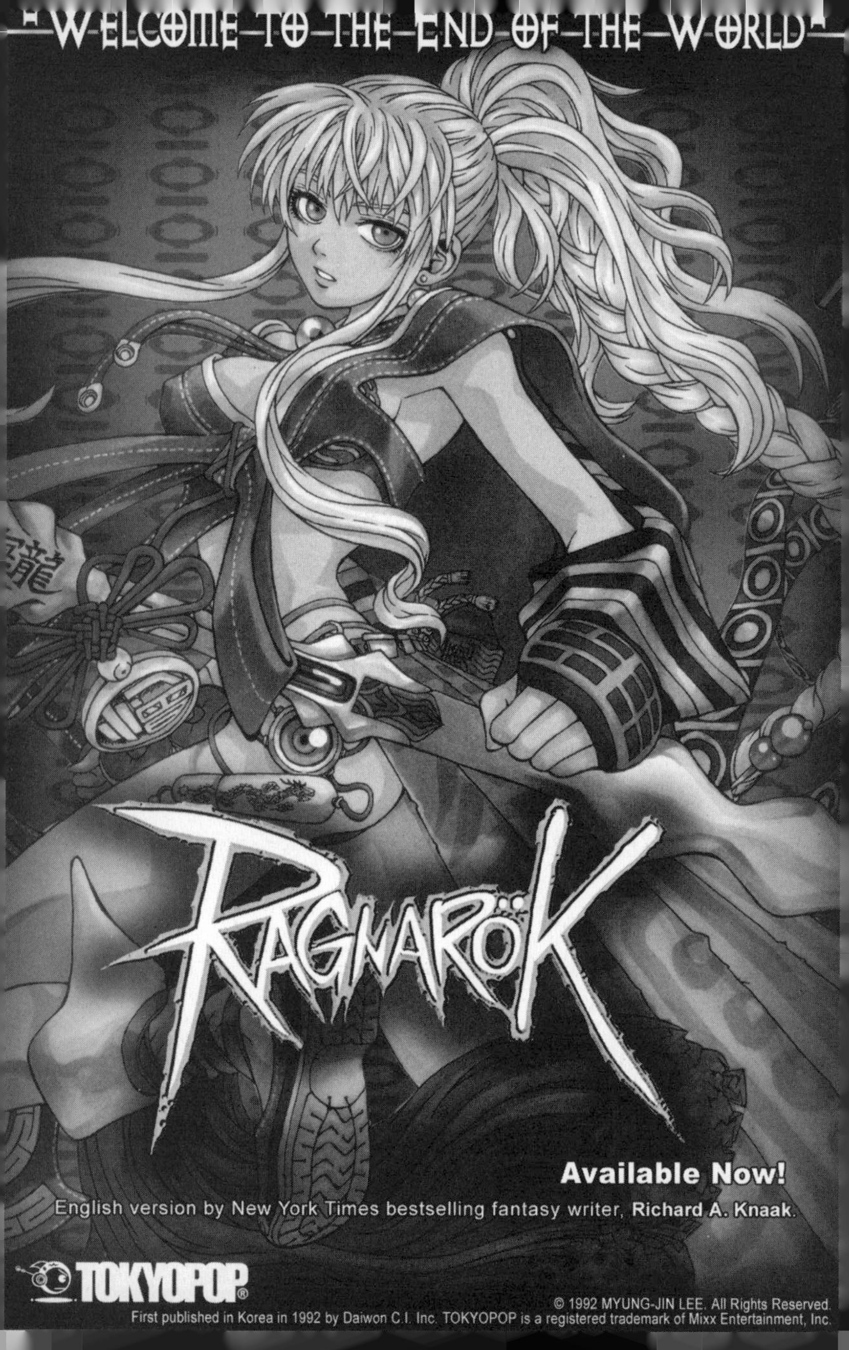

-WELCOME TO THE END OF THE WORLD-
RAGNARÖK
Available Now!
English version by New York Times bestselling fantasy writer, Richard A. Knaak.
TOKYOPOP®
© 1992 MYUNG-JIN LEE. All Rights Reserved.
First published in Korea in 1992 by Daiwon C.I. Inc. TOKYOPOP is a registered trademark of Mixx Entertainment, Inc.

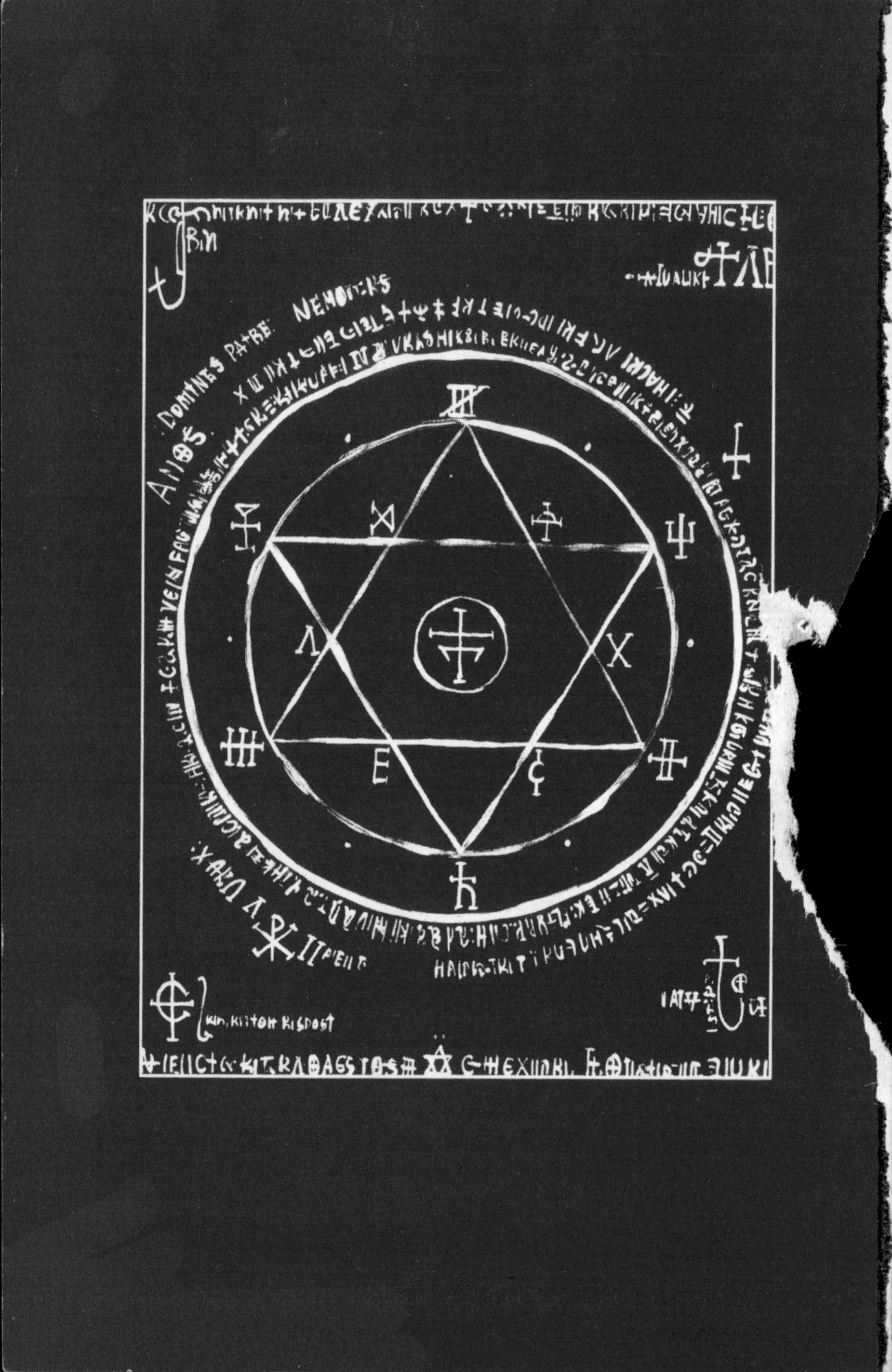